DATE DUE

DEMCO 38-296

GERMANY, INC.

The New German Juggernaut and Its Challenge to World Business

Werner Meyer-Larsen

Translated by Thomas Thornton

John Wiley & Sons, Inc.

New York • Chichester • Weinheim • Brisbane • Singapore • Toronto

love and patience sustained me
ation of this book

This book is printed on acid-free paper. ♾

Published by John Wiley & Sons, Inc.

Published simultaneously in Canada.

This publication is designed to provide accurate and authoritative information in regard
to the subject matter covered. It is sold with the understanding that the publisher is not
engaged in rendering professional services. If legal, accounting, medical, psychological
or any other expert assistance is required, the services of a competent professional
person should be sought.

Library of Congress Cataloging-in-Publication Data

Meyer-Larsen, Werner.
    Germany, Inc. : the new German juggernaut and its challenge to
world business / Werner Meyer-Larsen ; translated by Thomas
Thornton.
        p.   cm.
    Includes bibliographical references and index.
    ISBN 0-471-35357-4 (cloth : alk. paper)
    1. Investments, German—United States—History.   2. Corporations,
German—United States—History.   3. United States—Foreign economic
relations—Germany.   4. Germany—Foreign economic relations—United
States.   I. Title.
    HG4910.M38713   1999
    332.67'343073—dc21   99-33865
                                                                  CIP

Printed in the United States of America.

10 9 8 7 6 5 4 3 2 1

CONTENTS

PREFACE

E VEN WHILE THEIR CONTINENT is caught in a painful political
limbo, European companies are making the necessary preparations
for the future. They have acquired a place in the United States, they
have established company units *à l'Amérique,* and they have formed
transatlantic corporations with American companies as junior partners.
This development still has a long way to go, but the general direction is
clearly discernible. Germany's part in all this is the main topic of this
book. Specifically, it deals with German blue-chip companies that have
started challenging corporate America. Deutsche Bank and Volkswagen,
Bertelsmann and Lufthansa, and in particular, DaimlerChrysler (formerly Daimler-Benz) have a strategy that can be summed up in two mot-
tos: "Go West" and "Think big."

These and other large German companies have gone—floated,
really—through a cultural revolution so sweeping, it is doubtful they have
fully grasped it themselves. Nothing in that country is as it was a mere 10
years ago. The last time German business experienced such a sea change
was a century ago.

Such revolutions never erupt quietly and naturally. And in this case,
three events mark the cornerstones between which this new transatlantic world is forming: One, the Federal Republic of Germany turned
half a century old; two, the Soviet empire collapsed a full decade ago;
and three, the euro, Europe's unified currency, was launched with a marketing campaign worthy of any hot new consumer product.

From the start, this revolution has been determined not by politics
but by economics. The large companies act while the political machinery

remains hesitant. Caught in the middle of this upheaval, politicians are often still using the rusty tools of the Cold War. Where economic and social policies are concerned, it is difficult for them to change their style, which has become entrenched over the course of the twentieth century. Consequently, a country's policies are inevitably on a collision course with its industries, which have to deal with a radically new kind of competition they're not at all familiar with. Unless Germany redefines its identity with regard to the United States, it is in danger of maneuvering itself into an impossible situation. In a manner of speaking, during the Cold War, divided Germany was the center of the universe. The united Germany, however, is no more than one regular component of the whole, though a major one.

By external standards, Germany is stronger today than it ever was. It has become by far the most populous country in Europe, intended, with France, to form the heart of the European Union. For this reason the Germans do indeed have to begin to think less in Atlantic terms and more in Continental terms. Within the existing parameters, American and Central European concerns meet, but in a new way. Today, the United States no longer wants to control everything, but neither does it want to renounce its right to be the general leader. Europe, on the other hand, no longer wants to simply rubber-stamp everything the Americans do. Conversely, being a leader on a par with the United States would be too much to ask as well. Europe can hardly lead itself.

The managers of European corporations cannot afford to wait for new political blueprints to be drawn. Their early-warning system—the bottom line—has been sounding for years. It has taken German companies a little longer to respond, because the economy of reunification forced them to turn the alarm off temporarily. When it did sound again, it made all the more noise. Overnight, the European business dinosaurs found themselves at a gigantic, global bazaar of trade, industry, and services, without protection and facing a superior competitor—the United States. Managers had to very quickly learn what all this means for corporate policies. Consequently, expansion became the rule of the day, expansion at almost any price.

At the same time, Germany has particular disadvantages. Not only did it get started a little later than the rest of Europe, but politically it is in a far more precarious situation than, say, England, the Netherlands, or Scandinavia. As soon as the transatlantic business and commerce sky becomes overcast, German companies are sure to be the first to feel it. This often happens without noticeable warning signs. When Daimler-Benz and Chrysler began to work on finalizing their merger in 1998, no clouds darkened the sky; problems between Germany and the United States were nonexistent, and so the merger became the toast of the business world, and those responsible for it were celebrated for their keen vision.

Shortly thereafter, people who were driven to work for German corporations during World War II filed claims against these companies for unpaid compensation and for damages from bad treatment. Reportedly an unrelated issue, it nevertheless cast a dark shadow on every German company that tried to establish its presence in America. But there is a more bothersome fact: Before long, complex squabbling broke out between all of Europe and the United States. Though the disagreements were the result of frayed nerves rather than facts, this was precisely what gave them momentum.

Let's take a closer look. In mid-March 1999, the *Los Angeles Times* published an op-ed piece by foreign policy pundit Walter Russell Mead, a member of the influential Council on Foreign Relations. Europe, he complained, had stopped looking benevolently at anything the Americans did economically, culturally, or politically. "No matter whether it concerns trade, global economic management, or politics pure and simple—the United States and the European Union simply can no longer look each other in the eye."

What was going on? There was a rather minor contretemps about the reduction of tariffs on bananas from the Caribbean. Another, more serious, dispute concerned the export from the United States to Europe of beef containing high amounts of hormones and of genetically altered grains. Then there were arguments concerning the Balkans, the Middle East, and that long-term Cuban problem by the name of Fidel Castro. And the Americans didn't like Europe's financial and economic policies: As Mead wrote correctly, that continent was trying to regulate just about everything.

Blood began to boil on both sides. Some of the actions Europe takes, Americans find incomprehensible, and vice versa, resonating Mead's comments. Indeed, in some countries—including Germany after the coalition of Social Democrats and Greens replaced the Christian Democrats in 1998—there is a certain rebelliousness against U.S. directives.

This is not anti-Americanism à la post-Vietnam. Even during the more hellacious phases of the Cold War, America's ally France made a great deal more trouble than the entire European Union does now.

The average American sees it this way, too, at least for the time being. Mead writes that "as yet" the American people haven't noticed Europe's resistance to the United States' role as leader. But one day if public opinion in the United States were to turn against Europe, both continents would not merely drift apart, they would tear apart. That's what frayed nerves can lead to.

Perhaps it can all be chalked up to separation anxiety. After all, Europe still hasn't matured as a world power. When it comes to global policies, it is still dependent on America's assistance. It still has a long way to go on the path from complete independence as a junior partner to cooperation among equals. Politicians in all the major nations of continental Europe will have to acknowledge that no country in the world has amassed as much global know-how as the United States during its 45 years as the West's leader in the Cold War.

Fortunately, the leaders of industry have been proceeding more pragmatically than their elected government representatives. After the epochal shift of tides in 1990, they didn't hesitate long before following America's example, to establish themselves on the American market and to compete with American corporations. Rather than condemning America's economic philosophy, they began to apply it for their own good. (European politicians who endlessly gauge situations before they act are cordially invited to take lessons—if it's not too late.)

In the meantime, European companies are changing so quickly that their respective countries are being affected by these changes as well. The developments in German industry have been particularly extreme. From 1990 on, German companies with long and rich histories have been apprehensively trying to find their way around the firmly established rules of the old Federal Republic. Some of their top managers have spent years in the United States—years that invariably left lasting impressions. The rapid transformation of hick German companies into respectable global corporations is ultimately a testimony to the American system, even if that system—in the person of Walter Russell Mead, for instance—doesn't notice.

These are the cases that comprise this book. That many references are very personal cannot be avoided. I have spent decades observing economic, technological, and social developments the world over. I have, with interruptions, lived on both continents for 10 years. The cultural differences, and sometimes contrasts, between America and Germany are as familiar to me as are the similarities that link the two countries. I have routinely observed all the companies discussed and classified here under three different categories; and at some point or other, I have personally encountered many of the key people discussed here.

Unavoidably, my personal impressions have had an impact on how I present these cases. Certainly, I could have chosen to approach my topic in a more analytical and detached manner. But detached is not what this topic calls for. What makes all this so interesting is that stupendous illogic in many minor events led to extraordinarily logical results. Human beings act with emotions and passions no matter what the circumstance, and observing them while they are doing all this is often much more revealing than statistics.

In our current era, people who meet the unwritten requirements of the age make it to the top; and so, for a few years, they, with all their flaws, constitute our history.

Along with all the hoopla about mergers and acquisitions has come much talk about "corporate culture," whether a particular corporate culture is appropriate, or how it compares to another one. It has become a popular topic of analysis, and hefty consultation fees have been made on it. Simply, however, corporate culture is the extract of a company's history. The actions of major players such as DaimlerChrysler or Siemens, Deutsche Bank, Allianz, or Lufthansa have all been influenced by how it all began once upon a time, down to the smallest details.

Thus, a discussion of the horsepower or brakes in Mercedes race cars or the actions of Krupp administrator Berthold Beitz in Poland during the Nazi period are essential if we are to understand a company's spirit. These facts are what make it more palpable, more comprehensible, and perhaps even more human. Mercedes would not be Mercedes without race driver Rudolf Caracciola, and Krupp owes a great deal to the fact that a young Berthold Beitz saved Jewish prisoners during World War II.

That said, the romantic aspect of such stories should not be made too much of, either. Official histories of companies often are published specifically to pluck heartstrings. Ultimately what moves business are people's focus and foresight and the desire to make money. Some might call them obsessive. We will meet such people in these pages in all shades and colors. All of them, even if they've completely turned their companies around, have suddenly found themselves where their ancestors once were.

I focus on America. Why? Why should the fact that German companies are taking a position opposite American firms be particularly interesting? Philosophically, this may be viewed as an about-face, toward the values of a Western culture that were previously only parroted in Germany. These values have now been accepted in Europe, even though they became a bit altered and more complex in the process. Certain political parties and governments in Europe still prefer the old ways, though these are no longer viable. Competition makes its own laws; it is what makes the money, after all, and thus, taxes.

When it comes to making money, America, which was influenced by the British system, has always been superior to Europe. This aspect of the Anglo-Saxon world becomes clearer than ever in the new, almost depoliticized world. No other society is as blatantly determined by economics and money as the United States. A popular way to explain this phenomenon is as the result of Calvinism, which in its American permutation views economic success as a divine reward. But it isn't necessary to reach quite that far; a few simple facts will do. American pioneers might just as well have landed in the African jungle: Economically speaking, there was absolutely nothing there. To build a new civilization, they had to work hard, and they continued to do so. Unrestrained by the statutes of guilds and tax obligations to local princes, they amassed more income than they needed for their survival.

In 1776, both the American Declaration of Independence and Adam Smith's *Wealth of Nations* were published. It was a coincidence, but nevertheless has symbolic meaning. From that time on, Adam Smith was more influential than Karl Marx's predecessors or the author of *Das Kapital* himself. Walking down Wall Street at lunchtime, an observer can almost see dollar figures being computed in the minds of workers. Some might think this is obsessive. But it must be remembered that with the exception of their Civil War between 1861 and 1865, Americans have rarely had to deal with challenges on their own land other than those of economic origin. Unlike in Europe, in America not even the church objected to money, so American citizens have lived in a world driven by dollars. And what is wrong with it, as long as people don't cheat one another?

Europeans, in contrast, carry a lot of baggage. "Bondage to interest" was the phrase Protestants hurled against those dealing with money;

"exploitation" was the word Marxists used. Money is somewhat like love: If it's not associated with a guilty conscience, it's no fun. The Europeans' baggage included 2,000 years of feudalism, anarchism, theocracy, Communism, Fascism, and wars. Profit margins were small because there was always some damage to be fixed. Ruling and destroying seemed to be more important than producing and selling. The Age of Enlightenment brought about a change, but initially only as a counterweight, not as the only determinative force. There was still heavy baggage to carry for quite some time. Not until 1945 was it put down. Only the economic miracle awakened German sensitivity to the value of what they once despised.

America's advantage is that its economic values have always been democratic. Europe still has not caught up with this value system. When it comes to technology, however, things are different. Technology is something thoroughly European. Its origins are in poverty, bad weather, and the necessities of war. Technologically, Europeans have always been able to compete, and then some. A German conglomerate that wants to be an American company's equal draws its strength from precisely that source. It draws its identity much more from technological experiences than financial ones. In the days of old, Americans simplified European technology and made it available through financial large-scale operations. Today, the Germans peek at American financial creations in order to turn things around.

Thus, the gap between American and German economic thinking has closed since the demise of the Soviet Union. But make no mistake, this was not a matter of course. If German industry had listened to its supersmart cultural critics, it would be worse off than it is. Even now, those who despise America believe that globalization—allegedly a concept invented by the Yankees—is a new form of imperialism. Globalization today is probably something genuinely American, but whether or not it is imperialistic will be decided by the market.

Understandably, many Germans would have liked to erect a high fence around the idyll of the 1980s, but Germany's large companies did not choose to pursue that kind of romanticism. If they had, they would have forfeited their chance and been inevitably forced into an economic stagnation along with the rest of Europe. Instead, the large German companies are moving along at the same speed as their American counterparts, pulling along their sluggish consorts in old Europe—and one day perhaps even the forces of regress in the former East Germany.

German purchases in the United States are still far from the volume of American purchases throughout the Federal Republic of Germany. What propels Daimler, Siemens, Allianz, Deutsche Bank, and others is primarily the desire to make up for opportunities missed in the past. And the communication technology society—which was born in America as well—has so accelerated economic development that it has, ironically, enabled America itself to be challenged. As to who will meet that challenge, we'll have to wait and see.

Part I

Go West, Go Global

CHAPTER 1

The New German Challenge

MAY 7, 1998, will go down as a milestone in the history of industry. On that day two men, Daimler-Benz chairman Jürgen E. Schrempp and Chrysler chairman Robert J. Eaton, signed a merger agreement, the biggest industrial deal of all time, to form the fifth-largest car company (by volume) in the world, DaimlerChrysler Inc. The announcement was considered by many to be *the* economic news of the year.

Competing headlines from the world of commerce that year included an economic crisis in Asia and Latin America and the announcement that Russia's economy had dwindled down to a trickle. Rivals of currency trader George Soros estimated he had squandered billions and billions of dollars. Between July and October, the industrial averages at the international stock exchanges had plummeted so low there was serious talk about a new worldwide economic crisis. Oskar Lafontaine, Germany's new minister of finance, irritated the international financial aristocracy by conjuring up the specter of a planned economy.

But only a few months later, the various industrial averages had regained the highs of the previous summer, and Lafontaine was out. In fact, most of the major economic news reports turned out to be rumblings. But not the merger between Daimler-Benz and Chrysler. A short six months after Schrempp and Eaton had signed their declaration of intent, their armies of lawyers finalized the deal. Unlike Lafontaine's prophesies, the Daimler-Benz and Chrysler merger was a true sign of a new era.

For the first time in history, a transatlantic global conglomerate was in the making, one whose policies would be defined in Germany. Only

47 percent of the new company's shares were American; 53 percent were German. In terms of annual revenue, the joint concern has climbed to number three in the world's auto industry. When its internal strength is considered—capital and business know-how—it might even be number one.

It hardly need be said that the merger between Daimler-Benz and Chrysler would not be smooth sailing from beginning to end. But the potential for conflict between the two companies is less than for most other agreements of this kind. First, it was not a hostile takeover; it was a peaceful and voluntary agreement between two well-matched corporations. Unlike other arrangements of this sort, it was born out of prudence rather than of pressing necessity. In 1998, neither of the two conglomerates was so weak that it had to look for a strong partner; both had all the time in the world. Consequently, it came as a surprise that the American company so readily agreed to assume the role of junior partner and to submit to German business law with its stipulations regarding the supervisory board, the executive board, and worker participation. In short, there was little that was *not* unique about this merger.

Thus, DaimlerChrysler represents the model of a new challenge raised by Germany and confronting the United States. Economically, it is just as extraordinary as was Kaiser Wilhelm II's vast expansion of Germany's naval force to Great Britain's military strategists 100 years earlier. And there are some indications that the case of DaimlerChrysler marks not only the onset of a new wave, but constitutes its logical crest. It is hard to imagine that a transatlantic merger could be accomplished more resolutely, smoothly, or comprehensively. No doubt several major mergers will take place in DaimlerChrysler's wake, but the new conglomerate will be without equal for a long time.

That said, DaimlerChrysler found no shortage of business compatriots in America. After all, Frankfurt's Deutsche Bank, whose Fifth Avenue branch in Manhattan alone employed up to 700 at one point, had already taken over Bankers Trust in New York. Media conglomerate Bertelsmann, based in Gütersloh, Germany, had taken over Random House in New York, the largest book producer in the United States, thus becoming proprietor of such renowned imprints as Ballantine, Crown, Fawcett, Knopf, Pantheon, Times Books, and Villard. Already owner of two New York–based publishing houses—Bantam Doubleday Dell and Delacourt—this move catapulted Bertelsmann to the number one place among American book publishers. Occupants of Bertelsmann's high-rise offices on Sixth Avenue include Bertelsmann's subsidiary, BMG Entertainment, owner of American music businesses Arista, RCA, and Windham Hill, with Whitney Houston, Toni Braxton, and Puff Daddy just three of many star clients.

Likewise, publishing syndicate Holtzbrinck, owner of major German newspapers such as *Handelsblatt* and *Wirtschaftswoche,* had established itself solidly on the American book market by buying publishers Henry Holt, St. Martin's Press, and Farrar, Straus & Giroux.

And back on the merger front, Frankfurt's chemicals giant Hoechst (now Aventis) had joined with its American competitor Marion Merril Dow and the French corporation Roussel Uclar to become Hoechst Marion Roussel. This was soon followed by Hoechst's merger with the French chemicals company Rhône-Poulenc, which created strong competition for America's leading pharmaceutical companies.

In global passenger aircraft production, meanwhile, the European airbus industry (in which DaimlerChrysler's subsidiary DASA is a heavyweight) inched ever closer to American market leader Boeing. In 1999, Airbus landed more commissions for new jet airplanes than the Seattle-based corporation.

Among insurance companies, Munich's Allianz assumed the number one spot in the world, and it, too, gained a foothold in the United States when it acquired the American insurance company Fireman's Fund in 1990. Then there's Munich electronics firm Siemens, which publicly boasts of planning to allocate 6 billion euros—some $7 billion in United States currency—for acquisitions. Siemens chairman Heinrich von Pierer plans to invest the money mainly in the United States, if possible in the moneymaking branches of information and communications technologies. German pharmaceuticals company Merck KGaA in Darmstadt, a family business owned by the Langmann clan (until World War I, owner of the American pharmaceuticals giant of the same name), has earmarked almost $2 billion for purchases in the United States.

In short, as the end of the "American century" approached, German companies were flooding corporate America with bigger and better offers. Just as in the last century American oil baron John D. Rockefeller covered the globe with his corporate culture and as General Motors established footholds in the auto market all over the world (especially in Europe) since the 1920s, so German companies have begun to establish themselves in the United States and internationally. Only a small-town force until recently, today they are major competitors, which may strike some as "Teutonic furor." In the militant language of economic competitiveness, it has become a battle between Deutschland AG (Germany Inc.) and Corporate America. Is this an overstatement? Perhaps. It is, however, blatantly obvious that the collapse of the Soviet Union drastically changed the general conditions in the world's economic power centers. The global balance of power has shifted.

Not overnight, but step by step, the markets of the former power blocs, which used to be scrupulously separated, opened up. They became accessible and measurable entities; their potential could be appraised. And at times, alarm signals have gone off. The titillating but comfortable clubbiness between East and West, whose members all knew where the others stood and would ultimately protect the status quo, was over. Free markets here, an authorian economy there, bartering, supply quota, and fabulous currency exchange rates—how comfy was this fairy-tale world of well-ordered structures. Inflexibility had been the motto—and the goal—and corruption and gray or black markets the quietly tolerated side effects of this arrangement. No one wanted to hurt the others, after all. Everyone was in the trenches. Sure, they all fired a few harrassing rounds now and then, but basically they enjoyed the phony war.

There is no doubt that the Cold War had rigidified the West's structures as well. Of course, there was always much to-do about the risks of free enterprise, particularly in Germany. Enterprise was free, albeit a little curbed by government regulations. But that didn't make life terribly risky (not even for the workforce, by the way). Everyone was safely cocooned in a nice and cozy society, dynamic within reason but hardly ready to dare being innovative. The general modus operandi that was set in place at the top was one of consensus, which everyone enjoyed. As long as you followed the rules, you wouldn't bite the dust. And the rules were safeguarded by NATO; politics were according to then-chancellor Helmut Kohl and Deutsche Bank.

An economy based on patronage—corporatist, small-scale, and diligent, leisurely but solid—was the rule of the day. Electronics firm Siemens was so protected that it even functioned as its own bank, though that was hardly necessary because the Federal Ministry of Research habitually assumed coverage of its risks. And when it seemed inappropriate to claim R&D subsidies, the company was happy to hand its inventions over to the competition for development. Take the basics of fax technology, for instance, which the Japanese developed until it was marketable, earning themselves vast rewards in the process. Almost every large German company selling to the general public was a kind of Siemens.

Before the new era, Daimler-Benz was an integral part of this system, and the company's then-chairman Edzard Reuter its most eloquent spokesman. Backed by Deutsche Bank, the system's "politburo," Reuter had wanted to safeguard Daimler's traditional business, the production of heavy trucks and luxury cars, by obtaining federal subsidies for entering the weapons, aircraft, and spacecraft industry. Even though he considered this idea to be novel and brilliant, in fact, it was hardly an example of entrepreneurial vision. Quite the contrary; it turned free enterprise into "bossdom," making it dependent on the public sector. In short, it became a mix between market economy and planned economy. Thus, it was two-faced, contradictory, and in constant need of subsidies. Everything about it ran counter to the concept of risk taking. But then, Reuter was confident that the Cold War would never end. At the same time, he trumpeted the technological synergy between his company's two production centers. Even then, Chrysler Chairman Robert Eaton, now Daimler's partner, confessed that he had his doubts about these synergies. Any technology one wanted, he contended, could be bought cheaply.

In 1989, the year of political change, the former West Germany's incestuous system had essentially created the ultimate idyll of general prosperity: full employment and comfortable ways of making a living. Germany had become the new Switzerland of Europe; all it was lacking was numbered accounts. By that time, however, it had become so sclerotic that a halt in economic growth and a devaluation of the deutsche mark—that is to say, stagflation—were imminent. Unfortunately, nobody noticed that the IOUs were defaulting. The reunification of Germany simply prolonged this rotten state of affairs.

To be sure, the Kohl administration, remote-controlled by then–U.S. president George Bush, accomplished a brilliant political feat with the reunification of Germany. Economically, however, it tried to muddle along as before. Globalization? Thanks, but no thanks. Germany's entrepreneurs preferred doing business in places that were closer to them geographically, intellectually, and in terms of tax laws: If they wanted to grow, they looked to East Germany—which was helped along to the tune of 200 billion deutsche marks annually. Keynesian overkill—literally.

Skeptics such as then–BMW chairman Eberhard von Kuenheim immediately became worried that the convenient subsidy business with the former East Germany might keep businesspeople from meeting the true and immediate challenges of the new era. Not particularly interested in business ventures with the East, the British and the Americans had long since begun to adjust to the different reality. When the era of change actually turned into a new era, there was much wailing and whining. Politicians, the well-to-do, and bureaucrats committed to the modus operandi of consensus sought salvation by following the motto "what must not be true cannot be true."

From the catchword "globalization" was derived "globalization trap," a popular nonterm ideal for unauthorized use at home. A nostalgic book entitled *Globalization Trap* by Hans-Peter Martin and Harald Schumann (Rowohlt 1995) even became a best-seller. But reflections of that sort didn't really offer a path to bliss. Those who tried to avoid the trap of globalization were bound to get caught in the *real* trap—let's call it the trap of time. Surprisingly, it was German managers, otherwise so glib, who recognized that danger—just in time. Long before the political powers that be—under the presidential leadership of a chancellor to whom economy was a foreign affair—realized what was going on, management decided to pull the emergency brake.

It came as a shock to business leaders when they suddenly realized that German industry was doomed. Company size, productivity, return on revenue, wages, and work hours all were determined solely by patterns firmly established in four and a half decades of East-West policies. The Cold War had atrophied competition in the West not only politically, but also within its system of free enterprise. The West's market structures were obsolete, particularly in Europe and hence in Germany.

Now, suddenly, all markets outside of the Western bloc were wide open. That promised to be good for sales, but not in terms of costing. Not only did competition within Europe begin to increase on account of the euro and the European Union, but seemingly overnight, that market's internal walls, behind which it had always been possible to hide, had collapsed. Some 2 billion additional cheap laborers from countries as culturally diverse as Poland and China flooded the international job market just as quickly. Industry didn't have much time to respond to this challenge. It was forced to jump over its own shadow to make an instant switch from its provincial mode of thinking to an approach that employed global strategies.

In the "golden age" of the Cold War, an extended market back home had always been sufficient to guarantee the survival of even weaker companies. Now, global markets formed overnight, markets in which oligopolistic competition developed quickly, at least for high-volume transactions (most of Germany's industrial companies were too small to be serious contenders). In oligopolies, nothing remains a secret. Everybody knows how good or competitive each player is, and each is also eager for additional market shares; cost management is tight and international marketing calculations are subtle; profit margins shrink; downsizing and increasing productivity become number one priorities. "In the final analysis," Hermann Simon, a management consultant on both sides of the Atlantic, wrote in Hamburg's monthly *Manager Magazine* (November 1998, page 323), globalization means "being about equally strong in all the world's relevant markets." Management gurus offering expensive courses and conferences quickly realized that the solution was economies of scale. Conventional German managers found that hard to swallow at first. Size was not exactly what mattered most in their delicate, middle-class way of thinking. For a long time, the combination of sophistication in technological matters and leisureliness in business matters had been comforting in its own quiet way. Now perhaps this comfort zone was something to be missed, but in the global marketplace, there was no longer much use for it unless a company was the world's unchallenged market leader in certain specialized products such as cigarette-cutting machines (by Körber) or bottle-labeling machines (by Krone). In the mid-1990s, many German businesses realized that they were seriously lagging behind their foreign competitors.

American competitors were dealing with larger production units, for the simple reason that their internal market alone was the size of an entire continent. Conversely, huge conglomerates had developed in Europe for precisely the opposite reason: Their own market was way too small, so they had to acquire companies to grow big enough to compete on the international market. Psychologically, globalization had started decades ago for, among others, Switzerland's pharmaceuticals industry, the Nestlé corporation, and the Dutch conglomerate Philips. Globalization had become the normal way of life. That's the reason these companies today find it much easier than German or French companies to take the steps necessary to achieve the next economic level.

As we have seen, however, their competitors' more highly developed internal structures were not the only threat German managers faced in the international industrial marketplace. The new global labor market—an entity that had not existed since the beginning of World War I—promised to be far more devastating. Europe, with its unique social structures, was intellectually not the least bit prepared for it. European society had over the past decades been lulled by the knowledge that a qualified minority, the so-called social partners (i.e., labor and management), had a monopoly on wage regulation. Because of these mechanisms, a real labor market no longer existed factually. By being injected from outside, as it were, it turned out to be a revolutionary change with which European society was at first utterly incapable of dealing.

In contrast, German companies whose business routinely transcended borders, such as Lufthansa, soon realized that the new situation was an opportunity to significantly lower wages. In the meantime, those running the global oligopolistic companies no longer viewed the world solely through the eyes of a salesperson, but also through the eyes of a potential buyer. From there it was only a small step to the concept of shopping around on the international labor market. Very soon, Lufthansa chairman Jürgen Weber moved part of his airline's ticket sales operation to India, where highly competent computer experts make no more than one-tenth the salary their German counterparts typically command.

In the mid-1990s, when part of Germany's highbrow press, in a concerted action with the lowbrow press, merrily campaigned against the Maastricht Treaty, which laid the groundwork for the euro, the country's top managers were already forced to think far beyond Maastricht. From their Teutonic basis, they had to design a global company without a fatherland. Among those who recognized that early were Mark Wössner, then still head of Bertelsmann, and Deutsche Bank's Alfred Herrhausen, as well as his (sometimes misunderstood) successor Hilmar Kopper. Others, such as VW's Ferdinand Piech, a man obsessed with cars, simply had to follow their instincts to come to the same conclusion. In regard to the number of cars sold, Piech once said he wanted to get "on the three-tiered podium"—that is, the place where the medal winners stand at the Olympics.

What a goal: being number three behind General Motors and Ford but ahead of Toyota, especially considering that only three and a half decades earlier, VW's annual turnover had been no greater than General Motors' annual profit margin! In 1998–1999, VW did indeed sell some more cars than Toyota; and following these criteria, it now really *is* number three in the world. Though in terms of total revenue, Piech has not yet reached his goal, he does want to be among the automobile industry's Big Five in this respect as well. Who knows, perhaps there won't *be* many more than five large automobile companies 10 years from now.

Lufthansa director Jürgen Weber had early on globalized his company's operations as well, but inconspicuously. While Wössner is analytical and Piech is intuitive, Weber is pragmatic. He may not have had any grand visions of the future, but he certainly had no illusions, either. His advantage was that he became familiar with the deregulation of air traffic early—first in the United States and then in Europe. In 1991, Lufthansa, which had been re-founded in 1955, had financial difficulties, but technologically it was in tip-top shape. When Weber took over the company that year, he began to assemble the industry's most comprehensive system of allies. No less a company than United Airlines, one of the U.S. air traffic industry's Big Three, is a member of his *Star Alliance* network.

Compared to Wössner, Piech, and Weber, then, Jürgen Schrempp was considered a late starter. A trained technician like Piech and Weber, the Daimler chief soon proved to be in a category of his own. When it comes to linking ambitious goals and brilliant strategy, he is virtually unsurpassable. A longtime protégé of his predecessor Edzard Reuter, Schrempp abruptly abandoned his mentor's management philosophy and developed his own strategic concept, which he then set out to realize by rolling up his sleeves and pragmatically pursuing his plan with staunch persistence. His image was not that of a particularly sophisticated, but rather of a straightforward man—and that paid off nicely.

But before the payoff, Jürgen Schrempp suffered a number of serious setbacks in his career, all of his own making. For instance, he was personally responsible for a large portion of the losses Daimler-Benz suffered on account of Reuter's double-faced strategy. But Schrempp is not one for contrition, and Daimler is no monastery. Hardly had he settled into the chairman's office when Schrempp shifted gears to adjust to the new situation. He knew he had made mistakes, but now he was ready to do things right.

Part of his plan was to spread certain myths designed to create a personal aura for himself. Schrempp claimed that while sitting in front of the fireplace at his home in South Africa (which he purchased during his tenure with the company branch there), he suddenly realized that in order for Daimler to run smoothly again, everything had to be turned back. Each product line would have to show a minimum of 12 percent return on revenue. If it didn't, it was going to be strictly "fix it or sell it." However, what was most important, he said, was for Daimler to extend globally those core businesses it decided to keep. Daimler had to be among the world leaders in all branches of its business. If this sounds familiar, it is because esoteric Edzard Reuter had been replaced as Schrempp's spiritual foster parent by General Electric's Jack Welch, an American down-to-business type.

Welch had transformed the placid U.S. company General Electric into a flexible and enormously profitable corporation with many different product lines. Each of them, Welch decreed, had to advance to at least second place, and if possible to first place, within its field and yield accordingly large profits. GE's shares and its internal value soared so high that the company achieved the second-highest rating of all U.S. corporations, surpassed only by Coca-Cola. Wall Street analysts cheered. Welch pressed on and started preaching salvation through "shareholder values," that is, the highest possible dividends and share value—the ultimate management objective. Schrempp liked all this a great deal. Every other word out of his mouth was "shareholder values"—at least as long as he was abroad.

Schrempp soon realized that in Germany's society of consensus, this term was not considered politically correct. When at home, therefore, Schrempp talked about "business policies determined by values," which is just the song-and-dance term for shareholder values. The stockbrokers dug him, and it was their confidence that counted, after all. As far as labor was concerned, there was no outcry of indignation among the workers, much to the unions' dismay—not even after Daimler cut almost 90,000 of its 380,000 jobs within a five-year period. Only when Schrempp tried to realize his merciless austerity plan (called Dolores, for "dollar low-rescue" program) to put DASA back on its feet was there trouble.

Nevertheless, the Daimler workforce and its representatives realized that the new era called unmistakably for new measures. Schrempp then quickly dropped everything from the company that was in danger of losing money, and once again put all his stakes in the auto business. Still, he didn't plan to restructure the company from inside, as Ferdinand Piech had done; he intended to turn it into a company capable of merging with an attractive partner. The head of Daimler's automobile division, Helmut Werner, who had salvaged his product line in a tour de force and internally restructured his division, was ousted.

Schrempp pursued a simpler and, at the same time, grander design, in which there was no room for consideration of individual lives. He viewed himself as a more qualified leader than Werner, and that was all that mattered. Plus, he was the younger of the two, which was a factor taken into account by Daimler's supervisory board, including labor representatives, who share the seats with shareholder's representatives. And so this little detour contributed to the happy union between the myth of Schrempp and the reality of Schrempp: In record time, Daimler-Benz regained its preeminence as German industry's most distinguished name.

As so often happens, hindsight seems to justify everything, for without his about-face, Schrempp hardly could have pulled off his "mission impossible" with Chrysler. That deal, in fact, comprised chapter two of the Schrempp myth: During a casual conversation at the Automobile Salon in Detroit in early 1998, it is said, the idea of a merger between Daimler and Chrysler first occurred to Schrempp and Bob Eaton. But as is usually the case with tales told over and over again by the campfire, this story, too, has a few slightly different versions.

Whether or not one believes any of this, it does seem suspicious that Daimler's chairman was so remarkably well prepared for this "coincidence." In connection with this matter, he had read strategic studies, one of them by the American consulting firm Arthur D. Little in Cambridge, Massachusetts, which looked at the possibilities of an "ambition-given strategy." What could and what should a conglomerate such as Daimler-Benz do in an atmosphere of increasing globalization? Go with an overseas competitor. Period.

Schrempp, with his instinct for grand schemes, saw a green light to continue on his personal mission. This entire business could well propel him overnight to the position of a cult figure within the auto industry. Before the man from Stuttgart "spontaneously" talked things over with

Bob Eaton, he had already checked with market leader General Motors and with Englishman Alex Trotman, then head of the Ford Motor Company. Trotman, too, it soon turned out, was looking for a major fix for his corporation. Remember, at the beginning of his tenure he had vowed that by the year 2000, Ford would be number one in the auto industry—ahead of General Motors, the perennial number one for the past 70 years.

For Schrempp to go so far as to make these suggestions in the first place, the coordinates in world politics first had to shift. Put simply, Japan's image had waned, while Germany's had become more favorable. The Federal Republic of Germany had done an excellent job in the 50 years since it was founded. Outside of the country's borders, this was often more clearly recognized than at home, especially by the movers and shakers in the United States. After reunification, Germany had become America's most important partner in Europe. Previously "the world's greatest powerlessness" (as Deutsche Bank's Hermann Josef Abs put it), Germany was no longer restrained by occupation law. It once again had regained complete independence, within the framework of the European Union.

Japan, on the other hand, whose cockiness had thoroughly irritated the United States more than once, now seemed to be quaking. Its economic crisis was also a social crisis. That Japan was not ready to relax its rigid structures and build a truly modern society more often confused the Americans, to whom it seemed that the cultural gap between the two countries was wider than it had been in a long time. Concomitantly, Americans were pleased that Japan's industry had lost much of its bite. Japan was no longer intimidating.

Only a few years earlier even the renowned American economist Lester Thurow had referred to Japan as the most dynamic power of the so-called economic triad, insisting that any industrial superpower had to cooperate with Japan at nearly all costs—even if it had to grit its teeth—because the sons of Nippon were so difficult, because they were more interested in an economic war than in partnership, and because they were more concerned with increasing exports than with free trade. Once the Americans realized that the economic triad and Japan's dynamic strength were not all they were cracked up to be, their willingness to cooperate quickly began to evaporate. Freed of the Japanese nemesis,

America started to turn its sharp focus away from the Pacific. Germany became close again, and with it, all of Europe.

This was a natural turn of events. It is hardly necessary to point out that despite their differences, the Americans understand the European mind-set better than they do the Asian mind-set. After all, the foundation of American culture and the basic concept of American institutions is in the Old World (though more so in England and France than in Germany). And the Europeans had largely been following the advice America had been giving them since World War II. Consequently, as a huge bloc with its own unified currency, and perhaps even as a semipolitical union, Europe became much more important to the United States than it had been before.

The United States wants to be Europe's partner in many respects, without necessarily playing the lead. The prospect of establishing, along with the Europeans, an industrial position that is superior to that of the Far East is enticing enough. The more conventional rules of geopolitics—for instance, that neighbors on opposite sides of the ocean are all the more interesting the closer their shores are—are making a sort of comeback. The principal power on the other side of the Atlantic is once again Germany, now transformed by NATO and the European Union from its role as troublemaker into the great integrator.

The United States wants to take advantage of this transformation. With England's impact on the continent waning, the United States can exert its influence on the European Union's economic style only via Germany. Exerting its influence is an old political principle in Washington, one that serves to protect its political system at home. No one followed that principle more clearly than Franklin D. Roosevelt (from 1933 to 1945) in his crusade against German führer Adolf Hitler and his Axis powers. America, Roosevelt argued, could not defend its political system, which rested firmly on the freedom of its citizens, unless a large part of the developed world supported the same concept of liberty.

The present situation isn't nearly as dramatic as it was then, but the United States wants to nip in the bud any hints of a closed European economic fortress. For the United States, it is a matter of course that the more fully German-American and American-German concepts and values develop, the better it is for both sides. All of this understood, Washington simply could not oppose the DaimlerChrysler deal. The times of a tough "buy American" cross-country movement (with Chrysler being one of its main inspirations!) are over. So are the days of open or even subliminal antipathy toward Germany and the Germans.

Admittedly, many prejudices against the Germans remain inextinguishable—especially since the Hitler era. At the same time, there also exists a tradition of positive feelings, and these are more deep-seated, more profoundly rooted in the American people than the country's media would have us believe. In politics, it was mainly Republican presidents who dared exhibit support for Germany: Theodore Roosevelt (1901–1909), Herbert Hoover (1929–1933), and George Bush (1989–1993) each maintained a basic pro-German attitude, though one tempered by skepticism—the atmosphere was just a little overcast, and there was a slight northwesterly wind.

The reason for American support—albeit from a critical distance—for the Germans can perhaps be traced to the fact that, historically, many U.S. immigrants came from Germany, and as an ethnic group, they were distinct only during the first generation of settlers. They assimilated more completely and quickly into the Anglo-Saxon world than almost any other group. With the exception of the legendary Carl Schurz, they were not influential in politics. Among the 42 U.S. presidents to date, only Dwight D. Eisenhower (1953–1961) had a name clearly of German origin—though he didn't consider that an asset in gaining public viability.

Still, in a semianonymous way, the Germans exercised tremendous influence on the development of agriculture and the processing industries. It is fair to say that America's former main industrial area around the Great Lakes and in parts of New England was "German," a fact that was largely suppressed because of the world wars and Hitler. Against this backdrop, the Germans became respected as perfectionists and professionals, but that didn't win people's hearts, which were reserved for others. For instance, Americans love the French like good, albeit eccentric, friends; they love the English like cousins, family factotums whose whimsical behavior they have gotten used to.

The fact is, the Germans tested Americans repeatedly, and still do. In the twentieth century, the Americans had to confront them again and again, with the kind of intensity they were otherwise not forced to engage in. Throughout the entire century—which, following a statement by New York publisher Henry Luce, has been dubbed the "American century"—the Germans were the main concern of America's Western policies. (It would be worth analyzing whether the twentieth century has been a German-American century.)

Since the days of Theodore Roosevelt, there has been an ongoing dialectical process of thesis, antithesis, and synthesis between the two countries. Until 1945, Germany was a Mephistophelian contributor to the United States' emergence as a world power—in Goethe's words, it was "part of that force that always wants to achieve evil and always creates good." Incited and challenged by Germany's aggressive impatience, the deep-down somewhat isolationist United States found itself more directly involved in world politics, mostly in opposition to its natural impulses. That said, America sometimes liked it a bit: Theodore Roosevelt versus Kaiser Wilhelm II; Erich Ludendorff versus Woodrow Wilson; finally, Adolf Hitler versus Franklin D. Roosevelt in World War II. Germany always wanted everything and the United States always gained everything.

Between 1945 and 1990, Germany—geographically speaking, the principal dividing line in the Cold War—was newly created, shaped, and tamed by America. It became America's star pupil, its continental warrior, and eventually, even its defender of Atlantic values. Perhaps things wouldn't have gone that well if the United States hadn't found such a kindred spirit in West Germany's first chancellor. Konrad Adenauer, staunch anti-Prussian *haut bourgeois* from the Rhineland, tied Germany to the West for what must have been the first time since the decline of the Karolingian empire in the early Middle Ages, the Holy German Empire of the German nation. Adenauer had accomplished this by being tough, persistent, and clever—and it looks as if the bond has been forged for good.

But not until 1990 did America release West Germany into "adulthood." Reunification and the euro—a package deal from the get-go—turned Germany from America's main vassal into its partner, for better or for worse. Germany has not become a friend, as the French, nor a cousin, as the English; it has become a partner only, but in that role it is determined to be more important than anyone else. This relationship represents the synthesis between the two countries; it constitutes what today is considered normal.

Few understood and described this change in the geopolitical environment better than Zbigniew Brzezinski, a native of Poland who later served as security adviser (1977–1981) to President Jimmy Carter. "Germany's reunification," Brzezinski writes in his book *The Grand Chess-board* (Basic Books, 1998), "dramatically changed the real parameters of European politics. It was simultaneously a geopolitical defeat for Russia and for France."

Germany, Brzezinski maintains, has become a major European power and, in some respects, again a world power. It may seem hard to believe, but, as Brzezinski argues, Germany now serves as America's democratic bridge to the Eurasian continent. These are strong words. Too strong, really, for this book, though they precisely illuminate the political backdrop for the psychological bond that developed between the two countries and that now serves someone like Schrempp so well.

At the same time, Brzezinski provides the political explanation for how globalization came about; what's more, he analyzes lucidly the United States' future concerns. Brzezinski views the Federal Republic, with its key position in the united Europe, as a critical mass enabling America to successfully maintain its role as a superpower, however that role may be played. He sees Germany's part in this in an entirely positive light.

If Brzezinski is right, the United States will do favors for Germany in return—which gives the heads of German companies a great deal more room to operate than they could have ever gained for themselves during the first five decades after the Nazi era. Jürgen Schrempp, doubtless unfamiliar with Brzezinski's analysis, was the first to take full advantage of this new constellation. He neither wasted any time nor did he start a moment too soon; simply, his timing was perfect. Had he acted only months sooner, the American public probably would not have accepted quite so readily the takeover of its third-largest auto company by an even more reputable German car manufacturer. Subsequently, when Deutsche Bank took over Bankers Trust a short while later, the event did not create so much as a stir.

Really, though, who could protest, since apart from an embargo, the United States had no other option, specifically none involving Japan. Mergers such as Daimler-Nissan or Toyota-Chrysler may have looked promising just a few years ago, but whether they also would have been realistic is a different matter. Both Daimler-Benz and Chrysler already had experience with Japan—both of them, incidentally, with set pieces of the widely ramified Mitsubishi Corporation. But that was now history.

Today, Jürgen Schrempp, the trendsetter, is able to point out the stringent logic behind the DaimlerChrysler merger. There is virtually no overlap in the two companies' lines of business, so no part of production needs to be eliminated. This merger was close, bipolar, and dramatic—simply put, sensational. In addition, it makes it easier for all European—especially all German—companies to follow in Daimler's footsteps. And so mergermania (which originated in the United States) has only just begun. There will doubtless be new surprises—perhaps not quite as smooth and perfect, but comparable in size.

Needless to say, the mere hunger for size alone is not the only reason for these mergers and acquisitions (M&As). Part of it is also the need to play the traditional game of being present in other markets. But now the markets are bigger; in some cases, the whole world is the market. And where money is to be invested, you usually find sources of capital. Combining all the advantages of these various sources alone can be a major incentive for megamergers. It doesn't take a visionary to realize that the core region for movements of this kind, certainly in the not-too-distant future, will be North America and Europe.

At least psychologically, a generational issue also factors into this current German-American trend. The new generation of German managers—those between 45 and 55 years of age—clearly has grown up much more on Anglicisms, American management models, and private travels to the United States than have their predecessors. The "new Germans" typically speak English with only a slight accent. The corporate language of a German-American company can switch to English without much difficulty—which is a great convenience.

Another important difference between the generations is that the new Germans are less self-conscious of Germany's more recent history because they were not yet born during the reign of the Nazis; and in many cases, their parents were too young to be held responsible for involvement in it. The new generation knows neither the victims nor the perpetrators. Neither does it have to suppress anything: It can simply pass judgment. This also makes them more understanding when it comes to Nazi victims' financial demands made against their own companies.

Finally, the new generation of managers understands better than their emotionally charged predecessors that the point is no longer to answer for guilt, real or perceived; the focus is on identity and image of

the company—in other words, a tangible value in the international competition. This value is linked to the name of the company they represent,
even though the company may no longer necessarily be the direct legal
successor of the company carrying that name during the Nazi years.

Thus, Volkswagen (VW) has long since ceased to be the company of
the "strength-through-joy" car; Deutsche Bank is no longer the sponsor
of a repressive regime; and Lufthansa is no longer a cover organization
for the clandestine education of air force pilots. Between then and now,
there were years in which Lufthansa and Deutsche Bank didn't exist at
all and in which VW was owned by the British occupation forces. The
companies' names, however, didn't disappear; they returned, or were
resurrected, for well-considered reasons. There is a die-hard value connected with them that can't simply be separated from the past. Managers
like Schrempp, von Pierer, Schulte-Noelle (Allianz), and Middelhoff
(Bertelsmann) are in a position to see these things in their proper perspective, much more so than their predecessors and their predecessors'
predecessors.

Most German companies now setting sail in the direction of America
have troubled pasts. The larger and more important they were then, the
more it is assumed they were involved in the corporate system of the
Nazi regime. Not that this necessarily happened against their business
interests. Only companies such as Hamburg's Otto Versand—the world's
leading mail-order business founded after the war—do not have to carry
the burden of the past. The founder of that company, Werner Otto, had
been incarcerated by the Nazis for several years for his opposition to the
regime. Today's media conglomerate Bertelsmann, on the other hand,
was too insignificant at the time to have played a major role in the Hitler
movement. Yet it did align itself with the Nazis.

Now, more than half a century later, it is essentially the same companies that form the inner circle of Deutschland AG. Again it is their sheer
weight and power that drive companies like Daimler-Benz, Deutsche
Bank, Allianz, Siemens, Bayer, BASF, Hoechst, Lufthansa, Thyssen,
Mannesmann, Volkswagen, and BMW in the same direction, gathering
like lemmings to seek their ultimate union with Corporate America.

They are indeed a flock of lemmings, for they are not following some
grand design. Rather, they seem to be driven by inner necessity and, no
doubt, are propelled by fear of what the future might bring. Mergers and
acquisitions remain a tricky business, especially with American compa-

nies. Difficulties begin with financing. Those companies that have invested in the United States, such as Bertelsmann or Hoechst, have paid in a good German manner, with real money—that is to say, cash. The same goes for Deutsche Bank's takeover of Bankers Trust. Daimler-Chrysler was the first German-American megamerger that was transacted with the much more convenient payment method of stocks.

Stocks are Wall Street's tools, used to finance hundreds of American mergers and acquisitions, either by paying stockholders who already hold stocks in the takeover company or by trading stocks. Ideally, no cash is involved in these transactions aside from commissions paid to brokers and lawyers. The parties involved do not have to spend cash. But in the pre-DaimlerChrysler era, no German corporation that wanted to take over an American company was able to use its own stocks as a currency. It simply wouldn't have worked—because of Wall Street.

It is a fact of life that, until now, stock in German corporations has been valued far too low and that in American companies usually too high. This discrepancy is due, on the one hand, to the differences in social security and fringe benefits offered by European companies and, on the other, to America's rigorously capitalist entrepreneurial culture. In other words, until recently, the inner stability of European—specifically, German—firms has been ignored; when the value of that stability was acknowledged at all, it was as a social, but certainly not an economic value. Conversely, the rigorous capitalism of an American company, with all of its concomitant intrinsic instability, has been glorified.

In terms of numbers, this means that on the stock market, a European company's return on revenue is posted as lower than that of an American company, and that the market rate is still lower in relation to profit. Double jeopardy for German companies, so to speak. Because market rates determine a company's net worth, Europeans are doomed to do miserably when a merger is financed through stocks. Experts such as Hermann Simon can cite examples that are simply grotesque. On September 23, 1998, for instance—a day chosen at random—the Siemens corporation was worth 54.4 billion deutsche marks on the stock market according to the criteria, yet the U.S. company General Electric—by no means a bigger company—$441.8 billion. "If the two companies merged on this basis," Simon stated in *Manager Magazine,* "going strictly by numbers, current Siemens shareholders would get less than 11 percent of the new company GE Siemens. That's a joke."

Or take Bill Gates's Microsoft. While its turnover was only one-fifth that of Siemens, on the stock market it was worth eight and a half times as much as the German electrical company. The market value of BASF, Bayer, and Hoechst—the German chemical industry's Big Three—is fluctuating somewhere between 40 and 50 billion deutsche marks, while the much smaller U.S. pharmaceuticals company Merck is worth a whopping $288 billion.

Only the German auto industry could compare to its American competitors on the stock market—and only because German automobile shares were unusually high in 1998 and America's were particularly low at the same time. In this respect, too, circumstances worked in Daimler-Benz's favor. What was really significant, however, was that, since 1993, Daimler's stocks have been posted on the New York Stock Exchange alongside those of Chrysler. Thus, both companies have been assessed according to the same criteria.

It was Schrempp's much-maligned predecessor, Edzard Reuter, who introduced Daimler-Benz's shares on Wall Street, Germany's only stocks there at the time. This one move made up (almost) for Reuter's numerous blunders as a manager, which ultimately earned him the reputation as the worst squanderer of capital in the history of German corporations. Schrempp got all the credit for this brilliant maneuver. In all fairness, it is necessary to add that Schrempp's shareholder-values campaign was a tremendous boost to Daimler-Benz's market value and return on revenue. Both soared so high that, in the end, Schrempp's company was worth more than Chrysler on the stock exchange.

With this feat, Schrempp managed to eliminate for Daimler-Benz what constitutes any German company's worst handicap in the international game: the relatively low return on revenue. Those hopeful for future German-American megadeals still have some preliminary work to do, however. In 1997, for instance, Siemens just managed to get a 2.4 percent return on revenue, whereas General Electric got 9 percent. As already mentioned, Schrempp set the target at a straight 12 percent. The targets of modernized corporations such as Mannesmann are even higher (and, incidentally, are often met thanks to U.S. subsidiaries). Month after month, and very discreetly, Mannesmann as well as Krupp/Thyssen buy small but nicely profitable companies abroad, particularly in the United States. To avoid culture shock, they keep them on a long leash.

This represents another obstacle for progress-oriented strategist Jürgen Schrempp. He cannot keep DaimlerChysler on a long leash—which, incidentally, wouldn't be in keeping with his personality anyway. Instead, he has to streamline the new dinosaur. And finalizing a merger legally is not all there is to be done, even though the experts on the scene—the investment bankers—routinely leave the place of action as soon as that has been accomplished; once the legal finishing touches have been made, they're done with their job. But it is precisely at that point that the company's managers, suddenly abandoned, need serious, in-depth advice. After all, that is when newly enlarged, merged companies such as DaimlerChrysler really start growing together. Management is confronted with an overwhelmingly chaotic situation. During mergers, all participants are again and again forced to acknowledge that one plus one never exactly equals two. It might equal one and a half or even less, such as when the aerospace company Boeing took over the weapons manufacturer McDonnell Douglas, or when auto manufacturer BMW acquired its competitor Rover. On the other hand, it might equal three, as with the loose alliance between Lufthansa and United Airlines. The reason for this mathematical disparity can be accounted for by the difference in corporate cultures.

Though fitting the various assets thrown together during a merger into a comprehensive business plan is an academic exercise in bookkeeping, not even remotely is it a realistic undertaking. Anyone moving in and around the new structures runs into incompatible ways of "how things were always done"—sometimes due to regional or even national habits—ways that are ultimately incomprehensible to the newcomer. The previously computed synergistic effects, which often tipped the scale in favor of the merger, are sometimes quickly canceled out by the costs incurred on account of cultural obstacles on both sides.

The merged company's management has to choose between three different ways of approaching this problem. One, the principle of *laissez-faire,* wherein different cultures compete against one another until they ultimately blend; two, the *department* principle, in which the various divisions of the company that was taken over at first continue to work within their old cultural context; three, the *Stalinist* principle, according to which the stronger partner strictly forces its own culture onto the weaker one. Each principle has a huge potential for mistakes. Since it is almost a law of nature that emotions of jealousy and fear—of being patronized—arise in the new company, the problem is virtually unsolvable without sensitive outside consultation. Ironically, however, many don't want any advice. As "born victors," they prefer passing through this phase like an army.

The question of the cultural bridges that might be built during German-American megamergers is thrilling to ponder. Even though the basic setup seems promising for DaimlerChrysler, that company, too, will have to grapple with some serious internal differences. Let us not forget that, according to many sources, some 70 percent of all mergers don't make good on the promise they initially held. In other words, most of them turn out to be much more complicated and expensive than expected.

American business culture is very different from German business culture, for clearly discernible reasons. America has its shareholder values, and the New York Stock Exchange forces companies to post a profit every three months. Other important factors include the greater mobility of American society and its radically different education and vocational training systems. In Europe—especially in Germany—there are rigorous obligatory training programs, even for mechanics; students must pass them and get a diploma in order to land a well-paid job. A future plumber, carpenter, or electrician has to train as a modestly paid apprentice for three years while attending vocational school before he or she can graduate to become a journeyman or -woman.

Graduation doesn't necessarily translate into getting a job, but once found, a job does guarantee relatively high hourly wages, negotiated and protected by the union. Those who aspire to even higher orders must pass a Meister test, which often requires more academic knowledge than for an American bachelor's degree. Only a Meister certificate entitles someone to open his or her own business in the field of choice. The requirements for technical perfection are so high that journeymen and -women are reluctant to sell their prentice work, and more so their Meister pieces—even when they would earn top prices on the free market. If sold, such pieces by German carpenters are so exquisite that they would fall in the price range only someone like Bill Gates could afford.

For employees in trade companies, banks, and insurance companies, training lasts almost as long as that for mechanics. They, too, need a diploma to get a job. For this reason, it's very difficult for German managers to get used to the American principles of "hire and fire" and "learn by doing." Germans value constancy and professional competence. They are used to employees staying with the same company for many years— sometimes even in the same position for several decades. With the exception of postgraduates, managers, people in the military, top-ranking civil servants, and social climbers, a German with a job, no matter how cosmopolitan he or she may want to appear, would rarely consider relocating for a job.

On the other hand, because training for Germans in their respective fields is so rounded, they understand precisely what's going on in other departments of a large company, what the boss is doing, and what the company's profit and loss calculations are. This applies even to industrial workers, who also often undergo vocational training. Take the job of aircraft mechanic, for example. For a high-tech company such as Airbus, the thought of untrained or informally trained mechanics working in its highly sophisticated airplane production department is anathema. Such workers probably would not be allowed to count screws there. At competitor Boeing's plant, on the other hand, on-the-job training now is standard. New employees need only to watch an experienced worker long enough to learn by doing before taking over his or her job. In terms of quality, the results of the two methods differ much less than the methods themselves would suggest, yet they constitute different approaches between the two cultures.

Thus, assimilating European and American companies successfully is a time-consuming and costly process. German buyers have often seriously underestimated costs of purchasing American companies. After taking over the U.S. supermarket chain A&P, for example, the privately owned Tengelmann chain spent 10 long years pumping millions and millions into the enterprise. Grilled-chicken restaurant chain Wienerwald went bankrupt largely because of its acquisition of American restaurant chains such as International House of Pancakes.

The good fortune of Siemens and Germany's three large chemicals companies in regard to their acquisitions in the New World was likewise limited. A major reason was the casual manner in which they invested in the United States. For instance, they might base their decision to invest on certain advantages that existed only temporarily—say, currency exchange rates that were unrealistically favorable and therefore bound to change very quickly, or the acquisition of technology at what only appeared to be very good terms. Too often, these terms soon turned out to be much less favorable than they appeared. Very rarely were these investments part of a larger business plan. Even if it looked that way, it often proved to be an optical illusion.

As early as the 1970s, under its then-CEO Toni Schmücker, VW had acquired an old Chrysler manufacturing plant in Pennsylvania. That factory's purpose was to produce the U.S. version of the VW Rabbit. VW's managers had the brilliant idea of manufacturing the popular Beetle's successor near its customer base, for the sole reason that the deutsche mark had become prohibitively expensive. Due to the high exchange rate, production costs back home went sky-high, which made it impossible to export the cars at a profit. Therefore, the idea of producing them more inexpensively in the United States seemed to make perfect sense. But the advantage was canceled out when VW's managers decided to produce the Rabbit cheaply not only in terms of cost but also of quality. Rather than offering American car lovers a high-quality product made in Germany, VW surprised its potential customers with a crummy tin box, somehow convinced that this was what people really wanted.

This turned the entire operation into a disaster, and VW is still paying the consequences. With the factory operating at only a fraction of its capacity, VW sold the plant at exactly the point it should have been buying it. The deutsche mark had become so strong that VWs could be imported from Germany only at a significant loss. Soon the cars disappeared almost entirely from the American market. Not even the Beetle produced in VW's Mexican factory could salvage this situation, because the U.S. government had introduced stricter environmental policies and, consequently, it had become impossible to sell the Beetle there. At that time, Honda and Toyota were building large plants in the United States, and their products have since become market leaders in America within their category.

Other German-American companies also resulted from haphazard decisions, or at least decisions that often followed no discernible logic and sometimes seemed to be made in a haze. After the fact, it sometimes looked as though they were the result of grander schemes. This is true even for such industry icons as media giant Bertelsmann and insurance conglomerate Allianz. Even Lufthansa and VW's new managers, whom Ferdinand Piech had gotten to move forward, based their decisions to go global less on careful analyses and more because it seemed prudent from a strategic point of view. Only the airbus industry, which was established for political reasons as a mutually supportive club made up of French, German, English, and Spanish members, was designed from the start as a counterconglomerate. Hefty subsidies vouchsafed its survival during the long incubation period. Only now is it supposed to turn into a real company.

From this early, archaic way of dealing with Corporate America has evolved a sort of typology of Deutschland AG. Distinguished by varying degrees of density, intensity, and hegemony, there are three basic types: Transatlantic World Inc., the Pivot Strategy, and the Global Counter-conglomerate.

Let's look at type one. "World Inc." was the term DaimlerChrysler decided on from the get-go. Ever since, there is no way to circumvent this term, and so we comply, at least in part. But DaimlerChrysler, with its cosmopolitan air, has so far been only a Transatlantic Inc., serving as an umbrella for additional companies expected to be acquired—from the Far East, for example. Other binational companies such as Asea Brown Bovery, Unilever, and Royal Dutch Shell are just as entitled to call themselves World Inc.—as are all members of Big Oil, Exxon, Shell, and the like, when you come right down to it. After all, even the network of Standard Oil founder John D. Rockefeller extended across the entire globe.

To please the teachers of logic as well as DaimlerChrysler, we'll call the new structure *Transatlantic World Inc.* This term is also applicable to the second German-American megamerger, that of Deutsche Bank and Bankers Trust, and to the Bertelsmann conglomerate as well. No doubt the concept of the Transatlantic World Inc., which entails the full integration of forces, best satisfies the need to grow to a size befitting an American company and its interests. However, there can be no doubt that the new partnership cannot grow indefinitely. The above-mentioned snares in financing megadeals can hardly be solved overnight.

A strategy focusing on a company's location is both more popular and logistically easier to accomplish than the formation of entirely self-contained German-American units. It is a strategy whereby German companies are present on the United States' internal market, thus making sure they are among the global players. This can be accomplished via U.S.-based manufacturing plants and/or management offices. These also give companies a certain access to America's more flexible financial market and greater product variety, and they often reduce labor and management-relocation costs as well. In addition, the currency exchange rates tended to favor the dollar, and thus one's investment.

Early on, German chemical companies in particular pursued type two, the *Pivot Strategy*. Sometimes, they simply wished to acquire locations where large-volume production in, say, synthetic materials (Hoechst/Celanese) was cheaper. Other times, the main advantage was that the new location brought the company closer to its customers. On still other occasions, the reasons had to do with advanced strategies—which, one must add, might come in the wake of sheer panic. For instance, being present in the United States could simply mean having access to American R&D in areas of genetic engineering that were considered highly sensitive, if not politically incorrect, back home.

The Pivot Strategy is pursued with great finesse outside the chemical industry as well—for instance, in finance (the insurance company Allianz), publishing (Holtzbrinck), the processing industries (BMW, Mannesmann, Krupp/Thyssen), and commerce (Otto Versand). A number of German firms have already extended their Pivot Strategy to large parts of the world. This qualifies them for our third category, that of the Global Counterconglomerate.

The *Global Counterconglomerate* also has a strong foothold in the United States—perhaps even its strongest one. In this respect, it is also transatlantic. However, its concerns far transcend transatlantic limits, and this places it in dimensions that are not strictly pivot, or German American, but give it a downright universal presence. The Global Counterconglomerate views itself as the European mirror image of the American industry giant. Among German companies, auto conglomerate Volkswagen and electronics giant Siemens belong in this category.

Aside from these standard representatives of the Global Counterconglomerate, there are some more exotic cases. These include major strategic alliances such as Lufthansa's. Then there is the still somewhat nebulous Europa Inc., of which Airbus is a good example. Finally, there are certain producers of specialty products that operate globally, yet at the same time in an almost middle-class sort of way. The best example is Heidelberger Druckmaschinen AG, which is trying to become the world's market leader in the manufacture of printing presses.

In all companies, whether Transatlantic World Inc., Pivotal Strategy, or Global Counterconglomerate, decisions for or against something are closely connected with who is running the company. How closely the character of the top manager and his or her company match one another is really a phenomenon that should intrigue all those interested in social psychology. A company's annual report and press releases would have you believe it is facts, and nothing but facts, that determine the direction in which the company is going. But in practice, it is remarkable how often that decision is determined by chance or, more often, by the top manager's personal disposition, including most certainly his or her ego. Thus, facts become chance and chance becomes the rule.

The same holds true for those companies whose profiles were selected for the following chapters. No doubt there are dozens of other companies that exemplify the desire of German corporations to settle in the United States and the global market. Listing them here would be like trying to put together an encyclopedia—and a useless one at that, as companies are bought and sold every single day. "Every month I get a list of several dozen companies we have purchased," says the head of a foreign branch of Mannesmann, "and most of them are in the United States."

As mentioned, it is surprising the degree to which the character of most conglomerates continues to be molded by their top manager's personality type. Boss and company resemble one another like a dog and its owner. There are, however, exceptions to this rule. The airbus industry, for instance, would not have evolved as it did as a product of some central management with one single leader; and it wouldn't even have been conceivable that way. The reason lies in Airbus being a political entity behind whose facade strong individualities quickly disappear. They exist, but they're barely visible. Still, some stand out—a few of them Germans. Their personalities have broken through the general anonymity in the company.

In comparison, other leading figures of large companies have the image of lone combatants, *very* different from everybody else. And the same can be said for their companies. Ferdinand Piech, for one, is often considered a shark, and his reign as VW's sovereign has been very tough, whereas Lufthansa chief Jürgen Weber cultivates Lufthansa's Star Alliance reliably and methodically, like a son-in-law from a good family. Hoechst's Jürgen Dormann is considered a door knocker sitting in the director's chair—and not just because of his name. Gerhard Cromme of Krupp is the spider in the web of steel, the man who brought the former cannonsmiths together with the significantly more powerful Thyssen corporation and subsequently became the strongman of the merged enterprise.

Rolf E. Breuer of Deutsche Bank has been ever present for years as Mr. Stockmarket in Frankfurt. And since last year, Bertelsmann has been led by the young electronics enthusiast Thomas Middelhoff, a Mr. Spock who would love to have invented the spaceship if it didn't exist already. Jürgen Schrempp is more the contrast of him—not that sophisticated, more the Terminator type. Ten strong egos, three different strategies, and one major target. Enter Deutschland AG: Volkswagen versus Ford; Bertelsmann versus Time Warner; Hoechst versus Merck; Allianz versus Metropolitan Life; Lufthansa versus American Airlines; Airbus versus Boeing; and so forth. The contest is thrilling, intoxicating even.

Let's be clear that nothing like a systematic plan exists for an offensive by Deutschland AG on Corporate America. Virtually nothing in Germany's thrust toward America is reminiscent of Japan's global expeditions in the areas of shipbuilding, electronics, and auto manufacturing—expeditions that were directed by the political powers at the time. The Federal Republic of Germany does not act like a country that follows military concepts or even strategies issued by an imaginary central planning office. A mighty steamroller such as Japan's once-omnipotent MITI would be inconceivable in Germany, and in fact would have been inconceivable since the end of World War II. What makes German managers tick is neither mercantilism nor imperialism; rather, it is a defensive motive, regardless of the fact that pressure is put on American domains more unabashedly than before. Perhaps the Olympic spirit is playing some part here after all, and the whole thing can be seen as a sports event.

The transformation of the typical German industrialist from Mr. Moneybags to Citizen of the World will not only change the structures of Germany's society of consensus as we know it; it also implies the liberation of the large companies themselves from the tough but secure grip of the politburo of Germany's economic culture. Everyone is familiar with that culture; it is firmly established, and it is self-contained, even incestuous, so to speak. It will not simply disappear at the drop of a hat, for many potentates from the world of economics are enmeshed in it. The top of the pyramid consists of a few large financial institutions, most notably Deutsche Bank, the insurance conglomerate Allianz-Versicherung, and the the reinsurance firm Münchner Rückversicherung. Surely the names of these institutions alone couldn't conceivably exude a greater sense of security.

These institutions are connected not only through shared holdings; their closest circle consists of some 50 companies and 200 top managers. With few exceptions, the companies in this elite club are owned either directly or indirectly by the financial institutions just mentioned, which have always been joined by the second most important group, made up of the Dresdner Bank, the Commerzbank, the HypoVereinsbank, and the Westdeutsche Landesbank. Corporations and financial institutions have been intertwined to such a degree that they have been able to fend off any outside attack and regulate any internal disaster. Financially, self-regulation was made possible through mutual shared holdings, or because the large banks had an oligopoly in loans that was, in fact, a monopoly. In terms of human resources, it was accomplished through labor representatives who served as board members of this closed society.

This power structure has been fortified by the banks' exercising their right to vote by proxy, which is always certain to give them a majority at a shareholders' meeting (which by law is called a *general meeting*). This enables the network of banks to wield all the power in stock corporations in which the banks themselves don't own a single share. Needless to say, whenever necessary, via recommendations through their employees, banks can also influence the fate of stocks that are interesting to them. What is done separately in the United States by investment and commercial banks—and usually separated by geographic region—is all done on a national scale in Germany by its universal banks.

This was—and in part still is—the classic Deutschland AG, where nothing could go wrong, even when everything did go wrong. It was in keeping with its gilded self-image that the company wasn't very active beyond Germany's borders. Therefore, the opening of the global market is bound to diminish its influence. For financial operations, global companies such as Schrempp/Eaton's DaimlerChrysler AG, in which Deutsche Bank has a good 12.7 percent share, will probably use their international resources. Conglomerates that want to acquire other companies will only rarely do this via Germany's present banking system, opting instead to use Wall Street's investment banks. This puts considerable competitive pressure on Germany's universal bank, which has to embrace the outside world, cultivate contact with its shareholders, and streamline its business. Sitting on its share of holdings and acting like Deutschland AG's director of human resources is not part of its job description.

Now Deutschland AG is turning into Germany Inc. It is no longer aiming at the old, firmly established home base, but at the United States. To repeat, it is *aiming* at it, not combating it. Germany goes West.

Part II

TRANSATLANTIC WORLD INC.

CHAPTER 2

Case One: The Trident and the Terminator

Daimler-Benz

AMONG THE INTERNATIONAL LEAGUE of large companies, few are as steeped in glory as Daimler-Benz AG, based in Germany's high-tech capital, the southwestern town of Stuttgart. Both Gottlieb Daimler and Carl Benz, who invented the automobile, had their names in the company's logo, which arguably is today one of the most recognized worldwide. The Mercedes trident, the star, and Daimler-Benz came to be regarded as Germany's semiofficial national emblem.

From Hindenburg to Kohl—and including Adolf Hitler—the "big Mercedes" has been unchallenged as Germany's "state carriage." Vintage car buffs, in fact, refer to the Mercedes 300 from the 1950s as the "Adenauer," testimony to its famous early advocate. Konrad Adenauer, the first German chancellor, had complained that standard sedans did not provide enough room for him to stretch out his long legs. The Daimler-Benz line included an elongated model, and Adenauer ordered it, thereby setting a trend. To this day, when Germans want to impress, they drive a Mercedes. And the trend spread beyond Germany: Popes, industry magnates, athletes, Communist dictators such as Tito and Ceauşescu, and ostentatious third-world potentates have preferred to be chauffeured in a Mercedes.

It was not until the fall of 1998 that a German chancellor chose an Audi over a Mercedes. By that time, however, the manufacturer of the state carriage no longer went by the name of Daimler-Benz but Daimler-Chrysler. This is not to say that the two facts were causally connected, but it seems an odd coincidence. Clearly, Jürgen Schrempp, the great taskmaster, would have to watch out.

Daimler-Benz became adept at cultivating its image long before marketers thought in such terms. The company's Swabian home base has always focused on stability: stability through reliable and solid technology, shining car bodies, and—very important during the pioneer days—winning performances on the world's racetracks. Though frequently opposed, Jürgen Schrempp ultimately has prevailed. No matter what disrupted the company as the world changed around it, Jürgen Schrempp has maintained an innate sense of being at home with "Daimler's traditions."

That is something even the staunchest Swabian must admit, if reluctantly. Reluctantly, because Jürgen Schrempp is from the "wrong" side of the Mercedes' state of Baden-Württemberg. He is not from Württemberg, where Stuttgart, Swabia's capital, is located, but from Freiburg, in Baden, the capital of Alemannia. (The French and Spanish words for Germany—*Allemagne, Allemania*—derive from this name.) The two regions are like water and wine. The Baden influence has doubtless contributed to the car manufacturer's inventiveness, for like Baden-Württemberg, Daimler-Benz is a Swabian-Alemannian company. That was its identity from the beginning, arising from the birthplaces of the two men who gave the company its name. Gottlieb Daimler, the older of the two (1834–1900), a Swabian, was born in Schorndorf, Württemberg, and lived around Stuttgart most of his life. Carl Benz (1844–1929), on the other hand, was from Ladenburg, near Mannheim, on the Rhine.

Benz was only 35 years old when, on New Year's Eve 1879, he successfully started a two-stroke engine he had built himself. Three years later, he launched Benz & Cie. Rheinische Gasmotoren-Fabrik, a company whose official purpose was to build stationary internal-combustion engines. But what Benz was really after was to develop an engine-driven street vehicle for the public. In 1885, he attached a one-cylinder, four-stroke engine to a cart. It featured only three wheels. Axle-pivot steering for four-wheel vehicles would come later. By mid-1886, he was motoring that runabout through Mannheim's bumpy streets. Built as a motor vehicle, with a battery and a spark plug, it bore a remarkable resemblance to the automobile as we know it today, even minus the fourth wheel.

As early as 1888, Bertha Benz, the young entrepreneur's wife, dared take her children on a 110-mile ride from Mannheim to Pforzheim in the vehicle. And in spite of some mishaps, she safely negotiated her way along the road, which wound across mountainous terrain. In 1893, Benz added a fourth wheel and unveiled his Victoria, which in addition to the new axle-pivot steering also had a carburetor with a float and a two-gear transmission.

Benz focused not on speed, but on perfecting, refining, and simplifying his machine. His plan was to build a wide variety of different bodies for his cars. "Rather than participating in races that won't give me valuable experience, but do damage instead," he stated, "we will continue to focus on turning out solid and reliable touring cars."

Benz maintained that 30 miles per hour should be the top speed for automobiles, or else streets would have to be constructed specifically for cars. As early as 1899, the company had produced a 5.4-liter four-cylinder car with a 20-horsepower engine, which managed an average speed of up to 29.83 miles per hour—just short of the 30-mph ceiling Benz had established.

He was right, but what he failed to see was that these streets would indeed be built. Unintentionally, Benz started the biggest revolution in human society since Gutenberg rolled pages off his printing press.

The younger generation of Benzes, Carl's sons Eugen and Richard, did not share their father's views on the speed limit, and under their influence, by 1909, the Blitzen-Benz had a 200-horsepower engine and was able to do 125 mph.

But Papa Benz stuck to his philosophy of making cars that were practical. By 1902, he had sold no fewer than 1,200 of his four-wheeled Velos at 2,000 marks apiece. The Velo was the first true car "brand," and Benz was Germany's Henry Ford. The difference was that no one noticed, because at the time there was no market in Europe for mass-produced cars. Only the nobility, the merchant class, the financial aristocracy, and, most important, the imperial family, were interested in the automobile. In 1907, there were a measly 1,000 "fuel distribution places," and only one car per 2,300 people. Six years later, in 1913, only 17,162 cars had been built in Germany, compared to 491,500 (half of which were produced by Ford) in the United States. In Europe, driving a car remained a sport for the wealthy, who now wanted to race on wheels rather than on horses. Gottlieb Daimler extended that trend.

Daimler was much less spirited than Carl Benz. He did, however, have a more impressive resume. He had worked with Wilhelm Maybach (1846–1929)—arguably the most eminent auto engineer of his time—as early as 1869. He had also collaborated with Nikolas A. Otto (1832–1891), the inventor of the four-stroke engine (1861) that is still used today. In 1864, together with Eugen Langen (1833–1895), Otto founded N.A. Otto & Cie., which later became Gasmotorenfabrik Deutz. Otto sold 35,000 four-stroke engines relatively quickly. Between 1872 and 1882, Daimler was technical director at Otto. In 1882, he and Maybach founded their own factory in Cannstadt, near Stuttgart. The first four-stroke engine with self-ignition was built there, followed in 1885 by the first gasoline engine.

The two used their early gasoline engines on a bicycle—perhaps the world's first motorcycle. In 1885, Daimler rode one of the wooden "motorcycles" from Cannstadt to Untertürkheim. In 1886, the first Daimler "car" hit the streets, and was driven from Cannstadt to Esslingen. It was more like a horse-drawn carriage without the horse, built for Daimler by the royal court supplier W. Wimpff & Sons in Württemberg. The Swabian inventor finally founded his company, Daimler-Motoren-Gesellschaft, in 1890 at Cannstadt. Its original purpose was to build engines for cars, railcars, boats, and industrial installations. As suppliers to the French car manufacturer Panhard & Lavassor, Daimler and Maybach dealt with all the hotshots of the auto industry, who during those years were primarily French engineers, the industry leaders. In fact, German companies such as Benz would employ French design engineers in top positions for years to come.

French connections notwithstanding, Daimler remained staunchly German. Under Wilhelm Maybach as technical director, the Cannstadt firm soon began producing its own automobiles. Initially, production was slow. Technologically speaking, it did not become more sophisticated—in other words, faster—until 1896, when the Austrian businessman Emil Jellinek read a newspaper advertisement by Daimler-Motoren-Gesellschaft (DMG). As honorary consul and general agent of a French insurance company, Jellinek was not only rich but also had a wealthy clientele, which is why he was often seen in the popular European spas of his day, such as Nice or Baden, near Vienna. After seeing the ad, the 43-year-old traveled to Cannstadt to order a Daimler Doppel-Phaeton with a 6-horsepower engine.

The Doppel-Phaeton was a solid car, but it could go only 15 miles per hour. So one year later, Jellinek ordered four more Daimlers, but requested they be able to reach 25 mph. Maybach complied by using the company's standard two-stroke rear engine. Jellinek, however, had his own ideas; he believed a four-stroke front engine would be much more efficient, so he ordered six of those. Maybach gave him a 24-horsepower engine with a four-stroke cylinder, but because it was so large, it consequently gained him nothing more than notoriety.

Jellinek continued to up the ante. He now wanted a race car, pure and simple. Daimler's response to that request, the Phönix, bombed. Gottlieb Daimler didn't live to see the failure. On March 6, 1900, shortly before the Phönix was tested on the road, he passed away. In the aftermath, Jellinek became a kind of general agent for Daimler vehicles, a position he accepted with the stipulation that "a new engine shall be built by the name of Daimler-Mercedes." Mercedes was the name of one of his daughters. And so an international brand name was born. Jellinek requested that the first Mercedes be much lower and wider than its predecessor and have at least a 35-horsepower engine.

The future of the automobile corroborated that Jellinek, an outsider, had a good instinct for the physics of fast cars, and he gave the company its technological direction. He immediately strengthened his position by ordering 36 new cars—which in the early twentieth century was an extraordinarily large order.

Jellinek's next car had a top speed of 54 miles per hour, and it won first place in all categories during an event in Nice, though in more important races it failed to win any first prizes. In 1903, the triumvirate of Daimler-Maybach-Jellinek introduced a race car with a 60-horsepower engine that could go almost 75 miles per hour. In the hands of Belgian driver Camille Jenatzy, it immediately won the prestigious Gordon Bennett Cup, named after the editor of the daily *New York Herald*.

Even though race car drivers had to finance the sport themselves in those days, auto manufacturers began to pay closer attention to car races. Later, the Daimler-Benz AG reputation would develop within the triangle of racing, wealth, and influential people. Daimler-Benz would turn high-quality cars into an integral part of contemporary culture. What Benz and Daimler created eventually caused an upheaval they could not have foreseen. More immediately, they had invented most of the automobile's basic technology in their own factories. What's more, they had a keen sense of how to market a brand name. In this effort, they had help, and from the highest circles. Kaiser Wilhelm II, for one, had a passion for research, development, and technology; specifically, he was a car aficionado.

With a car buff leading the empire, the industrialists' hunger for new speed records became insatiable. At first, this pushed the development of the European automobile into a very narrow direction. The public was not able to enjoy this new product of modern technology. In Munich, former home of the Wittelsbach dynasty, the Royal Bavarian Police Department decreed that no more than 25 motorcars would be allowed in the city. Of course, your regular burgher wouldn't have been able to afford such a handmade and expensive toy. And no one in Germany was even trying to make the automobile cheaper by mass-producing it the way Henry Ford was doing in the United States. The price for a Benz with a 5-horsepower engine that could go 15 to 20 miles per hour was 4,500 to 6,000 marks. In sharp contrast, an industrial worker's hourly wage was 50 pfennig (half a mark).

Consequently, even the firm of Carl Benz, who was so averse to racing, entered the contest, feeding the wealthy's hunger for faster cars. From 1903 on, the French designers Merino Barbarou and, later, Louis de Groulart developed fast touring cars for Carl Benz to compete against Daimler. At Daimler, Paul Daimler, the founder's son, replaced technical director Wilhelm Maybach, who had done such great service to the company. The younger Daimler subsequently astonished the experts by producing faster and faster cars. In 1910, red-bearded Belgium Jenatzky drove a 17.4-liter Mercedes in Ostende at an unheard-of 107 mph. Then came the Blitzen-Benz from Mannheim.

Within the world of automobiles, the Blitzen-Benz was a sensation comparable to the aerospace industry's space shuttle 70 years later. Propelled by a 21.5-liter, 200-horsepower engine, on March 16, 1910, the slender car with a weight of more than one and a half tons reached a speed of 131.71 mph after a flying start. On April 11, 1911, on the track in Daytona, Florida, American Robert Burman drove at a speed of 141.35 mph for over one mile. The Blitzen-Benz record speed was between 150 and 155 mph, stupendously fast for those days. (Even 90 years later, the Mercedes-Benz S-600 doesn't exceed the speed of that Blitzen-Benz.)

For many years this wonder car remained the fastest means of transportation in the world. In 1910, it was three times faster than the fastest airplane; and though train technology was highly sophisticated, even the speediest rail vehicles, at 130 mph, could not keep up with it. Nowhere was it more popular than in the United States, where its name, Blitzen—German for "lightning"—originated. Record-holder Bob Burman, a former test driver for Buick—along with racing fans—didn't want see the end of the 200-horsepower Benz, the star of the race car circuit. From 1912 to 1916, Burman drove a modified Lightning-Benz he called Jumbo-Benz, until his fatal car accident in 1916 (in a Peugeot). His Jumbo-Benz was taken over by Ralph "Pappy" Hankinson to use in his dirt track group. It was disassembled at the end of 1917 by some carnival group, never to be seen again.

In 1922, a Blitzen-Benz won the difficult Semmering race in Austria, but its fame had begun to pale. That same year, the Daimler-Motoren-Gesellschaft rang in the era of the compressor car. It was also the era of Rudolf Caracciola, a Rhinelander who was arguably the best race car driver of all time. Between 1922 and 1924, when Caracciola won his first races in a Mercedes compressor car with only a 1.5-cubic-liter engine, the new German republic had gone through its infamous hyperinflation, at the end of which a citizen needed 4,000 billion marks to obtain a single dollar. Banknotes were shipped by the truckload to stores, restaurants, and payroll departments. Wages were paid twice a day, because money lost its value by the minute. The London *Daily Mail*'s Berlin correspondent reported on July 22, 1923, "I was surprised to realize that a ham sandwich was 24,000 marks when the previous day it had been only 14,000 marks in the same café."

Under such conditions, the auto industry could neither expand its product line nor improve production. Those who wanted to buy cars were dependent on foreign currency, and those who wanted to make money on cars had to export them. Still, business was not dead. There were some genuine luminaries in the financial world who made good investments with money that was soon devalued. Berlin financier Jakob Schapiro, for one, became Benz & Cie. AG's largest shareholder, owning 42.3 percent of the company's stocks. Subsequently, 30 percent of all Benz cars had their bodies produced at Schapiro's Berlin factory, Schebera AG. At Daimler, a significant shift in personnel took place in 1923: Paul Daimler, the founder's son and head technician, moved on to the Horch plants in Saxony. His successor at Daimler was Ferdinand Porsche, until then Austro-Daimler's CEO. Porsche's entrance marked the beginning of yet another era.

Market experts believed that both Daimler and Benz were close to bankruptcy. As early as February 1924, the management and supervisory boards of both companies received a letter from Carl Jahr, a member of the board of Mannheim's Rheinische Creditbank, suggesting that the two companies merge. Deutsche Bank's director, Emil Georg von Stauss, even envisioned uniting the entire field into a single national auto corporation, comparable to what had been done in the chemical industry. This did not come to pass, however. On May 1, 1924, Daimler and Benz signed a pooling agreement, and soon thereafter expanded their supervisory board to the size of two soccer teams. (Deutsche Bank had major holdings in Daimler even then, while Schapiro owned 60 percent of Benz shares at that time.)

The following year, Daimler and Benz presented trucks at the German Auto Show in Berlin under the new brand name Mercedes-Benz. Finally, on June 28, 1926, the two companies' annual meetings approved a contract, merging the two companies into Daimler-Benz AG with headquarters in Berlin. The company was financed by the Daimler-Motorengesellschaft AG (joint stock value: 36 million reichsmarks). Deutsche Bank became the principal stockholder, whereas the Schapiro group gradually withdrew from the merged company during the next few years. The new firm's top management was consolidated in Stuttgart-Untertürkheim. Coincidentally, around the same time—in 1925—Walter Chrysler founded the Chrysler Motors Corporation in the United States.

At the next auto show in Berlin, Daimler-Benz exhibited new passenger cars under the names of Stuttgart and Mannheim. Priced at half the cost of the luxury models 400 and 630, these cars targeted members of the upper middle class. The company also offered the K model, which at the time was the fastest touring car in the world. This series delineated the basic program of Mercedes cars for decades to come: At the top of the scale were luxury sports models, whose technological parents were the upper-class prestige cars. Below that were two smaller and cheaper series of models for a more down-to-earth audience. In the language of cubic capacity of cylinders this meant 2, 3, 4, and 6.3 liters. (Sounds familiar, doesn't it?)

Despite its racy K model, after the merger, Daimler-Benz eased off its emphasis on car racing. Not even a man as obsessed as Ferdinand Porsche, who had taken over as the person in charge of technology and development at Daimler-Benz, could change that. Papa Benz had his revenge—albeit belated. "Considering the financial strength of their former company, the members of Benz's supervisory board had less power with the new top management," wrote automobile historian K. B. Hipfinger in a Daimler-Benz brochure, "but still, they could torpedo every proposal of the Mercedes people. Actually, it was the Benz managers who successfully prevented the production of race cars prior to 1934."

Probably, it was more the Great Depression that sabotaged the production of race cars after 1929. In the meantime, Daimler-Benz had again become so weak that BMW figured it had a chance of investing in the Stuttgart firm. But no later than 1933, the racing aficionados at Daimler sensed that their second chance had come. Adolf Hitler, the new man in the chancellor's office, was even more of a car buff than Kaiser Wilhelm had been. No company profited more from this than Daimler-Benz AG.

The self-titled führer did not have a driver's license (*Führerschein* in German), but he found riding in a car intoxicating, particularly when the car was a Mercedes: ". . . in a compressor-engine car, we made 95 mph," he once gushed enthusiastically to Albert Speer, his chief architect and, later, minister of armament. "How much fun we had when we passed the big American cars! We always stayed close behind them, until they tried to shake us off. These American cars are junk compared to a Mercedes" (Albert Speer: *Erinnerungen*, Ullstein, 1969).

Hitler's Mercedes mania dated back to his years in Munich, before his failed Beer Hall Putsch of 1923 landed him in the fortress of Landsberg. When his confinement was over, Hitler was picked up by his triumphant vassals in a rented Mercedes. Rumor has it that Jakob Werlin of Munich's Mercedes branch was behind the wheel. Later, after Hitler's party had collected both money and votes, the big, black, open Mercedes cabriolet was never missing when the führer appeared in public places. After he came to power, photographs of Hitler in a Mercedes appeared on millions of propaganda leaflets.

Other highlights of free publicity for Mercedes were Hitler's convoys to the Reich Chancellery in Berlin and to the openings of sections of the autobahn, where he was always accompanied by legions of cars. Only rarely was a Horch among them, which at the time was the more elegant car. Daimler-Benz returned the favor by using major Nazi events as an opportunity to publish huge ads that expressed the company's devotion to Hitler. One ad read, "We are serving the nation." Notably, the Mercedes star pictured in the ad was just a tad larger than the swastika.

Hitler's phrase "big American cars" was a reference to the fact that in 1928, 35.5 percent of the 124,000 newly licensed cars in Germany had been produced by foreign companies. Most American auto manufacturers had built German production plants during the 1920s: General Motors, Ford, Chrysler, Hudson-Essex, and Willys Overland in Berlin, and Durant and Studebaker in Hamburg. In the fall of 1929, General Motors had taken over Adam Opel AG, which had been the unchallenged market leader in Germany, producing 44 percent of all cars. One year later, Ford began building its own plants in Cologne. The auto industry had undergone a distinct consolidation period: In 1924, 86 percent of German companies produced 146 different types of automobiles; in 1929, there were only 17 companies and 34 automobile types. Daimler-Benz climbed toward the top, and stayed there.

The least-expensive Mercedes, which had a 2-liter, 6-cylinder, 38-horsepower engine, was priced at 6,000 marks at that time; the most expensive one, an SS cabriolet with a 240-horsepower engine, cost some 44,000 marks. The cheapest Opel, on the other hand, was priced at around 2,500 marks; and Hanomag's pontoon-shaped two-seater with a rear engine cost less than 2,000 marks. As the supplier of 9.2 percent of newly licensed cars in Germany in 1930, Daimler-Benz was in fifth place. With its 19.8 percent share of the combined value of cars, it was number two, behind Opel. Then, in 1932, the auto industry again changed drastically.

In Bremen, a small company by the name of Borgward & Tecklenborg acquired the larger Hansa-Lloyd plants, a deal that laid the foundation of the Borgward Corporation—which today is where DaimlerChrysler's sports cars and C-class cars are manufactured. In Saxony, two companies, Horch and Audi, both founded by August Horch, merged with Zschopauer Motorenwerke (DKW cars and motorbikes); along with Wanderer-Werke AG's auto departments, this became Auto Union AG. Later, the four rings in its logo would decorate only the Audi grille, but initially they stood for the four brands of Horch, Audi, Wanderer, and DKW.

The smallest DKW (front-wheel drive, synthetic plywood body, and two-stroke engine) cost only 1,685 marks. Though unconventional, the car became a huge success. The largest Auto Union vehicle, a 6-liter, 12-cylinder Horch, cost 22,500 marks. In terms of design elegance, the Saxon vehicles were soon regarded as superior to their German competitors. Furthermore, from the viewpoint of their competitors, it took the Saxons disconcertingly little time to start manufacturing race cars. Mercedes people in particular were perturbed, as behind it all was none other than Ferdinand Porsche, who had left Daimler-Benz in 1928 in a fit of anger. Now he ran his own design company, Dr.ing. Ferdinand Porsche GmbH. Even before the Auto Union was founded, Porsche had designed an elegant 2-liter Wanderer that would have fit perfectly into Auto Union program.

Porsche, who was known for his quick temper, had spent five and a half rocky years at Daimler and Daimler-Benz, often in contention with his colleagues on the board of directors under Wilhelm Kissel's chairmanship. While there, the fairly large cars that Porsche developed were marked by a somewhat stiff elegance, and their success on the market was limited, so his attempts to produce smaller vehicles were blocked by the other members of the board. After Auto Union was founded, they may have come to regret their resistance. But at least they were consistent: Mercedes was intended to be in a league of its own, so it was important that its designers create models that, in technological terms, intersected in terms of luxury, touring, and racing—like the cars in the previously mentioned K series and their offshoots.

On July 11, 1926, 24-year-old Rudolf Caracciola won the Grand Prize of Germany, driving a 2-liter compressor racing car, setting a new lap record on a wet track. From 1927 on, things developed exponentially. The giant compressor cars (6.8 or 7.1 liters, respectively) designated S (for Sport), SS (for Super-Sport), SSK (for Super-Sport-Kurzchassis—short chassis), and SSKL (for Super-Sport-Kurzchassis-Leichtbau—lightweight construction) had been developed by Porsche. Caracciola won one trophy after another with the SSK, especially in flatland races. In 1932, he was joined by a second star, Hans Stuck, who turned out to be virtually invincible in mountain races. They were joined by Manfred von Brauchitsch, son of a well-to-do Prussian officer. Brauchitsch privately drove a Mercedes SSK, in which he became the surprise victor on the Avus in 1932.

When plans were later drawn to introduce a new racing formula with weight limitations in 1934, the big Mercedes models were recivilized. In

February that year, the racing car department released a new 750-kg model with a 3.8-liter motor. Its design would leave its imprint on racing for most of the next 20 years and would lead to the legendary Silver Arrows. In response, the Auto Union came up with a spectacular new Porsche design, weighing the same weight as the new Mercedes and with a 16-cylinder rear engine. Because the Mercedes still contained a large number of Porsche elements, races between the two brands soon turned into a brisk rivalry. With increasing frequency, Mercedes and Auto Union left the Italian Alfa Romeos, Lancias, and Maseratis in their dust.

More significant was that the two German companies' competitions on the racetracks were turned into promotional battles for the Third Reich, which used these races to demonstrate what it could accomplish. In return, the Reich gave subsidies to the manufacturers and premiums to their victors. The German people were soon caught up in radio reports of the races. Everyone was talking about Mercedes and Auto Union. The toy company Schuco even got in on the act: It introduced a Mercedes Silver Arrow in miniature; children could change its tires and wheels in racing boxes set up on the living-room floor. In short, Mercedes was everywhere.

The 1930s were the German auto industry's most creative period, during which structures were developed that formed the industry's image for 50 years following World War II—when globalization would change everything again. Germany also experienced something of an automobile boom during the decade, though nothing to match that in the United States. Still, the construction of the autobahn was a portent of things to come. It didn't hurt that Hitler eliminated the automobile tax for all cars built from 1933 on. Volkswagens, marketed as "strength-through-joy" cars (after "Kraft durch Freude," an organization intended to make the German people happy), became available for under 1,000 marks. This had Opel and Auto Union scrambling to come up with competitive prices.

Gradually, the middle class began to buy cars. This prompted Daimler-Benz to produce 1.3- and 1.7-liter cars in a lower price range. In 1938, it astonished the automobile world with a four-cylinder model, the 170 V, which was to be Mercedes' first mass-produced car. Between 1933 and 1938, Daimler-Benz's sales quadrupled, reaching 396 million marks. At the same time, the number of Mercedes sold in Germany jumped from

7,844 to 20,899 annually. Though Auto Union sold twice as many and Opel four times as many, Mercedes led the others in sales figures for trucks of all categories.

After the 1936 Olympics in Berlin, which had gone so well for Hitler, Germans became increasingly focused on establishing records in as many areas of competition as possible. For the auto industry, this translated into numerous speed duels between Mercedes and Auto Union. Besides cars, Daimler-Benz also built multiple-use aircraft engines. One of these, the DB 601, a 12-cylinder model, in production as early as November 11, 1937, was put into a Messerschmitt Bf 109 V13, which set a new speed record for airplanes at 379.38 mph (610.55 km/h).

That was the engine Auto Union's Hans Stuck wanted for his next race car. A blond giant with a casual, carefree attitude, he had set the one-hour-race world record for motorboats, and to add to his list of accomplishments, he now wanted to capture the world land-speed record for Germany. "The absolute world record on water as on land, that would be perfect propaganda for us," Hitler reportedly told him. But Englishman Malcolm Campbell stood in their way. He had already achieved a speed of 298 mph and surely had a few more surprises in store. Stuck was determined to launch a major effort to reach his goal.

The only problem was that it was too big an undertaking for his employer, Auto Union, so Stuck talked to his friend Porsche. This resulted in a plan to build a streamlined race car with a 2,500- to 3,000-horsepower engine capable of reaching a top speed of 342 mph. To achieve this, Stuck wanted two of the new DB 601 airplane engines, which he intended to get through another friend of his, World War I pilot Ernst Udet. Udet, now director of the procurement office in the Reich Aviation Ministry of Hermann Göring, came through for Stuck. This meant that the 90,000-mark engines were paid for by the government. Ferdinand Porsche was so keen on the project that he did not charge anything for his participation, either.

Stuck informed his former employer, Daimler-Benz, about this "no-cost" enterprise. Now all that was needed was someone to build the car. Daimler's Chairman Kissel squirmed at first, as he didn't want to have anything to do with Porsche, but in the end, money and fatherland won out: Porsche would design the car, Daimler-Benz would build it, and Stuck would drive it. Unfortunately, while the triumvirate was busy working on the project, George Eyston, another Englishman, reached

311.99 mph in his 4,600-horsepower Thunderbolt, which contained two airplane engines. Eyston soon set another new record at 356.42 mph. Stuck's T 80 had lost even before it was assembled.

The stakes were again raised. Now Porsche wanted a car that would go 372.82 mph, which needed at least a 3,000-horsepower engine. Mercedes was willing to supply two DB 603 aircraft engines, improved versions of model DB 601. But even on the brink of World War II, the new engines still were not powerful enough to accommodate 1,500 horsepower each. In any case, eight days prior to Germany's invasion of Poland, another Englishman, John Cobb, had done 369.71 mph in his Railton Mobil Special. Thus, the T 80, a streamlined car with three axles that could only drive straight ahead, remained an expensive folly (which today can be seen at the Daimler-Benz Museum in Stuttgart, but without the engines). After the war, the corporation, by then the project's sole owner, no longer dared revive it, as in 1947 Cobb had reached 394.2 mph.

When the T 80 was still under development, Mercedes had, however, set one record. In early 1938, two top drivers, Caracciola and Bernd Rosemeyer, dueled for the absolute street-speed record—a public street, that is. This contest would change car racing in Germany dramatically. Even the preparations became something of a race. Both Mercedes and Auto Union had produced, for the first time in automotive history, futuristic streamlined bodies. The race itself was to be run along a section of the autobahn between Frankfurt and nearby Darmstadt, where every fall, a "record week" took place. On October 28, 1937, an Auto Union car driven by Rosemeyer had been clocked at over 250 mph; Caracciola was clocked at only 246 mph in his Mercedes.

Clearly, the Mercedes staff had to rework their 12-cylinder car with its more than 700-horsepower engine. In doing so, they took particular care to consider wind tunnel measurements made by the German Testing Institute for Aviation (Deutsche Versuchsanstalt für Luftfahrt, DVL), as first-rate aerodynamics were meant to ensure a maximum speed increase. On January 28, 1938, at 8:00 A.M., Caracciola started his first trial run in the streamlined car, which was adorned with a Mercedes star and a swastika.

The result was sensational. The autobahn was dry and Caracciola's speed was measured at 268.56 mph over the course (about a mile). The pressure was now on the gutsy, blond Rosemeyer, who had to risk a great deal if he was to best Caracciola. Sadly, at an underpass, gusty winds caused Rosemeyer's car to lose its road grip, and he lost control. The car crashed against a pillar, and Rosemeyer was killed on impact. Caracciola's record would survive for years.

After Auto Union lost its best driver—the Nazi archetypal Aryan man—competition for new records lost much of its allure. The era of car races and the idolizing of drivers was coming to its close. But not before Mercedes drivers Rudolf Caracciola, Manfred von Brauchitsch, Hermann Lang, and Richard "Dick" Seaman (a Brit) concluded the 1938–1939 season with a series of spectacular successes. In early May 1939, Lang and Caracciola chalked up a remarkable double victory in the Race of Tripoli in two previously untested 1.5-liter compressor cars. Six weeks later, on June 25, 1939, the Englishman Seaman lost his life during a race in Belgium. On September 1, 1939, Hitler started World War II.

Hitler's attack on Poland forced Daimler's racing department to acknowledge that they had been too cozy with the devil, which had made it possible to accept certain privileges conferred on them by the Nazi regime. Rudolf Uhlenhaut, a race car designer and driver, later described the eeriness of the situation: "We always worked very hard and weren't very interested in politics. The outbreak of the war pretty much surprised all of us."

In retrospect, it is difficult to believe they could have been surprised by Germany's aggression. Uhlenhaut, his technicians, and his drivers had been present at almost every Grand Prix. They had traveled abroad widely and had more contacts around the world than the average German citizen. Had they really not suspected what was brewing? If they did, apparently they chose to ignore it, perhaps because it would have interfered with their work and personal achievements.

Explanations or equivocations aside, their narrow focus served them well postwar. The reputations of the elite among the technicians went virtually untarnished after World War II, enabling them to rise to the most powerful positions at Daimler-Benz. Rudolf Uhlenhaut was given responsibility for Mercedes' entire auto construction, design, and development. Chief technician Fritz Nallinger remained as strongman of the board of directors until long after the war. Werner Breitschwerdt, one of their most docile students, became the company's CEO in 1983.

The first 60 years of Daimler and Benz had evoked a Mercedes "spirit," which was incomprehensible to outsiders; the six decades to follow would intensify it. In fact, the Daimler image became such a presence that it threatened to jeopardize the future well-being of the company. The Daimler-Benz style was determined by its Swabian birth, so much so that even first-rate staff without at least a touch of the Swabian dialect were accepted only with qualification. Global its reach became, but the company remained, at its core, Swabian. It didn't hurt that the major players in Germany's mechanical industry had settled in Swabia. Suppliers, machine-tool factories, and owners of midsize companies who had earned a good reputation all were nearby. Even the Swabian accent came to be regarded as an element of power.

The point is, the Daimler-Benz phenomenon is inseparable from its culture, meaning that any plan to merge with another company would have to factor it into the equation. That was the dilemma facing every Mercedes chairman who wanted to accomplish something beyond growing the company from the inside.

Roughly speaking, Daimler-Benz's history between the "golden" thirties and its merger with Chrysler can be divided into three phases: the war period and time of occupation between 1940 and 1950, the great consolidation between 1950 and 1980, and the era of experimentation between 1980 and 2000. Compared to many other companies, Daimler-Benz mastered the transitions between periods brilliantly, thanks to its tight corset. Its fame from the days of car racing and its steadfast refusal to build a line of cars below a certain level continually restabilized its image. Ultimately, not even the company's involvement with the Nazi regime could tarnish the well-polished image significantly. The Mercedes star seemed to be coated with Teflon.

Beginning in the fall of 1939, the company became almost completely ruled by Germany's need for arms production, though since 1934 Hitler's militarization program had been up and running very steadily. Between 1926 and 1932, the company's military production increased from 8 to 19 percent; between 1933 and 1938, from 26 to 51 percent; and between 1939 and 1944, from 65 to 93 percent. The company's war-related revenues had climbed from a little over 5 million reichsmarks in 1926 to 900 million reichsmarks in 1944. From 1933 on, Daimler-Benz produced four types of jeeps with engines between 45 and 100 horsepower. Messerschmitt's Me-109 fighter plane had Daimler-Benz engines, as did several German army tanks and ships. This arguably made Daimler-Benz Germany's most significant armament plant.

All German car companies contributed to Hitler's war machine (with production being organized first by Fritz Todt and then by Albert Speer), including Opel and Ford, even though both were owned by American companies. The production of trucks focused on four models: the Opel Blitz, the Ford V 3000 S, the Magirus S 3000, and the 8.5-ton Mercedes L 4500 R. Altogether, Daimler-Benz built some 429,000 trucks, 39,000 tractors, and 187,000 cars between 1940 and 1945, primarily for the German army. In addition, the company produced 60,000 vehicles specifically for military use. Consumer-oriented car production decreased to 7 percent in 1944. On the home front, where fuel was scarce, Daimler-Benz developed wood-gas producers for trucks and cars. Between 1942 and 1945, 44.6 percent of Daimler-Benz employees—36,147 total—were non-Germans, not including concentration camp inmates and POWs.

In 1944 and 1945, Daimler-Benz's plants were seriously damaged during air raids: The factory in Berlin-Marienfelde was completely demolished; the plant in Sindelfingen suffered 85 percent damage; the one in Gaggenau, 80 percent; and in Untertürkheim, 70 percent. Only the plant in Mannheim remained 80 percent intact. The company's material losses—including approximately 7,500 tools—were assessed at 141 million reichsmarks. Later, the total damage was assessed at 194.4 million marks.

In keeping with its Teflon image, the chaos at the end of the war and during the early occupation years barely affected Daimler-Benz AG's managers and shareholders. Wilhelm Haspel, an engineer and chairman of the company since 1942, stayed in office until his death in 1952. The system set up by the Allies of checking the big industrial companies didn't work for Daimler-Benz because no one could figure out who the major shareholders were. Deutsche Bank, the company's constant companion since it had merged, had ceased to exist in 1945. This freed Daimler-Benz to start again almost immediately, with only external obstacles to overcome. Expediting the company's resurgence was the fact that the manufacturing plants for the 170 V, the smallest and latest Mercedes car series, could be rebuilt without much trouble.

Truck production wasn't entirely dead, either. As early as 1945, the Gaggenau plant was manufacturing 290 L 4000 vehicles—under American supervision; the Mannheim plant was turning out 474 units of the type L 3000. The 170 V was reissued from 1946 on, as a passenger car and an ambulance, with few changes. In 1948, the year of the German currency reform, 6,225 units of that type were shipped. Before the reform, the 170 V model cost 6,200 reichsmarks, but could be purchased only with a permit. On the black market, it sold for 100,000 to 120,000 reichsmarks, which later turned out to be a fairly realistic exchange rate. Since the company was in the American occupation zone, it was not burdened with reparations. Competitor Opel, on the other hand, had to ship the entire production equipment for the 1.1-liter Kadett to the Soviet Union, even though the company was really owned by General Motors.

In other respects, too, Mercedes was under a lucky star. Its traditional competitors were paralyzed. All of Auto Union's plants, including those of its distinguished Horch brand, were in the Soviet occupation zone. So were BMW's auto manufacturing plants in Eisenach, Thuringia. Mercedes had an open field in which to reestablish itself as the industry leader for state limos and prestige cars. Only Opel entered the contest when it reissued its prewar model Kapitän. It had a six-cylinder engine long before Mercedes put one back on the market. Daimler-Benz began to release six-cylinder cars in 1951: the 220 (11,925 marks and up) and 300 series (19,900 marks and up), and later the Adenauer, then the coupé 300 S, which was priced at 34,500 marks. A large number of cars were exported, the most expensive ones to the United States.

With the release in 1950 of the new 7.3-ton diesel truck L 6600 with a 445-horsepower engine, Daimler-Benz became Europe's largest truck manufacturer. There were still no major shareholders. Only the industrialist Quandt clan had a sizable package, with 1.4 percent of shares. As major shareholders of battery-producer Varta, understandably the Quandt family was also interested in the auto business. Later, they were to become major shareholders of Daimler competitor BMW.

Board member Fritz Nallinger, a technician, established Daimler-Benz's business policies. Under Nallinger's direction, Daimler-Benz gradually evolved into a company where unit price was determined by production cost, not the other way around. The company adhered to this policy for almost half a century. And once the initial clearing work was done, sales skyrocketed. In 1953, the company recorded earnings of 688 million marks, almost twice the figure for 1937, the last "normal" prewar year. In 1955, earnings doubled again, to 1.44 billion marks. Ten years after the war, the company was again offering three types of cars as if nothing had happened. A successor to the SSK racing car was also on the test block. And soon, a major shareholder emerged. After purchasing a few personal stock packages, Friedrich Flick KG in Düsseldorf, which had been founded in 1937, held a blocking minority in the firm. As a Nazi collaborator, Flick had been incarcerated after the war and had been ordered to sell his large shares in Germany's coal and steel industry. Unlike others similarly punished, he complied immediately, then invested the money from the sale in the far-more-promising processing industries. Deutsche Bank, too, "reappeared," with 15 percent of Daimler shares. In the meantime, the Quandts had accumulated 10 percent of shares.

After 1951, racing again became a sizable part of Daimler-Benz business. The influential Alfred Neubauer, former head of the racing department, made sure of that. He intended to revive the 1.5-liter, eight-cylinder model W 165, which had been so successful at Tripoli. Five of these cars were to be manufactured in Stuttgart. Now, however, these cars faced major competition in the form of the new Alfas and Maseratis. Caracciola, along with Stuttgart's new star driver, Karl Kling, gave the W 165 another try on the Nürburgring, but they were not terribly impressed. Consequently, the board of directors decided to design an entirely new car for the next Grand Prix formula in 1954: a W 196 with a 2.5-liter, eight-cylinder engine.

The W 196 dominated the Grand Prix racetracks for two years, 1954 and 1955. Its loose shape, not unlike the classic Silver Arrows, and streamlined body made it the car of choice for racing stars from all over the world, including Argentinian Juan Manuel Fangio, Englishman Stirling Moss, Italian Piero Taruffi, and German Karl Kling, all of whom performed brilliantly in the new car. As a result, multiple victories became commonplace: In one race, there was a quadruple victory; in another, a triple victory; and five double victories were recorded. Unquestionably, Mercedes was the world champion brand name again, as in the 1930s.

History again seemed to be repeating itself when Daimler-Benz began to reestablish its dominance in touring sports cars with the release of the famous 300 SL "Gullwing," later offered as a roadster as well. Technologically, the 300 SL was an offshoot of the Adenauer Mercedes, but its drag had been reduced to almost nothing. Ironically, however, the resurgence of the 300 SL spelled the beginning of the end for Mercedes' involvement in racing.

The 300 SL was the last car used in the 30-year career of star racer Caracciola, who had won three German and six European championships for Mercedes without a single accident. After the brakes in his black 300 SL locked and he ran into a tree, "Carratsch" quit. Then, on June 11, 1955, at 6:27 P.M., during the 24-hour Le Mans, a more disastrous accident occurred that changed everything for Mercedes and its racing department. France's independent race driver, Pierre Bouillon—who called himself Levegh—was driving a 300 SL when he brushed against an Austin Healey whose driver did his best to get out of Bouillon's way. But at a speed of 149 mph, a brush was all it took. Bouillon and his car bounced straight up into the air and came down on the spectators seated in the boxes to the left. The aftermath was horrifying to calculate: 82 people dead, 110 injured. Mercedes, whose Fangio-Moss team had a two-lap lead, stopped the race.

When the dust had cleared, the company's directors heatedly discussed the value and risks such events carried for the Mercedes image in particular and for Germans in general. On October 22, 1955, at the close of the season and after winning the world championship for sports cars, Daimler-Benz announced its decision to unconditionally retire from the Grand Prix "for years to come."

The years to come became decades. By the early 1960s, Daimler-Benz had as good as vanished from the world of car racing, though this, too, would change with Jürgen Schrempp and the impact of Helmut Werner. Until then, Mercedes would focus on production—of both quantity and dollars. In September 1962, the one-millionth car since the end of World War II left the assembly line. In April 1968, the two-millionth car came off; four years later, in February 1972, the three-millionth; and in February 1975, the four-millionth. By 1977, Daimler-Benz was producing 401,255 cars annually, passing a mark long considered an absolute limit. In addition, it was manufacturing 248,100 trucks, four times as many as in 1965. Moneywise, at 25.86 billion deutsche marks, the company's sales were four times that of the 12 prior years.

Daimler-Benz also became focused on its reputation, establishing itself as the expert on expensive cars and heavy trucks, which in those days was like life insurance. The company became one of the three largest firms of German industry. Its success, however, was not entirely self-induced. Luck was on its side, too. Bremen's Borgward company (in the early postwar years, considered to be Europe's most innovative auto manufacturer) had collapsed; a number of heavy industrial conglomerates had retreated from truck production; and finally, the Flick clan had gradually begun to shed its holdings. These three factors furthered the growth of Daimler-Benz AG tremendously.

The first, the collapse of Borgward, was particularly meaningful. Entrepreneur Carl F. W. Borgward had been director, sole owner, and chief designer of this company that dated back to the 1920s. Some of Borgward's products—such as Germany's first pontoon car, Hansa 1500, and its successor Isabella—with their dependable high-performance engines, were unparalleled in their day. From the compact Alexander to the Big Borgward with air suspension to a precursor of the minivan, Borgward was far ahead of his competitors. Since he also built trucks, race cars, and helicopters, he was a direct competitor of Daimler-Benz. The difference was that he had no access to the financial cushion that Germany's banking system could provide. Borgward had declined an offer from the Chrysler Corporation to buy his company for approximately 200 million deutsche marks. Then, when too much inventory caused cash-flow problems in the winter of 1960–1961, he found himself in serious trouble. The Bremen state government's intervention only made matters worse; the unions were not prepared to help him, even though they could have; and the banks were more interested in cleaning up the market in favor of Daimler-Benz and BMW.

By 1961, Borgward, which in number of cars sold had, on occasion, been fourth behind VW, Opel, and Ford, disappeared from the market. (A few years later, most of Borgward's creditors received most of what they were owed from the company's estate, meaning that the firm had not been bankrupt at all; infamy and incompetence had wiped it off the market.) Daimler-Benz and the others helped themselves to Borgward's customers, its know-how, and ultimately to its assets as well.

The second factor—the retreat of competitors from truck production—gave Daimler-Benz significant leverage in this area. As early as 1957, Daimler-Benz had garnered more than 50 percent of German sales of heavy trucks and buses. Then, within two decades, reputable companies such as Hanomag, Henschel, Krauss-Maffai, Büssing, Krupp, Vidahl, KHD, Faun, Ford, and a few others either sold or discontinued their truck production since they couldn't reach profitable production numbers and lost money. Most of that business, particularly that of Hanomag-Henschel, which had set up its factory on Borgward's former estate in Bremen, eventually went to Daimler-Benz. By 1968 Daimler-Benz sold twice as many trucks as it had eight years earlier; and only three years later, in 1971, it doubled its sales again. Though growth in the following years would slow somewhat, in 1997, Daimler-Benz was the world's largest manufacturer of full-sized trucks.

The third factor—the Flick family's release of its Daimler-Benz holdings—would be the one to free the company to grow. In the 1960s and early 1970s, the Flick family, which at times owned almost 40 percent of Daimler-Benz's stocks, resisted the company's fast expansion. The Flicks did not support major investments; they preferred hidden reserves, plus the distribution of bonus shares. This assured them of tremendous risk-free earnings. As late as 1960, the total nominal value of Daimler-Benz stock had been 180 million deutsche marks, which by 1974 had grown to 1,189 billion marks. The company's Swabian managers loved this kind of financial conservatism.

All this began to change in the 1970s, when the Flick heirs went head-to-head, and the shah of Iran moved to take over their shares. The situation was all the more critical because the oil sheikhdom of Kuwait had already taken over the Quandt group's Daimler shares. Now the fatherland was in danger. The other major shareholder, Deutsche Bank, had to step in and save it. At the time—in early 1975—the bank owned 28.5 percent of Daimler-Benz's stocks, among them many preferred stocks, with 30 votes per share. The bank's director, Franz-Heinrich Ulrich, quickly declared that further blocks of Daimler-Benz shares would not be sold abroad. This brought him in conflict with Friedrich Karl Flick, who after his father's death had inherited billions of deutsche marks. He wanted cash in order to buy out his nephews, with whom he was on bad terms.

Flick eventually dropped his insistence on dealing abroad and agreed to negotiate with Ulrich. Flick sold him 29 percent of Daimler-Benz's shares and kept the remaining 10 percent. Ulrich sold a smaller part of these new Daimler stocks to third parties and founded a Mercedes automobile holding company to administer the larger part of it. This gave the bank more than half of all Daimler-Benz stocks, which were distributed as follows: 28.5 percent to Deutsche Bank, 25.25 percent to Mercedes-Automobil-Holding, 16.5 percent to Kuwait Investment Company, 10 percent to Friedrich Flick KG, and 20 percent to independent stockholders.

Deutsche Bank was the leading power on the supervisory board, which had been joined by rocket pioneer Wernher von Braun in March 1975. Chief executive of the company at that time was the lawyer and former chief financial officer Joachim Zahn, though the strategy of the company was heavily influenced by the chief technician Hans Scherenberg, whose 1972 S-class set new standards in safety and comfort. The rising star of the company was Gerhard Prinz, who came from VW. He was keen on expanding Daimler-Benz truck and car business to unmatched dimensions.

In order to expand the heavy-truck business in the United States, Prinz orchestrated the acquisition of Euclid Inc., a subsidiary of White, the American truck manufacturing company. Euclid built superheavy (almost 200 tons) commercial off-highway vehicles. On March 1, 1981 Prinz purchased the U.S. truck manufacturer Freightliner Corporation of Portland Oregon. Being Zahn's successor since 1980, he handled the expansion of the company's product line at the lower end. Daimler-Benz was directed to produce a "little Mercedes," a type below the 200-class.

This made sense in that Daimler-Benz offered cars with cubic capacities between 6.9 and 2 liters, but made only two basic bodies for them: one for the S-class and one for the 200-class, which was used for everything from taxicabs to managers' cars. Munich's BMW, on the other hand, which also manufactured luxury cars, adhered to its so-called niche policies and offered three basic bodies. Daimler recognized the need to reach that sector of customers who wanted a prestige car but in a smaller model. Thus, Prinz's board decided to manufacture the 190, which later became the C-class.

Since the Stuttgart plant's capacities had reached their limit and there was no additional labor force to speak of available in Swabia, management decided to transfer the production of the new model largely to Bremen so that those designated for export could immediately be shipped via the city's port. On December 8, 1982, CEO Gerhard Prinz and his technology director Werner Breitschwerdt introduced the new class, which became a huge success for the company and for Gerhard Prinz personally.

The Euclid acquisition turned out to be less successful. The company's losses approximately equaled its revenues. Obviously, this state of affairs had to be put to rights. But who could do it? Prinz decided on the technological director of his South African subsidiary, United Car and

Diesel Distribution (UCDD). Only 37 years old, the man had the reputation as a truck buff. Prinz assigned him the job of putting Euclid Corporation back on its feet.

The man given the assignment was Jürgen Schrempp, and though he
believed he was embarking on a suicide mission, he also realized he had
no choice. In September 1982, he started his new job—in Cleveland,
Ohio. He quickly concluded that it was impossible to put Euclid back on
its feet. To prevent matters from worsening, he recommended to the
company managers in Stuttgart to sell Euclid—and quickly. During long
telephone conversations with Schrempp, Prinz kept trying to save the
unprofitable subsidiary. After all, it was his baby.

In the end, Prinz threw in the towel. Euclid's sale was finalized at the
end of October 1983, but Prinz was not the one to put his signature on
the dotted line. A couple of days earlier, on October 29, the beleaguered
Daimler-Benz chief died while exercising in the basement of his home in
Stuttgart.

Daimler's Schrempp

Jürgen Schrempp was born in Freiburg on September 15, 1944, the second of three sons. His father worked as a low-level administration official at Freiburg University. Like his brothers, he attended the local
Rotteck-Gymnasium, where he was kept back one year for failing
French. He later dropped out of high school, thereby earning no more
than the preliminary degree automatically conferred upon German students after successful completion of six out of nine high school years. His
plans didn't require any high school diploma, he allegedly shouted out at
his angry father.

Since then Jürgen Schrempp has had only one real home: Daimler-
Benz. He served his apprenticeship as a mechanic at the firm's local
branch, where his unusual interest in trucks did not go unnoticed. (To
this day, Schrempp is one of the few top managers who can take an ordi-
nary diesel or Otto engine apart and put it back together.) Schrempp also
became known for his musical talents which, true to his nature, he
expressed on the trumpet. Even if he had failed in his career in the automotive industry, he would have been able to make a living with his
music. Perhaps surprisingly, these two diverse talents would serve him
well in his early days at Daimler-Benz.

In Freiburg, Schrempp met the first of his sponsors, all of whom had specific things to offer him. The city's Mercedes branch was headed by Karlfried Nordmann, a former air force major who had earned a string of medals as a fighter pilot in World War II. Many of the planes he had flown had been equipped with Mercedes-Benz engines. He asked Schrempp to play the trumpet part in taps during get-togethers with his air force friends. After completing his apprenticeship as a mechanic, Schrempp used his musical skills to pay his way through engineering school in nearby Offenburg, the seat of the newspaper and magazine giant Burda.

In 1967, immediately after he graduated, with assistance from Nordmann, 23-year-old Schrempp landed a job at Daimler-Benz's headquarters in Stuttgart's district of Untertürkheim, where he started out as a specialist for technical matters in the commercial vehicle department, now called Central Customer Service. Nordmann soon advanced to the position of director of that department, so for the time being Schrempp was happy to stay put. But when in 1971 the company promoted Nordmann to president of Mercedes Benz of North America, the coveted royal throne of all positions abroad, Schrempp wanted to join him right away. However, he had to wait.

Relief didn't come until 1974, when the company finally offered him a new job—not as he had hoped in the United States, but in segregated South Africa, which at the time was a paradise for powerful foreign companies. Germans enjoyed special privileges there. Their past as colonial masters in neighboring Namibia was partly forgotten and partly glorified. What was not forgotten, however, at least not among the South African Boers, were Germany's wars against the former colonial power Great Britain. Daimler-Benz's subsidiary United Car and Diesel Distribution (Pty) Ltd. was located in Pretoria, the capital situated in the predominantly Boer (Afrikaans) part of the country.

When Schrempp took over the company's customer service at just 30 years of age, he felt he had found his own personal paradise. Given the country's clear-cut separation into rich and poor, his job instantly placed him among the rich and powerful. He began living the high life, one in which all servants were easily recognizable by the color of their skin. His peers had luxurious urban villas—mostly in nearby Johannesburg—and second homes by the Indian Ocean, preferably around Durban; once in a while, they traveled to attend a congress in British Cape Town or the Dutch vineyard region around Stellenbosch. Many of the upper class also had farms in the northern—warmer—part of the country. And for excitement, there were safaris in the jungle. Naturally, the prestige car of choice was a Mercedes.

South Africa with its incomparable sky impressed Jürgen Schrempp right away; the Alemannian found the experience unforgettable. Right or wrong, he felt this was his country. Still a management novice, already he was a member of the elite. Nevertheless, South African life had a temporary feel to foreigners. Europeans like Schrempp sensed that their life of luxury wouldn't last forever. They knew that the present social structure could be abolished at any time.

Europeans were, in a sense, torn. On the one hand, they had to woo the government; on the other, they had to send signals to the opposition that they were really on *their* side. When European companies started cooperating with blacks, giving them more responsible jobs, they were violating the government's apartheid laws. But they didn't do so without protecting themselves: Harry Oppenheimer, the famed diamond mogul, argued that if companies didn't start employing blacks in responsible positions, South Africa would be unable to fill middle management positions as early as the turn of the century.

Clearly, Jürgen Schrempp had to be both very sensitive and extremely tough. Running a company in South Africa required the ability to respond quickly, to proceed spontaneously, while being strict. In this environment, German branch managers became used to making decisions independently, without interference from their faraway control center. In this climate, a self-confident group of young turks soon made headlines as the "Springbok Mafia," and Schrempp was one of the gang. His timing was right. Having South Africa on one's resume at the end of the 1980s was as impressive as a degree from Harvard Business School. It was said that anyone coming from the Cape had management potential. VW, BMW, and Daimler were where the troops were trained. Springbok member Eberhard von Koerber was named director of the board at Brown Boveri; Bernd Pischetsrieder achieved the same at BMW; and Jürgen Schrempp did it at Daimler-Benz. When apartheid was abolished at the Cape, this trend fell out of vogue, and Jürgen Schrempp turned out to be its last great example.

During Schrempp's tenure in South Africa, the country was a protected market for Germany's auto industry. Competition from outside was deflected through tariffs. Auto parts (and sometimes production parts) were shipped from Germany, just as in other companies. Machine tools that were regarded as obsolete at home could be used in South Africa because they were not expected to contribute much to productivity, for labor was cheap. Furthermore, cars cost more than in Europe. The customer base—limited to begin with—was wealthy, and there was neither demand from the masses nor cheap imported cars to compete with. It was an idyll—provided it was viewed from the top. Whenever there was a slump in sales, it was not because of the competition or management incompetence, but invariably because something was not functioning properly in the country in general.

The republic at the Cape depended on the world's raw materials market, which meant on the Western world's economy. White South Africans wanted nothing to do with the Soviet empire, if only because it interfered with their gold and diamond business. As long as they had all the power, South Africa was not a volatile country, and thus offered safe ground for companies such as Daimler-Benz. When there was a sales crisis, management couldn't do anything about it anyway. The only action was inaction, during which everyone indulged in drinking local wine and going hunting. That was the general situation in 1980, when 36-year-old Jürgen Schrempp became a board member of Daimler-Benz's South African branch, leading the technology department.

His horizon broadened. Now he knew not just the powerful people in South Africa, but also those at the Daimler-Benz headquarters in Stuttgart, Germany. Just one more promotion—to general manager of Mercedes-Benz of South Africa (MBSA), as the branch was now called—and he would be on equal footing with his first mentor, Nordmann. At the time, there was a new string of Schrempp sponsors: CEO Gerhard Prinz, CFO Gerhard Liener, technical director Werner Breitschwerdt, and last but not least, Edzard Reuter, the corporation's strategist—each with a long future ahead of him.

They all considered Schrempp to be straightforward, stable, and tough, a man who could—and would—roll up his sleeves and clean things up, if need be. A terminator. The only roadblock to his future was that he wanted to remain at the Cape. South Africa excited him. He wanted to own something there so he could stay forever. So he purchased a farm in eastern Transvaal, very close to the beautiful Krüger National Park. This, too, he managed to do at the right time. He gave his mansion, which was built in the Boers' horizontal style, the name Crocodile.

Gerhard Prinz's marching order to Schrempp to relocate to Ohio tore into this idyll. But practical-minded Schrempp realized that by being moved to Euclid, he had effectively been advanced to the position of chairman. Any future position at the Daimler-Benz corporation would therefore have to be at a higher level. He had already told his secretary in Pretoria that he would return as director—or not at all. When his "adventure" at Euclid ended, he was 39 years old, and essentially, he had just fired himself. Though the corporation's long-term human resource plans were vague at that point, Werner Breitschwerdt, Daimler's new chairman, credited Schrempp with elegantly untangling the Euclid jam. In 1984 Breitschwerdt granted Schrempp's wish to return to South Africa—not, however, as the boss, but as his deputy.

From that point on, Jürgen Schrempp's career was inextricably linked with the frequent changes Daimler-Benz went through. In 1985, when poor health forced MBSA head Morris Shenker to resign after 26 years at the helm, he recommended Schrempp as his successor; Gerhard Liener, the board member in charge of partnerships, approved. Barely in his early forties, Schrempp's dream had come true. If, as he originally hoped, he remained the head of the South African branch for as long as his predecessor, he would have a number of years in paradise until his retirement. Then, his goal within reach, he suddenly realized he wanted to go somewhere else. His constant dealings with Daimler's top managers in Stuttgart had convinced the self-confident Schrempp that he had it in him to rise to the top among Daimler-Benz AG's central board of directors.

Schrempp's management capabilities were not, however, regarded as highly by others. His critics pointed out poor staffing choices. Financially, his one and a half years as the branch boss were noted to be among its worst. And his straddling the fence on apartheid—opposing it at headquarters but not doing anything about its proponents' "superman philosophy" in the company's East London factories—was difficult to overlook. He also spent a great deal of time traveling, while neglecting, some said, daily business.

Schrempp definitely is no paper pusher. He is the hands-on type, someone who follows his instincts. This is especially true in his choice of people with whom he has to interact and work. He sensed early on that at headquarters a revolution at the top was in the making. Werner Breitschwerdt, the technician under whose leadership car production had earned enormous revenues, was proscribed by Deutsche Bank, the major shareholder. The bank's director, Alfred Herrhausen, declared that the filthy rich company had to position itself differently. Simply selling heavy trucks and expensive cars would soon no longer be sufficient.

Behind the strategic reorientation was Edzard Reuter, the unconventional but great intellect on the board of directors. Reuter had repeatedly been considered as the new CEO in Untertürkheim, but he lost twice, first as successor to retired Joachim Zahn, and second to the recently deceased Gerhard Prinz. Reuter always believed that he had been passed over because he was a member of the Social Democratic Party, in solidarity with his father, Ernst Reuter, Berlin's famous postwar mayor at a time when the city constituted the major front facing the Soviet bloc.

But there was more to it than that. Reuter had always been something of an outsider in the company. He was not even an automobile buff— almost the opposite, in fact. In his estimation, the car would not play a major part in the transportation of the future. He predicted that for a variety of reasons it would give way to other means of transportation. Therefore, he maintained, Daimler-Benz should start involving itself in a number of new "business areas," as he put it, that would make up for the anticipated losses in auto production and that would support each other synergistically. To finance that transition, he argued, Daimler-Benz had only to tap its enormous financial resources.

Deutsche Bank's Alfred Herrhausen had similar ideas. At the time, it was rumored that Daimler-Benz was earning much more than the 1.5 billion deutsche marks posted on its balance sheet. The number that circulated was 7 billion. Herrhausen was determined to make Reuter the boss even before Breitschwerdt's contract expired. Along with auto technician Werner Niefer, Herrhausen began to figure out a legal maneuver whereby Breitschwerdt would simply no longer be necessary and be forced to resign.

All this maneuvering was to Schrempp's liking. He assumed that the chaos that was bound to ensue would propel him to the top. At the same time, Reuter was looking for unconventional managers who could be useful during such a period. The two met when Reuter was on an inspection tour in South Africa. Schrempp did his utmost to please his visitor, showing him all the country had to offer in the way of entertainment. Despite their differences, he and Reuter became friends.

Around that time, the Stuttgart board of directors was even debating whether to close the Daimler-Benz South African branch, considering the country's heated political atmosphere. The Republic of South Africa was becoming increasingly isolated from the rest of the world. The Soviet Union had aligned the other African countries against South Africa, while the West was in fear of a bloody rebellion within the country and so put pressure on South Africa by imposing economic sanctions. Western companies, particularly American firms, began withdrawing from South Africa. Schrempp, who still loved it there even though his ambition was pushing him toward Stuttgart, convinced the board of directors that Daimler-Benz's retreat would not help the country's disenfranchised. In fact, he argued, it would cause even more unemployment and still more misery. Furthermore, he argued, it would be advantageous to be there when the other companies returned—which he was sure they would.

Daimler-Benz stayed in South Africa; Schrempp left—just in time to avoid a disastrous strike in East London's factories, which his successor, Christoph Köpke, then had to deal with. In 1987, Schrempp became director of distribution for commercial vehicles, and deputy member of the board of directors in Stuttgart. Helmut Werner was CEO. By this time, Reuter and Herrhausen had turned the company completely upside down. Daimler-Benz had become a holding company whose subsidiaries included Mercedes-Benz AG, Deutsche Aerospace AG (DASA), Debis, and AEG. In a series of acquisitions designed to cover a wide variety of markets, Reuter, Niefer, and Herrhausen had purchased not only the by-then comatose electrical company AEG, but almost the entire aeronautics and astronautics industry in Germany. It had cost a great deal of money, and—more significantly—it had fatefully changed the longtime culture of the Swabian company.

Because there were national concerns linked with the aeronautics and astronautics industry, it became government-subsidized, which did not prevent it from suffering significant losses. In this industry, a limited number of lobbyists had to work on an even more limited number of major customers. In the auto business, it was the other way around. Furthermore, where it was standard in aeronautics to guarantee a profit for government commissions that grew in proportion to the order's cost—in other words, the higher the cost, the higher the profit—in the auto business the rule was the lower the cost, the higher the profit. Thus, the rules of business and economics were virtually turned upside down. This conflict forced Daimler-Benz's holding company's board of directors to become industrialists who had to think duplicitously, spending much more time on the new business areas than on their core business, automobiles. The cultures of public financing and the free market economy clashed. For the first time in the history of Daimler-Benz, the development department, the company's jewel, was given a budget. Money was needed elsewhere.

Guiding this business development was Edzard Reuter. He deputized Niefer—whose background was in cars—promoting him to chairman of the board of Mercedes-Benz AG, the by far biggest subsidiary of the Daimler-Benz holding and its ultimate cash machine; AEG, in contrast, was swallowing more and more money; Debis was constructed by many acquisitions as a software house and financial service organization at least for Daimler-Benz itself but with outside customers as well; DASA was an unmitigated disaster. Schrempp was asked to repair the damage. On May 1, 1989, he became chairman of the aerospace company and, simultaneously, a member of the board of the holding company. At the age of 44 he was now Edzard Reuter's most important ally. Schrempp's job at DASA was to sort out the potpourri of companies between Lake Constance and the North Sea. He soon discovered that DASA was a microcosm of the entire corporation: What happened at DASA was also bound to happen at Daimler-Benz if action wasn't taken to stop it.

Thanks to Reuter and Schrempp, DASA soon combined such well-known firms as the old aircraft company Dornier, turbine manufacturer MTU, and Telefunken Systemtechnik, which was really an offshoot of AEG. Then it followed with the acquisition of the Bavarian engineering, armament, and aerospace company Messerschmitt-Bölkow-Blohm (MBB) for DASA. MBB was considered to be a German high-tech gem that promised to garner many public commissions. Reuter didn't, however, like it when the federal government urged DASA to also take over MBB's subsidiary Deutsche Airbus.

Everything or nothing, the government insisted, because it wanted to get rid of its obligation to subsidize the commercial aerospace industry. In Reuter's opinion, any involvement in Europe's Airbus program was doomed. Ironically, Airbus, the only acquisition Reuter didn't want, proved to be the only successful one. Schrempp, who subdivided the various parts of DASA into different areas of production, decided right away to make the company the third-largest aircraft company in the world—an effort that required he go head-to-head with the company's Airbus partner, France. In October 1992, he completed this undertaking by purchasing a 78 percent share of the Dutch Fokker Holding NV, which owned 51 percent of Fokker NV, whose stocks were posted on the stock exchange. This made DASA number one in its area in Europe. But what Schrempp had overlooked—or didn't know—was that the Dutch sell a national "treasure" such as the Fokker aircraft plants to a foreign country only when it is irreversibly headed for bankruptcy.

One year later, Schrempp's DASA recorded an annual loss of 809 million marks. Even though Schrempp abandoned six DASA locations completely, folded three individual plants, and laid off 16,000 employees, he still had to deal with another loss of 438 million in 1994. Fortunately, during that time Mercedes-Benz chairman Helmut Werner had increased the auto business sufficiently so that Daimler-Benz didn't crash entirely. In spite of the losses, Reuter stood by Schrempp, supporting him as his successor. Daimler's supervisory board followed his recommendation and put Schrempp, rather than the successful Helmut Werner, in the corporation's driver's seat.

The first year of Schrempp's tenure as director of the holding company was an unqualified failure. In May 1995, Reuter, getting set to resign, promised attendees at Daimler-Benz's general meeting that they could expect a handsome profit that year. But at the end of the year, despite a good turnover in the auto business, Daimler-Benz posted a loss of 5.7 billion marks, the highest annual loss a German stock company had ever reported. Nothing had sold except cars. There were plenty of reasons for this, and they all had to do with Reuter's strategy of turning Daimler-Benz into a slim and synergistic technological company. The end of the Cold War had led to a 30 percent decrease in commissions from the Department of Defense as early as 1991, and that figure had not improved since. Aircraft production, too, had run at a loss because of the grotesque rise in the exchange rate of the deutsche mark to the dollar. Finally, AEG virtually had not developed any new technological products. It was, simply put, comatose.

As a result, the remains of AEG were either sold, mostly to Scandinavia, or ended up in other segments of the Daimler-Benz conglomerate. DASA was subjected to the previously mentioned (see Chapter 1)

Dolores program. As for Fokker, Schrempp let it go bankrupt after putting no less than 5.5 billion marks of Daimler's money into it. Reminiscent of what he had done at Euclid, Schrempp essentially fired himself. Though he was still chairman of the board at Daimler-Benz holding, most of that company's subsidiaries had disappeared; and what remained—DASA—seemed anemic for years to come.

Thus, the holding company Daimler-Benz AG was almost identical to its subsidiary Mercedes-Benz AG, and the former's board of directors presided like a meaningless House of Lords over the immensely busy automobile board led by Helmut Werner. This created a dichotomous situation: Helmut Werner could survive only if the holding company was dissolved, while Jürgen Schrempp's survival was possible only if the holding company devoured its own child. Naturally, Schrempp suggested the latter, and the supervisory board, still led by Hilmar Kopper, went along. Again, Schrempp emerged victorious, though he had done nothing but fix the damage Reuter and he himself had caused. Conversely, Helmut Werner lost the game, even though he had salvaged and widely expanded the company's core business—and thus, saved the company itself.

Schrempp's career prior to his victory over Werner needs closer examination. Schrempp's modus operandi was always the same: In a critical situation, he acted immediately; when things were going smoothly, he stuck to his wait-and-see philosophy. Until Schrempp's last career step, it was this stop-and-go principle that secured his advance. In the United States, he sold Euclid before he got burned, in spite of the fact that it cost more than 100 million marks. When Daimler-Benz had to be put back on its feet, Schrempp adhered to the company's tried-and-true values. It was not imaginative or visionary, but it was clever.

Schrempp exhibited similar prudence during his advance to the top of the conglomerate. In South Africa, he sat back until his predecessor retired after a little over a year. In Germany, he agreed with everything Edzard Reuter said for five years, until Reuter's time was up. Doubtless, at Daimler-Chrysler, he won't have to wait long until Robert Eaton leaves. Of course, Schrempp loves a challenge, especially while he is waiting, impatiently, for something to happen. But it is doubtful whether Schrempp, whose focus is on the future, truly appreciates the risks of extreme situations. Even if he does, he's convinced he will master them. This is his strength.

Schrempp's brawny Gary Cooper demeanor plays better in the Anglo-Saxon world than in Germany. It doesn't hurt that he is a big fan of all things Anglo-American. American Jack Welch made him his disciple, and South African Nelson Mandela, his honorary consul. As for Robert Eaton, Chrysler's chairman, he must at least have believed him.

Daimler-Chrysler

As it turned out, only 1995 was bad news for Daimler-Benz—and for Schrempp. The fiscal years 1996 and 1997 looked much better, and Jürgen Schrempp began considering a merger. Daimler's revenues had climbed to 124.05 billion marks in 1997 from 104.113 billion the previous year. More than two-thirds (66.9 percent, compared to 62.8 percent) came from foreign sales, with increases particularly high in the United States. Debis, the car and truck business, which Helmut Werner had greatly expanded, and DASA both reported increases, too. Only Daimler's major shares in companies such as Adtrans, Temic, and MTU posted losses. Roughly speaking, car and truck sales had increased to 77 percent of the corporation's total business; aeronautics and aerospace moved to 11 percent, and software to 8 percent.

Furthermore, the major shareholders were standing pat. Deutsche Bank owned some 25 percent of all Daimler-Benz shares, and the Emirate of Kuwait, 15 percent. Schrempp again began to focus on clearly distinguishing Mercedes-Benz cars from other brands, and his goal was to increase production from about 710,000 units in 1997 to 1 million by the beginning of the new century. (A million units was generally considered to be the approximate break-even point, above which production would become profitable.)

But even such a distinguished company as Daimler-Benz could not count on achieving that level of sales volume. Schrempp knew there were three possible routes to achieving this goal. Edzard Reuter had tried number one: to seek the company's growth potential in other highly technical areas, thus smoothing out economic fluctuations in the automobile business. The attempt failed, not only because Reuter had aimed too high and his approach had lacked sufficient analysis, but also because his timing couldn't have been worse. Helmut Werner dared try route number two: popularizing the Mercedes-Benz brand and, if necessary, doing it by creating a new brand of subcompacts. Attempts such as the A-class cars and the Smart proved problematic. VW had too much of an advantage in this area. The third possible route was to merge with another large manufacturer. That's the route Schrempp chose.

In 1997, Schrempp, sole company head since the beginning of the year, paved the way for that merger, both in terms of the company's production plans and its finances. This type of solution suited Schrempp: It was big and it clarified everything in one fell swoop. Schrempp, however, had remarkably few options. He needed a company that could produce high volume with a popular brand. In another time, VW would have been the ideal partner. As early as the 1960s, Friedrich Flick, the major Daimler-Benz shareholder, and Heinrich Nordhoff, VW's powerful coruler, had tried unsuccessfully to initiate some form of cooperation. But now that Ferdinand Piech had turned VW into a fierce competitor, such attempts would have been futile.

Other large European companies—mainly Fiat, Peugeot, and Renault—occupied large market segments in Europe but had nothing to offer for the U.S. market or Asia. In partnership with one of them, Daimler-Benz would have become a Eurocentric company, not the global giant Schrempp had in mind. That still left the Asian companies. Among them, Toyota would have been the ideal partner—it was market leader in the Pacific region and strong in the United States. The Japanese, however, are a bit like the Dutch: They tend not to sell or merge healthy companies, preferring to expand on their own. And at the time, Japan was in a crisis, so Toyota's management wanted to do neither. Thus, Schrempp turned his attention to America's Big Three: General Motors, Ford, and Chrysler.

General Motors was quickly eliminated, as the company was undergoing a cumbersome reorganization that wasn't anticipated to be completed until 2003 at the earliest. Ford was a possibility, as it had completed its restructuring and was capable of a merger, and its management was seen as "thinking big." After all, its longtime goal was to push General Motors from the number one spot. In concert with Daimler-Benz, this would have happened overnight. Schrempp and his director of strategy, Eckhard Cordes, arranged what was called Operation Beta: talks with Ford. During these talks it became clear that the U.S. company was able but unwilling to merge. Ford wanted to become number one as Ford, not as Daimler-Ford or even Ford-Daimler. Talks were discontinued. One important realization resulted from the otherwise fruit-less negotiations: Both companies were pursuing the same goal—to become the largest company. Chrysler was now the only possible, and soon actively courted, partner. Operation Gamma was on: talks with Chrysler.

Successful as it had been at times, Chrysler Corporation never quite made it as a member of the upper nobility of the American auto indus-try. Nevertheless, it has survived beside the leading duo of General Motors and Ford. Walter Chrysler, who gave the company its name, was a railroad man who had previously worked for the General Motors Cor-poration, founded in 1908. He resigned from his secure position as one of the company's top managers in 1919 in order to implement his plan to put the troubled Maxwell Motor Car Company back on its feet. After succeeding, he rechristened the firm as Chrysler Motors Corporation in 1925. Walter Chrysler was an innovative technician with a pronounced instinct for styling. His cars soon stood out from the other mass-produced look-alike products. As early as 1929, he had advanced his company to number three in the hotly contested U.S. auto business.

Three years later, Chrysler made news when it was the first company to install brake boosters in its cars. Two years later, the streamlined model Chrysler Airflow was on the market, which not only made Walter famous, but earned him the honor of supplying the lead car for the Indi-anapolis 500. Still, Chrysler Corporation never managed to close in on General Motors and Ford, and it remained in a financially weaker posi-tion, particularly after World War II.

In the 1950s and 1960s, General Motors totally dominated the mar-ket, capturing a share of up to 55 percent. GM determined the size of motors, the length of car bodies, and the basic elements of styling. What-ever GM did, Ford and Chrysler followed. As market leader, GM pro-duced the largest series at the lowest unit cost and the highest profit per unit. Its financial power grew while the other two companies became more vulnerable.

Especially at Chrysler, productivity fluctuated greatly. In 1955, the company produced 1,371,736 cars; a year later only 870,623 rolled off the line (which, by the way, was still more than in 1997). This pattern was repeated several times. In 1960–1961, car production plummeted from 1,019,295 to 648,671; between 1978 and 1980, total production decreased from 1,914,348 to 758,206. When Chrysler, undaunted by the second oil crisis of 1979–1980, continued to put its stake in the big tin lizzies that got 12 miles per gallon or less, the end seemed near, propelled by the influx on the American market of reliable and economical Japanese subcompacts.

Nothing appeared to work at Chrysler: By 1982, car production had dropped to 722,418 units. Then President Jimmy Carter prevailed against his Republican congressional opponents in getting federal backing for certain Chrysler loans. Behind this decision was Chrysler's new chairman, former Ford president Lido Anthony "Lee" Iacocca. Shortly before, the company founder's grandson, Henry Ford II, had fired him because he could "no longer look at his face," a flimsy cover-up for Ford's concern that Iacocca wanted total power over the company. He was not being paranoid. Iacocca later had to leave Chrysler for the same reason. First, however, this son of Italian immigrants put the comatose company back on its feet.

Iacocca, marketing man and supersalesman, retrieved from among the buried treasures of Chrysler's development department the so-called K-car platform for small to medium-range cars with front-wheel drive, as well as the design for a minivan. Chrysler was the first of the Big Three to offer cars with front-wheel drive by varying the K-car platform. With the minivan—technically a K-car as well—the company created an entirely new market, one that grew very quickly and one in which Chrysler remained number one for the time being.

By 1983, seven years earlier than it had to, Chrysler had paid back its government-sponsored loans. In 1986, all divisions of the firm were consolidated under the new company name, Chrysler Corporation. One year later, at Iacocca's instigation, Chrysler acquired American Motors Corporation (AMC), fourth-largest car manufacturer in the United States, from Renault, the French auto manufacturing company. The French did, however, keep AMC's heavy-truck company, Mack Trucks. Iacocca couldn't have cared less; all he was interested in from the deal was the Jeep. In possession of that historic brand, he grabbed large segments of the market for what are now commonly referred to as sport utility vehicles (SUVs). It was one of his most winning inspirations.

With small cars, minivans, and jeeps, Iacocca had given Chrysler Corporation completely new standing in the market. Structurally, the company was now ahead of everybody else. Even today, the market structures Iacocca instituted at that time underlie America's entire auto industry. Then, toward the end of the decade, Iacocca the Savior almost crashed the company against a wall because he didn't want to spend much money on technological development. Chrysler's products by then had started getting a bad rap as primitive and obsolete jalopies. Iacocca was forced to give his blessing to a comprehensive cost-reduction plan and a revolutionary model policy.

At first, subsidiaries extraneous to the auto business were sold, subsidiaries Iacocca had acquired as his success became assured. They included Gulfstream Aerospace, Electrospace Systems, FinanceAmerica, E. F. Hutton Credit, and no fewer than four rental-car companies. For Iacocca, who liked to move in fast company, parting with Gulfstream, an important producer of management jets, was most difficult. Next he formed the so-called platform teams, responsible for the entire life cycle of their products, from design to distribution and even customer service. Costs and production time shrank dramatically, while product quality—often a problem for Chrysler—significantly improved.

As Ford had done with its first Taurus model, Chrysler now freed itself from the traditional cost structure developed by GM. Soon the company achieved the highest profit rate per unit sold in the world. In 1998, it was $2,266, clearly better than Ford's $1,872 and GM's $874. A considerable part of this success can be attributed to the wide variety of products offered. Small trucks and SUVs, which are particularly profitable, accounted for 71 percent of Chrysler's production, compared to 61 percent at Ford and only 47 percent at GM. Small trucks especially, which use set pieces and are easy to manufacture, raked in money, as did Jeeps, whose more expensive models bring in five-figure profits per unit.

Finally, in 1991, Chrysler opened a large technology center in Auburn Park, near Detroit, with the express purpose of catching up in the area of auto technology, which the company had long neglected. Though Iacocca had no particular interest in this project, one of his designated successors did: Swiss-born Robert Lutz. Although Lutz was not an engineer, he had always been intrigued by race cars and jet fighters. Before he came to Chrysler, the ex-Marine and elite corps officer had worked at General Motors as director of distribution at Opel; at BMW as director of distribution; and at Ford as director of the Ford plant in Cologne, then as director of European operations, and finally as vice president of the Dearborn branch. His nose for the numerous aspects of the auto business was renowned.

After Iacocca had lured him to Chrysler, Lutz created sexy new products, from the 8-liter, 10-cylinder Viper sports car to the subcompact Neon. Suddenly, Chrysler's unusual styling was causing a buzz. Lutz also released three entirely new basic models, with cab-forward design, and exhibited several ultramodern or, conversely, nostalgic concept cars at auto shows. Many of them, like the Viper, later became huge hits. This time it was Lutz who saved Chrysler Corporation.

Bob Lutz, son of a well-off Swiss family, soon became more popular than Iacocca, which didn't go down well with the proud Italian American. Iacocca wanted to be the company's sole savior; he wanted to be "Mr. Chrysler" forever. Consequently, Iacocca recommended General Motors manager Robert Eaton, not Lutz, as his successor. At the time Eaton, an engineer, was head of General Motors of Europe in Switzerland. Everybody, and most of all Iacocca himself, expected Lutz to take his hat and leave the company. He did not. Furthermore, much to everyone's surprise, Eaton and Lutz agreed to lead the company together. Lutz did not retire as vice-chairman until 1998, when he was 66 years old.

It was, in fact, Iacocca who was forced to step down from Chrysler's board of directors following Eaton's intervention with the stockholders' representatives. From then on, Eaton and Lutz proceeded in an increasingly European manner of running the company. To survive the next industry-specific crisis, they hoarded huge capital reserves. This displeased major shareholder Kirk Kerkorian, who, in a sort of coup d'état, tried to force the company to give out dividends up to the amount of the new reserves. The leader of Kerkorian's move against Chrysler management was none other than Lee Iacocca. He simply couldn't let go. Eaton and Lutz fended off the attack, and Iacocca's reputation was ruined.

In 1997, Chrysler Corporation, with a profit of almost $4.6 billion on a return of $61.1 billion, did better than the two other leading American car companies, and much better than Daimler-Benz ($2.5 billion profit on a $72 billion return). In automobile production, Chrysler posted a 9 percent profit, and Daimler-Benz, 6.5 percent. In 1997, Chrysler had 121,000 employees worldwide compared to Daimler's 300,000. The German company has 21.2 billion deutsche marks ($12.3 billion) in capital reserves, and Chrysler has 14.1 billion marks ($8.2 billion).

Chrysler's strength was its productivity, whereas Daimler's was technology and size. What one lacked, the other offered. No other companies of this size could have been more suitable to one another. According to official historiography, Schrempp and Eaton met during the auto show in Detroit on January 12, 1998, to discuss precisely this point.

Eaton may have been speculating that Chrysler's present strength—its large profits on the American market—might soon turn into a fundamental weakness. The company owned only a few bases abroad, and therefore had few foreign markets. And though Chrysler had been making big money with its minivans, Jeeps, and light trucks, all of which sell particularly well in the United States, that, he may have feared, might change if regulations for exhaust fumes for most of these vehicles became stricter or if oil prices started to climb seriously. Furthermore, at the time, Chrysler's average of 860,000 passenger car units sold was lower than during the 1950s, 1960s, and 1970s.

What must have persuaded the cautious Eaton to go with Daimler was not just mathematics, but the potential future threats to the auto industry and the growth of other car companies. The deal also enabled Eaton to reduce the power of bothersome major shareholders such as Kerkorian. Most stocks in the new DaimlerChrysler Corporation are owned by Deutsche Bank, which has a 12.7 percent share, followed by the Emirate of Kuwait with 7.5 percent; Kirk Kerkorian has only 4.5 percent.

But what were the advantages of the merger for Daimler-Benz? Naturally, there were certain purely practical benefits—for instance, through discounts on supplies. DaimlerChrysler's managers estimate them to be around $3 billion per annum, which at a turnover rate of $150 to $180 billion translates into 2 percent tops. In addition, the corporation would be able to save certain plant costs by using, either alone or in conjunction with Chrysler, already existing Chrysler plants, such as the Jeep factory in Graz, Austria. But all that was peanuts, really. The more important advantages lay in strategy and are difficult to pin down in numbers.

There is no doubt that Daimler will save the expense of developing its own brands and models for affordable mass-produced vehicles. To be sure, it is unlikely that it will be easy for Chrysler cars to succeed in Europe, but Daimler will save major expenditures trying to penetrate the American market. Furthermore, in the United States, Daimler can share Chrysler's megaprofits. This frees the Stuttgart base of the company to continue building on its prestige in the high-end car market, with, for example, the new Mercedes Maybach.

Much depends on this model. Its name harkens to Daimler's famous head designer, Wilhelm Maybach. In the 1930s, the Maybach Motoren-werke, which the designer's family had founded, produced the May-bach *Zeppelin*, which was something of a super-Mercedes, a German Duesenberg. Today, DaimlerChrysler owns the rights to that name, for in 1960 Mercedes-Benz had acquired the majority of the Maybach Motorenwerke. Now Schrempp is banking on the new Maybach mak-ing the Rolls Royces and Bentleys—brands that were acquired by BMW and VW—look obsolete.

Jürgen Schrempp is also counting on being able to prevent the rup-tures that typically accompany any merger by quickly moving ahead. After all, there is quite a difference in the philosophies of Stuttgart, Ger-many, and Highland Park, Michigan. The fact that Eaton and Lutz have injected more European elements into Chrysler Corporation than is usual in the American auto industry doesn't change that. The clash of top managers with different philosophies can lead to frictions and losses in transcontinental day-to-day business.

It is, however, possible that requisite cultural assimilation may be confined to top management. Should there be fits of jealousy within the corporation, the directors can then act as mediators. The company's basic focus on the automobile will ultimately heal many wounds, espe-cially with the figures in the corporation's annual report acting as ban-dages. They constitute the principal advantage of this merger, anyway. If shareholder values are tended to, the entire corporation's value can increase even more, as can its overall solvency. Thus, DaimlerChrysler is in a situation comparable to that of the Getty Museum in California: It can participate in any major auction.

Whether such auctions are still worthwhile for DaimlerChrysler remains an open question. No other car company in the world has as many equally strong bases in the United States and in Europe. It also leads in the most lucrative market segments in both major auto markets: the prestige car in the Old World and the robust SUVs and light trucks in the New World. Yes, everything changes, favorable markets included. But for the time being, the DaimlerChrysler Corporation looks so strong that industry leaders General Motors and Ford have reason to worry.

CHAPTER 3

Case Two:
Mr. Stockmarket and the Politburo

Deutsche Bank's System

HARDLY HAD JÜRGEN SCHREMPP finalized the Daimler-Chrysler merger when the new auto giant's largest stockholder, Deutsche Bank, announced a similarly imperial plan. Prior to the announcement, a dozen other major bank mergers in America and Europe had raised the question: Why wasn't Deutsche Bank making a move? With no answer forthcoming from the bank, observers decided it was because the bank had turned into an institution—and a thoroughly German one at that. So, when on November 23, 1998, the bank board's spokesman, Rolf-Ernst Breuer, announced that Deutsche Bank was acquiring New York's Bankers Trust for $9.2 billion in cash, it caused a sensation in the financial world. On the balance sheet, this meant that Germany's largest and America's eighth-largest bank would form the world's leading financial institution—just ahead of Switzerland's UBS Bank, and far ahead of the United States' Citigroup and Japan's Bank of Tokyo Mitsubishi.

Deutsche Bank the largest bank? The second Transatlantic World Inc. in a single year? Rumors had been circulating for a while, but nothing had materialized. As was customary, mediators on both sides had ordered their respective colleagues not to breathe a word to anyone outside the companies. Negotiations took place entirely behind the scenes, sometimes in the war room of Wachtell, Lipton, Rosen & Katz, the New York law firm, and other times in the private home of big boss Breuer.

Public amazement at the German takeover was quickly replaced with predictions of failure. Even retired top managers of Deutsche Bank believed that their former employer had made a mistake. One of them told German journalists that the whole deal made as much sense as attaching a state-of-the-art computer to Russia's Mir space station.

The main players, Rolf Breuer and the American Frank Newman, attempted to rise above the naysayers. They talked about synergistic profits of about $1 billion per annum and of a total profit of some $5 to $6 billion by 2001. In *Manager Magazin* (January 1999, pages 69ff), Breuer assured his interviewer that "Bankers Trust is even better suited for us than we had figured previously."

Without a doubt, optimist Breuer piggybacked Jürgen Schrempp's publicity about his company's merger. DaimlerChrysler's boss, like Breuer, insisted that Daimler and Chrysler suited one another in all aspects, like two sides of a zipper. But where Schrempp never had any trouble supporting this statement, and it was virtually impossible to disprove him, in Breuer's case, the identical arguments seemed a little forced, no matter how emphatically they were put forth.

First, in terms of the bottom line, capital resources, and number of employees, Deutsche Bank is about four times as large as Bankers Trust. Second, the New York bank's business cannot fill the gaps in the German bank's services—though Bankers Trust does offer Deutsche Bank an enormous customer pool for the administration of property and securities and, for the first time, direct access to the complicated world of Wall Street. But as far as share issuing and investment banking are concerned—two activities of particular interest to Breuer—the new acquisition cannot help much: The merger with Bankers Trust will not bring Deutsche Bank much closer to the main players on this field—Goldman Sachs, Lehman Brothers, or Merrill Lynch. Breuer, in response, claimed that he wasn't trying to do that. He insisted that his goal was for his bank to become as quickly as possible a "real global financial services business." Whatever that may mean.

As with Jürgen Schrempp and Chrysler, Breuer did not have a lot of time to plan this venture, nor were there many alternatives available. And he was not able to pique the interest of the really large companies. His dream partner, J. P. Morgan, the most distinguished name in American banking, didn't even want to discuss a fifty-fifty merger. Founded in New York in 1861, J. P. Morgan and Company was nine years older than

Deutsche Bank. J. P. Morgan and his son had single-handedly helped the American economy through several serious financial crises. And though no longer America's largest financial institution, Morgan was still so solid and held in such high esteem that a merger with Deutsche Bank would have been regarded as a sellout, if not high treason.

Pressured, Breuer went after Bankers Trust. The New York bank, whose motto was "no risk, no fun," had posted a staggering loss of $488 million for the third quarter of 1998. The fact that it seemed to be recovering from the slide gave Breuer his window of opportunity. Otherwise, the deal couldn't possibly have gone through. Breuer could breathe a sigh of relief.

Throughout its history, Deutsche Bank had conducted business in the same way, with fashionable variations, as did Daimler-Benz, its pet company among those in which it owned stock. Until 1990, German markets had always been surrounded by formidable barriers. In this environment, as Germany's largest bank, Deutsche Bank had always carried the most weight and had the greatest success. When the German empire was at the zenith of its international glory, during the reign of Kaiser Wilhelm II, the bank—whose headquarters were then in Berlin—was even the *world's* largest financial institution for a while. Its connections to the other major institutions of Germany's economy, such as Siemens and Allianz, date back a century. Likewise, it had been a major stockholder in Daimler-Benz from day one and, before that, in Daimler-Motoren-Gesellschaft.

Since capital markets had become global, however, the bank had failed to keep up. Breuer, a member of Deutsche Bank's board since 1985 and its spokesman since 1997, had long ago realized that it would have to eliminate some of its antiquated practices if the bank were to escape looking as outdated as England's royal family. He was also aware that the rule of grow or go applied even to a giant like Deutsche Bank. But disentangling the bank from its outdated traditions would prove difficult. Breuer was called upon not only to revamp an enterprise that had been almost synonymous with German money, but to turn it into a cosmopolitan enterprise in the process. Or, as he put it, the bank had to metamorphose "from a universal bank into a bank with multiple specialties." A linguistic subtlety only Germans were likely to comprehend.

That Anglo-Saxon houses of finance doubted the feasibility of the merger is understandable. Deutsche Bank practices have long been foreign to the Americans and British. In all likelihood, too, the world couldn't fully realize that even after the collapse of the Communist Eastern bloc, Deutsche Bank remained an almost unequaled citadel of power, universality, and solidarity; a sponsor of the arts and adviser to governments; feared and respected by everyone from window cleaners to industry giants. Even if Europe went through another financial disaster of historic proportions such as the one in 1931, in all likelihood, Deutsche Bank would survive it, perhaps not alone, but as one among a select few. The market value of its stocks in other companies alone is greater than its own value if stated in terms of market capitalization.

For some 100 years, Deutsche Bank had been Germany's largest bank, as well as number one on the stock and credit markets and in terms of savings and checking accounts of the general public and of the managers of large companies. Hermann Josef Abs (1901–1994), an organ and solitaire player who presided over the bank in the early postwar years, had once and for all determined the direction the bank was going to go and grow. More than any other financial institution, it was called upon to design and build Germany's economic landscape.

Designing and building were always corporate activities, not elements of a market economy. Germany's economy was formed by Deutsche Bank's—or, more generally speaking, the large German banks'—structural policies. However, the other banks—Dresdner Bank, Commerzbank, Westdeutsche Landesbank, or Hypovereinsbank, and others—never moved and shook as much in concert as Deutsche Bank did alone. True, they could call themselves universal banks, but they had always been mere cogs in a system built by Deutsche Bank.

Deutsche Bank's system was one of omnipotence and omnipresence, of quiet domination. It was ruled by a web of managers, none of them radical, each moderately conservative. It preferred its staff to adhere to a strict diet, to part their hair properly, and, ideally, to be six feet tall, married with two or, better yet, three children. Step by step, sometimes with the subtlety of a steamroller and sometimes with popelike diplomacy, Deutsche Bank evolved into the country's most powerful financial institution.

No bank in Germany, or in Europe for that matter, was ever as large and comprehensive as Deutsche Bank, and none held its respective country's financial or industrial key positions the way "the Deutsche" has done. At the height of its power, in the late 1980s, Deutsche Bank clandestinely achieved the status of a semiofficial constitutional institution for financial affairs that could monitor everything, including itself. "I'm not a general manager," patriarch Abs put it bluntly and succinctly, "I appoint general managers."

In his 35 years as member, spokesman, and chairman of the board, Abs ("My name is Abs, A as in Abs, B as in Abs, and S as in Abs") a dedicated member of the Catholic Church, refined the bank's gradually developed rules into a code of law, which no one who wanted to make it in banking dared to oppose. The rules of this order soon spread to other parts of the system until they became universally valid within the Deutsche Bank cosmos. Supported by cross-connections between different people and their functions, this system led to the development of a certain species of people who became distinct and easily recognizable.

This was not natural selection à la Darwin. Quite the contrary: At work were Mendel's laws—the laws of artificial breeding. They resulted in that particular quality of moderate dynamism characteristic of Germany's upper industrial class, who prefer not to rush things, to double-check everything, to avoid mistakes of their own, to exploit those of others, and to offer and accept support against any outsider. It was a highly sensitive, hierarchically structured reinsurance system. It was a control center of the old Deutschland AG. It was also a kind of politburo whose knowledge became a power that could not be weakened by democratic institutions— which in fact took advice and learned from the wisdom of the arbiters of this supreme authority.

It was not only the conservative-liberal school of Wilhelm Röpke, Ludwig Erhard, and Alfred Müller-Armack that made Germany's economy after World War II so strong—seemingly invincible—it was also the rules of Deutsche Bank. The system was beneficient as long as everyone obeyed, but it became dictatorial as soon as anyone rebelled. Reliable and steadfast in the chancellor's as well as its customers' eyes, it developed into an enlightened feudal core within Germany's social democracy, comparable to Frederick the Great's rule. Each spokesperson in the institution's board, comfortable moving in the highest circles, was designated to give the chancellor to-the-point, elegant, and free advice, a responsibility each naturally passed on to his successor.

Abs, the Rhinelander, so superbly advised the like-minded Chancellor Adenauer that the latter wanted to appoint him foreign minister. Abs certainly was no newcomer to the international scene. In 1952–1953 he had negotiated the London treaty concerning Germany's debt to its erst-while enemies, in which the original claims of 20 billion marks against the Federal Republic were trimmed to 14 billion. Abs's two successors, Franz Heinrich Ulrich and Karl Klasen, both from Northern Germany, advised the two northern German, Social Democratic chancellors Willy Brandt and Helmut Schmidt. Later, when Klasen, a Social Democrat himself, became president of the German National Bank and Ulrich was approaching retirement age, the role of adviser was assigned to successors Friedrich Wilhelm Christians and Wilfried Guth.

Initially, Helmut Kohl, too, the eternal chancellor, relied on such an ordained pundit by the name of Alfred Herrhausen. The two had met during a vacation near Salzburg, before Herrhausen had moved into the bank's executive suite as Christians's successor. Only after Herrhausen was killed in a bombing on his way to the office in the fall of 1989 was the direct contact between Deutsche Bank and the chancellor's office suspended. The bank no longer wanted to make headlines, opting to better protect its managers.

In any case, it elected Hilmar Kopper director, a man as stocky as he was competent, and a member of the Mennonite Church. Kopper owed his appointment to selection principles reminiscent of those used by the Catholic Church. From a modest background, he did not have a college education or even an honorary degree. Hilmar Kopper had begun the old-fashioned way: as an apprentice. He was part of Deutsche Bank's system from the beginning of his career.

It's another distinguishing characteristic of Deutsche Bank that a preeminent name or one's parents' social rank don't count for very much. It breeds its own elite, and careful selection starts with apprentices. Smaller banks may hire blue-blooded employees, but Deutsche Bank doesn't even particularly care about higher education credentials. At the time of this writing, the bank's 12-member board of directors included one aristocrat and seven Ph.D.'s; and the former is not one of the latter. The 20-member supervisory board was made up entirely of members of the middle class, though handpicked in regard to their financial background.

Hiring the bank's top personnel is strictly the boss's job. Here, too, the rules according to Abs apply. In this case, the boss is not the spokesperson of the executive board but the chair of the supervisory board. At Deutsche Bank, this office—with only one exception since World War II—has been held by the person who is about to resign as spokesperson of the executive board. To become spokesperson, the candidate must have served as a regular member of the board of directors for at least 10 years. Given this kind of inbreeding, the supercontroller is presumed to know best who deserves to be sitting in the highest chair. Remarkably, it isn't necessarily only ability that counts. Following the bank's "Abs-olute" rules, the board must always consist of three age groups comprising as much as possible equal numbers of members: those between 40 and 50, those between 51 and 60, and those over 60. To preserve the balance, a spokesperson of the board may retire before the age of 65, but never later. Thus, Hilmar Kopper, who forcefully secured the bank a place in the international business community, made room for his successor Rolf Breuer (considered important for the bank's further development) before reaching retirement age. To date, Kopper chairs the supervisory board, from which he can resign after five years to make room for Breuer.

Continuity has been key. Deutsche Bank has had only eight spokesmen since World War II, including two simultaneously a few times between the Abs era and the Herrhausen era. While these gentlemen were different from one another, they all shared the pursuit of one goal: the preservation of their bank as universal, and thus Germany's banking system in general. As a universal bank, it may do almost anything that has to do with money: Not only may it trade stocks and bonds, but it may introduce them to the market. It may grant loans to local businesses, to countries for their national budgets, to small savings account holders, and to buyers on installment plans; it may even lend itself money. It can trade with money, gold, and foreign currency; it may invest in companies, and in many cases, dominate them.

In this way, Deutsche Bank has become number one in most of these areas. To some extent, its customers rarely have a choice but to become dependent on it. For example, many German workers must open a checking account at Deutsche Bank and the like to get paid by their employers. It is no different for homeowners, entrepreneurs, and smaller companies that need loans. It is even true in a wider sense for Germany's large stock corporations, the inner belt of the Deutsche Bank system, for which the bank often acts in three different roles: as creditor, as stockbroker, and as stockholder.

Whenever regarded as prudent, Deutsche Bank sends one or two of its staff to join a company's supervisory board. This gives it control not only over the company's money and strategy, but also—as with Daimler-

Benz—over who runs the company. The bank also has a say with its many smaller securities customers, which give it the right to vote by proxy at the annual meeting. This translates into enormous power. If the stocks of corporations are spread widely—as are those of Germany's three largest chemical companies—the right to vote by proxy often suffices to obtain a simple majority. Only very mobile stock corporations such as Mannesmann that don't want banks to meddle in their business affairs took the precaution of instituting strict voting restrictions in their bylaws, stipulating that no one may represent more than 5 percent of the company's total capital at the annual meeting.

The right to vote by proxy is sacrosanct, not least because it is an advantage to the bankers within their own company. With their customers' powers of attorney in their pocket, not only can they conveniently check on each other, but they also determine who becomes a member of their board of directors. Grassroots democracy and elitist thinking are perfectly complementary. To date, Deutsche Bank's grand masters have painstakingly prevented any stockholder from becoming big enough to approach the 25 percent ceiling for stocks that might end their idyll by way of a blocking minority. The largest stockholders of Deutsche Bank are Allianz AG with 5.03 percent and the Münchner Rückerversicherungs-Gesellschaft AG with 1.5 percent. Conversely, Deutsche Bank owns 9.4 percent of Allianz's stocks and 10 percent of Münchner Rück. Tit for tat.

Arrangements like this are typical of the Deutsche Bank system. They are enhanced by employee involvement in different companies. In the days of old, when Abs alone had more than 30 proxy votes, this was obvious: You join my supervisory board and I'll join yours.

But because this consolidation of power was limited by the so-called Lex Abs (or "law of Abs"), which restricted the number of powers of attorney one could hold and prohibited crossover powers of attorney, these complex interlockings have existed only very indirectly. Take, for example, Deutsche Bank's connection with Cologne's large insurance company, Gerling. Deutsche Bank and Gerling each own 15 percent of the investment firm Deutsche Beteiligungs AG's stock. Deutsche Bank also owns 30 percent of Gerling's stock. Michael Otto, a member of Deutsche Bank's supervisory board and head of Hamburg's Otto Versand, and thus a fairly independent man, is also a member of Gerling's governing board, which convenes discreetly. Another member of that committee is Manfred Bischoff, chairman of the board of Daimler-Chrysler's subsidiary DASA and thus part of Deutsche Bank's system.

Bischoff's boss of bosses, Jürgen Schrempp, is a member of the Allianz advisory board. Marcus Bierich, Bosch's chairman (Bosch is one of DaimlerChrysler's most important suppliers), is a member of the supervisory boards of both Allianz and Deutsche Bank. Ditto for Klaus Liesen, director of Ruhrgas for many years, who, in addition, is chairman of the supervisory boards of VW and Mannesmann. Heinrich von Pierer, head of the electrical corporation Siemens, is also a member of the supervisory board of VW. These are only a few examples from 1996 to 1998.

But it has always been this way. Twenty years ago, Allianz and Münchner Rück were interconnected. Along with Daimler-Benz, they formed the hard inner core of the Deutsche Bank system. Since Daimler's merger with Chrysler, Deutsche Bank has continued to hold 12.7 percent of the company's stocks, totaling 19 billion marks. The bank's combined shares of Munich's insurance duo is worth 20 billion marks. At almost 40 billion marks, these three stock packages constitute the bank's basic portfolio, whose equity capital is estimated at 45 to 50 billion marks total.

Less directly, but for an even longer period of time than the car and the insurance companies, has been Siemens's relationship with Deutsche Bank. The difference is that Siemens's capital is still clearly under the influence of its founding family. One of its early members, Georg von Siemens, was Deutsche Bank's director for 30 years after its founding. Another case in point is Robert Bosch GmbH in Stuttgart, which is governed by a foundation (and, incidentally, is Siemens's partner in the appliance business). The credit of Hans G. Merkle, Bosch's director for several decades, with the bank was so good that he advanced to chairman of its supervisory board in the mid-1980s. An "outsider," he was the one famous exception to the rule.

Next to the bank's hard core of old-timers comes the inner circle. It is made up of Frankfurt's Philipp Holzmann AG, the leading company for large construction projects, in which the bank owns 25.1 percent, and Cologne's machine manufacturer Klöckner Humboldt Deutz (KHD), in which the bank owns 47.7 percent. Then there are Heidelberger Zement AG, Linde AG, Mannesmann AG, and Südzucker AG, in which the bank owns 10.1 percent each. Smaller players are Hannover's tire manufacturer Continental AG (8.4 percent), Dortmund's power company VEW (6.3 percent), and Aachen-Münchner Beteiligungs AG (5 percent). True, these are merely statistics that could change any day, but they are representative of the contents of Deutsche Bank's portfolio.

The next level in the system consists of corporations to which the bank is connected neither historically nor through large stock packages. These include Veba, which was Germany's largest company for a long time, and Volkswagen, which is still Europe's largest car manufacturer in terms of number of units produced. The three large chemical companies BASF, Bayer, and Hoechst also belong into this category.

The core, the inner circle, and the outer ring of the system also can be used to chart with some precision the movements of Germany's industrial complex after World War II. Until the end of the war, Berlin had been the country's major industrial center, ahead of the Rhine-Ruhr region. Stuttgart, Frankfurt, and Munich were less important than Germany's coastal towns. Then Deutsche Bank left Berlin to reestablish itself in West Germany. For a while, it maintained major branches in Düsseldorf and Hamburg, but soon focused more on Frankfurt, hometown of the Rothschilds. Dresdner Bank and Commerzbank had no choice but to follow suit, as, eventually, did others, most notably Germany's National Bank and, as the big finale, Europe's Central Bank. In a sense, Deutsche Bank became the City of Frankfurt's second founder.

Throughout history, those in power like to represent it in stone and art treasures. Deutsche Bank was no different. It spent 465 million marks to build Germany's most expensive financial "cathedral" at the time, with not one but two towers reaching into the sky. And to mark the two-story difference in height between the two, they were promptly nicknamed "Debit" and "Credit."

In 1985, the bank's high priests and their believers moved into the new cathedral, which had been enriched by contemporary art. But, as is often the case, no sooner does an entity erect a monument to itself than it turns into a monument itself. Deutsche Bank's system had reached the pinnacle of its success. It had emerged unscathed from an unexpected financial crisis in Germany, which its competitors had survived only by selling huge chunks of their portfolios and buildings and by reactivating old top managers. On the other hand, the bank's dogmatic policy of avoiding risk had so overregulated Germany's business landscape that its entire topography had shifted. There were productive areas in Germany where Deutsche Bank's system did only what was absolutely necessary.

Though the bank's move from Berlin to Frankfurt was one of the many consequences of the outcome of the war, and thus, almost inevitable, it had turned Deutsche Bank into a *Westdeutsche* (West German) bank. What followed were independent decisions by the system's leaders that were, like that move, politically motivated but *not* inevitable: The grand masters of Adenauer's republic on the Rhine had turned their backs on northern Germany, glanced at East Germany with disgust, and looked straight down south. There, in Baden-Württemberg and Bavaria, the conservative state governments were firmly established, whereas the north was almost equally solidly "red," which means social-democratic or, in U.S. terms, liberal. Wilfried Guth, Erhard's nephew, stated unequivocally that a conservative government "pays off better economically."

The move also had an impact on the Deutsche Bank system itself, which encompassed the entire area of what was then the republic on the Rhine. Members of the system's hard core and inner circle extended into Bavaria's "bratwurst border" in the east and south. North of Frankfurt, governments were mixed; north of Cologne, they were red. With the exception of VW, which was already considered to be an endangered corporation, nothing was possible there. Neither did northern Germany have anything to offer. In the final analysis, then, the "German bank" was only a "southern German bank." It actively tried to separate from those regions in Germany that it simply didn't know how to handle.

Such a strategy can work for awhile, and it may even go unnoticed; eventually, however, a counterproductive process starts. This process is what the bank had to avert as soon as the country's insulation—which ensured profits—became porous. That was the phase the bank was in when Alfred Herrhausen, of a modest background from the Ruhr region, became Deutsche Bank's new president. His supporters had wanted a modern version of patriarch Abs, someone to be the board's sole and long-term spokesman again. Herrhausen was a man with a special charm, who at times seemed less interested in the inner workings of the bank than in what was going outside it. He also was strategically and politically minded, a characteristic that would ultimately profit the bank. It was obvious that he would extend the bank's limits and free it from its golden cage. Telegenic, Alfred Herrhausen directed his game from outside—which meant in part via the media.

Herrhausen wanted to turn Deutsche Bank into a European universal bank; he wanted to extend investment banking. He worked hard on

the acquisition of the British investment bank Morgan Grenfell, which
had been founded in 1910. This didn't pan out as planned, but it did
mark the beginning of a new way of thinking. In the meantime, Herrhausen's universe was still the world of the Cold War. He, like many
others, considered Germany the "greatest powerlessness in the world."
Initially, he refused to think beyond the borders and limits of Europe.
Consequently, he, too, was surprised by the East's collapse. Although he
had the advantage of being close to the chancellor and always getting the
scoop on new developments, he had never envisaged a united Germany.
Subsequently, however, when he publicly reflected on German affairs,
his comments implied the wisdom of his strategy and his political
courage. This strategy, as far as he and Deutsche Bank were concerned,
might mean a return to the place where Hermann Josef Abs had come
from as Deutsche Bank's youngest director: Berlin.

The old Berlin as Germany's new financial center, Herrhausen figured, would quickly change everything. Indeed, the major political
events would transform a southern German bank with clipped wings
back into a real German institution. Herrhausen couldn't have foreseen
the package deal between German unity and a European currency. Not
even his friend Helmut Kohl saw that clearly at the time; perhaps not
even then–U.S. president George Bush and his secretary of state James
Baker were fully aware of it, either. And what about France's François
Mitterrand? At that time, the package deal was the last option he had for
taming the larger Germany by way of integration.

In retrospect, Herrhausen still believed that acquiring Morgan Gren-
fell was an act of genius, but Rolf Breuer less than 10 years later stated:
"From what we know today, we should have had the courage to go to
America back then," adding, "But nobody did."

Rolf Breuer's Escape Forward

Rolf-Ernst Breuer, the man who did have that courage, was from the
country's western region, like Abs and Herrhausen. He was born on
November 3, 1937, in Bonn, a somewhat insignificant town with a university, known largely as Beethoven's birthplace. Breuer's family was not
exactly *haute bourgeoisie,* even though his father had advanced from
merchant's apprentice to member of the board of directors of the

famous chocolate company Allgäuer Alpenmilch AG. Apparently, however, the atmosphere at home opened a window to the great wide world
for Breuer. After his graduation from high school, he passed the difficult
selection process at Deutsche Bank and subsequently became an
apprentice, first in Mainz and then in Munich.

At the time, people of Breuer's generation who were too young to
serve in World War II and too old to be drafted into the postwar German
army, were able to advance uninterrupted in their careers. With his college education completed, things were bound to happen even faster,
especially since the financial hard times were over back home. Breuer
moved to Lausanne, Switzerland, then back to Munich, and from there
to Bonn to go to law school, where in 1967 he earned his J.D. A law
degree and a certificate as a bank employee were the perfect combination to launch a successful banking career. During semester breaks,
Breuer traveled to London and Paris, where he worked as an intern. At
the age of 29 he had done everything that was necessary and returned to
Deutsche Bank to work at the Karlsruhe branch in southern Germany.

Breuer initially got caught up in the noisy gambling-hall atmosphere
of stock trading, so three years later, he joined the Deutsche Bank headquarter's stock exchange department, where he encountered Hans Feith
and Robert Ehret, who would determine the course his life was to take.
The former had been a member of the board since 1959, the latter since
1970. At the age of 35, Breuer, an admirer of stock exchange specialist
Ehret, became director of the bank's stock exchange department. It was
the kind of job that reinforced his way of thinking—which had led to that
job in the first place.

Breuer was not like Herrhausen, Ulrich, or Klasen; nor was he as
flamboyantly dramatic as Hermann Josef Abs. And he didn't have
Hilmar Kopper's down-to-earth burliness. The man he resembled most
was Ehret, his role model and boss, who was 12 years his senior. Perhaps
he worried that if Ehret followed the bank's unwritten laws and retired
at 65, he, at 53, might be regarded as too old to succeed Ehret on the
board. But Breuer needn't have worried, because Ehret did what he had
always promised he would do: He quit his post as a board member
before he was 60.

It was during 1985, when Herrhausen made sweeping personnel
changes, that Breuer knew his time had come. Ehret had moved to the
supervisory board, where he became a member of the powerful loan

committee, the center of Deutsche Bank's administration of capital. Breuer, then 47, was promoted to member of the board of directors. For the first two years, he was only a deputy with responsibility for taking minutes at meetings, but in 1987, he became a full-fledged member of the board. He became preoccupied with Herrhausen's plan to develop investment banking in Germany, which compelled him to closely study how this was handled in the United States. Consequently, Breuer soon lost his shyness with the Wall Street crowd. Besides, things were different there since the crash of October 1987.

That same October, Breuer gave the speech that would earn him a controversial notoriety. In front of the Frankfurt financial elite, he called for vast reforms and the complete computerization of securities trading in Germany, all but saying that unless this was done, the influence of the German stock exchange would be history. Not surprisingly, traditionalists resented him deeply, but Breuer's farsightedness soon made him the leader of Germany's stock exchange reform. He organized the founding of the German Futures Exchange (Deutsche Terminbörse, DTB) and of the electronic trading system IBIS (Inter-Banking Trade and Information System). In short order, "Mr. Stock Exchange" was awarded a number of honorary positions—though sooner than he would have liked, as they threatened to diminish his presence at the bank.

In early 1993, Breuer became stock exchange president in Frankfurt and chairman of the supervisory board of the national stock exchange association Deutsche Börse AG. Breuer continued to eloquently champion Frankfurt's significance as an international financial center and, his long-term goal, an electronic European stock exchange. Unfortunately for him, he and the bank's new director, Hilmar Kopper, a certified merchant banker, were worlds apart. The only thing they had in common was a mutual interest in investment banking.

Hilmar Kopper was the man behind the bank's current strict internal structure. He had it working much better than it had under the extroverted Herrhausen. Kopper took a hands-on style, and was known to surprise many, both within the bank and in the world at large, by his moves. The Anglo-Saxons liked him because he spoke English without an accent. And because he was no dictator but more the wait-and-see type, his calm nature kept the bank from making many a rash decision. On the downside, it also hindered him when he needed to make quick decisions. He gave the British money jugglers at Morgan Grenfell too much rein, for instance. And during the restructuring of Daimler-Benz, whose supervisory board he chaired, he failed to hold Reuter, the company's director, in check from launching his ambitious armament, aeronautics, and aerospace plans, even though the end of the armament department was obvious by then. More significant, Kopper was blind to the warning signs of the worst disaster confronting him: the bankruptcy of Frankfurt's big-time construction company Jürgen Schneider.

Schneider had let his real estate empire, which depended on bank loans, collapse, then clandestinely escaped abroad. Deutsche Bank was one of his major victims. The details were very embarrassing for Kopper's board of directors. Jokes started circulating to the effect that the bank was hiding Schneider in one of its guesthouses and planned to keep him there until no one could recognize him any longer. The jokes stopped when, one year later, Schneider was apprehended in Florida and extradited to be put on trial in Germany. Though the trial was as embarrassing for Deutsche Bank as its directors feared, mercifully for them, it was quickly forgotten. What was not forgotten, however, was a major public relations gaffe Kopper made. At a press conference, when asked about the small businesspeople whose bills Schneider hadn't paid, Kopper promised that Deutsche Bank would help out with 50 million marks; then he unwisely added that the sum was peanuts. The public was outraged, and Peanuts and Kopper became synonymous.

Kopper had less trouble smoothing over the Daimler-Benz situation with Reuter, but it, too, revealed one of Kopper's weaknesses: He was not an experienced man of the industry like his predecessor Herrhausen, but a merchant banker. Herrhausen, many believed, probably could have stopped Reuter in time, whereas Kopper succumbed to Reuter's considerable persuasiveness. Or perhaps Kopper simply wanted to avoid having to listen to Reuter's endless speeches. Probably, however, Kopper didn't really know what Reuter was up to, or what the consequences would be for Daimler-Benz. Could he realistically have gauged the implications of the end of the Cold War for Reuter's armament department plans? We will never know.

What is known is that the DASA disaster, caused jointly by Reuter and Schrempp, in particular the acquisition of Fokker, did not alert him either. When the full extent of the Daimler-Benz debacle became known, Kopper's reputation was damaged. Nevertheless, he made no objection to making Schrempp—the accessory—Reuter's successor. In spite of Schrempp's involvement with the DASA debacle, Kopper just got along better with Schrempp than with the other top contenders for

Reuter's position. Thus, Schrempp found it very easy to convince Kopper of his take-no-prisoners plan for putting Daimler-Benz back on its feet. Besides, Kopper recognized that Schrempp had done the bank much more good than harm. Furthermore, by mid-1996, it looked like Daimler-Benz's problems were soon to be solved.

It came as a big surprise, then, when Deutsche Bank announced in October 1996 that as of the date of the annual meeting in May 1997, its director was being transferred to the supervisory board. Breuer's time had come—in fact, it was his last chance. Only two years Kopper's junior, he was lucky a second time when one of his superiors left office early. So when Kopper left at age 62, Breuer, almost 60, arrived. He was now the man Deutsche Bank was counting on to accomplish what Herrhausen hadn't been ready to and Kopper was no longer able to: expand to the United States.

Breuer's first attempt was not a success. Deutsche Bank, ever faithful to its system, had tried to turn the merger of Thyssen and Krupp—the steel trusts of Germany's founding years—into an American-style takeover battle. Krupp, the smaller of the two partners, was supposed to acquire the Thyssen group, one of the largest steel producers in Europe and approximately twice as large as Krupp, in an unfriendly takeover. Behind this was the rather bold assumption that while Krupp had a few large shareholders, 80 percent of Thyssen was owned by small stockholders who would be susceptible to a good offer.

Breuer optimistically explained, "It's very important to me that this first big case set an example in the financial center, Frankfurt." That it did: Chancellor Kohl's conservative administration, the Social Democratic state government of North Rhine–Westphalia, along with the unions, drummed up public opposition to the former cannon factory's plans. It didn't work out for Krupp, and *that* became the example. Rolf Breuer had hardly warmed his new chair as Deutsche Bank's spokesman, and already many wondered if the writing was on the wall.

Deutsche Bankers Trust Co.

Despite the Krupp failure, in the final analysis, Deutsche Bank maintained influence. In part this is because the bank has always grown from the inside, even while it expanded through the acquisition of numerous smaller financial institutions. Its first glorious period encompassed the four and a half decades between the foundation of the second German Empire in 1871 and the beginning of World War I in 1914. During those years Deutsche Bank became notable both for its remarkable internal drive and for its hundreds of acquisitions. What Breuer now was charged with doing—acquiring another large institution without jeopardizing the bank—was something the bank's founders had managed to do again and again in situations that were much less stable. What's more, no matter how large the takeovers and mergers had been, the company's name always remained Deutsche Bank.

Deutsche Bank and the German Empire were born together. The company conducted business out of rented quarters at a time when the first unified German currency was established. Thirteen decades later, with the euro replacing the national currency and the European Union beginning to take shape, Deutsche Bank is facing its most significant transformation ever. Such transformations will undoubtedly affect the clout of the bank's name. In Germany, Deutsche Bank automatically elicits images of solidarity and brand identification. Beyond German borders, however, the bank must prove itself to be a first-rate house of finance. But this the bank cannot do alone. It is dependent on Germany's economy and the way other countries view it. Consequently, the bank today has a new, powerful incentive to help German companies finance investments abroad, which in turn means that it will have to compete with foreign banks and their offers. The acquisition of an all-American institution such as Bankers Trust can only make things easier in this regard. A German bank cannot be easily separated from German history. By the time the bank celebrated its 75th birthday in 1945, a once-proud German history was now steeped in shame, and the nation's largest financial institution had some blemishes as well.

In Deutsche Bank's early days, however, everything was going with the flow of general industrial development in Europe. Private banker Adalbert von Delbrück from Berlin, who had degrees in law and divinity, was one of Deutsche Bank's founding fathers. It was the era of Otto von Bismarck, of railways and iron boats—risky investments that required healthy banks for financial backing. The typical private banker—who existed in every midsize city in Germany—was not powerful enough for this, unless his name was Rothschild, Bleichröder, or

Bethmann. At the time, companies were essentially invited to take advantage of German stock law, in the investment business as elsewhere. Distributing stocks was a source of additional capital resources for new companies that were on solid economic footing and wanted to grow fast. Myriad such "joint-stock banks" were founded in the 1870s. Between June 1870 and February 1873, 35 new banks were established in Berlin alone. Naturally, not all of them were healthy.

Prussian King Wilhelm I (later, Kaiser Wilhelm I) issued Deutsche Bank's license on March 10, 1870. On April 9, the bank opened its doors in Berlin. The following year, the bank's first branch was opened in the port town of Bremen. Beginning in 1872, the new institution had a web of branches all over the world, from Shanghai to Constantinople.

Order and perseverance ruled in the new enterprise's executive suite. Two kindred spirits jointly led the bank for no less than a quarter of a century: Georg von Siemens, who was only 31 years old when the bank was founded and who had previously worked in London and Tehran for his family's firm of Siemens & Halske, and Hermann Wallich, who was 37. Unlike Siemens, Wallich—a well-known banker's name in the United States, too—had had many years of banking experience. Where Siemens often acted rashly, Wallich tended to be hesitant and cautious. The mix was perfect. Siemens would be director of the bank for 30 years.

The two of them quickly consolidated the bank's property. Soon after it was founded, they acquired Berliner Bankverein and Deutsche Union Bank. They also randomly collected numerous sluggish local banks, as well as medium-size joint-stock banks and their branches. In retrospect, this helped the company rise to the status of universal bank. Over the years, more than 400 banks merged with Deutsche Bank, most of them during the Siemens-Wallich era.

Early on, the young bankers also got together with the representatives of institutions of political power who wanted the bank's support for their various endeavors, especially in foreign policy. Once in a while this led to major deals, but it often resulted in big flops as well. It was with the "help" of German authorities that Deutsche Bank got involved in risky deals in the Orient and the Balkans. It built the Anatolian railway, acquired the operating company of Turkey's Oriental Railways, became a partner in the Romanian railway, and financed Vienna's Tramway. And when the U.S. company, Northern Pacific Railroad, collapsed in 1893, it was Deutsche Bank that helped it back to its feet by

1896. In Germany, Wallich and Siemens also founded the Deutsch-Überseeische Electricitäts-Gesellschaft, an international power com-pany, and the Deutsche Petroleum AG. All these ventures were risky and progressive. Never again would Deutsche Bank do as large a part of its business with venture capital as it did then. But if it wants to remain in first place in the finance business, it will have to pick up where it left off during that period.

When World War I broke out, Deutsche Bank's dynamic era ended, to be followed by decades of retreats or consolidations; the bank became defensive and conservative. At the end of the Great War, several of the empires with which Deutsche Bank had formed good business relations had been erased from the map: the Ottoman and the Hapsburg Empires, to name two. Russia, too, with its vast need for financing had turned into the Soviet Union. The former world power Great Britain was becoming economically tight; and the new world power, the United States of Amer-ica, didn't need to be financed by a bank in Germany. The German empire itself—now a republic—lost a fantastic amount of middle-class property, while new major industrial property was being accumulated. In other words, foreign business was as good as dead, while inner-German business was shrinking.

Clearly, in the 1920s, the German banking system had to rearrange itself, whereby it became much more "deutsch." Those remaining in the financial world were the four large "D" banks: Deutsche Bank, Dres-dner Bank, Darmstädter und Nationalbank (Danat), and Disconto-Gesellschaft. Then, at the end of October 1929, when Wall Street crashed, Deutsche Bank and the Disconto-Gesellschaft frantically merged in a one-to-one ratio. The deal, which also involved the acquisi-tion of four large regional banks, resulted in a house called DeDiBank for the next eight years—Deutsche Bank und Disconto-Gesellschaft. After taking over a few additional local (private) banks in 1930, it was by far the largest bank in Germany. The following year, Jacob Gold-schmidt's Danat-Bank went belly-up in a major crash, leaving only two of the four D banks standing.

During the global economic crisis, Deutsche Bank held tightly to the so-called Russian business. It was a time of large-scale industrialization for the new Soviet Union. Altogether, 27 German banks under the lead-ership of Deutsche Bank became part of the loan syndicate newly estab-lished by the government and the Reichsbank. To their capitalist business partners' delight, the Soviets paid up promptly. Still, both Deutsche and Dresdner Bank needed federal subsidies to grant these loans, and the two were moving toward each other again. Enter Adolf Hitler.

It hardly need be said that the Nazi period did not stimulate Deutsche Bank's foreign business. Its defensive phase continued. The bank became even more German, if not entirely a Nazi institution. It was now by far the largest individual bank in Germany. It held onto some of its holdings, such as the portfolio of Daimler-Benz AG, which was important to the Nazi government. Though during the early Nazi period, Hitler's yes-men launched a propaganda war against large banks and capitalists, the banks knew they simply had to wait for it to blow over, for the truth was, Hitler needed them for his armament program, which was openly discussed in so-called informed circles in Berlin. Like all large and many small businesses at the time, Deutsche Bank aligned itself with the Nazis. Perhaps they couldn't be said to be having a full-blown affair, but certainly they were involved in something of a compromising relationship.

At least that's how today's Deutsche Bank managers prefer to see it. To that end, in the 1990s, they commissioned a committee of scholars led by German historian Manfred Pohl to research the bank's activities during the Hitler era. According to their findings, Deutsche Bank continued to go about its business during the Third Reich. And because it was a large company, so were its deals. The new government regarded it with suspicion at first, not least because there were many Jews and Catholics among its top managers. Most of the Catholics were allowed to keep their jobs, but all Jewish members on the board of directors and on the supervisory board were forced to resign in 1933 and 1934. One of their most prominent representatives, board spokesman Oscar Wasser-mann, who left in late 1933, publicly decried the injustice.

Georg Solmssen, a member of the boards of Deutsche Bank and the Disconto-Gesellschaft since 1911, also became "no longer tenable" to the Nazis. He lost his post in 1934, but remained a token member of the supervisory board until 1937. Solmssen knew exactly what was coming. He wrote to a colleague, "I'm afraid that this is the beginning of a well-planned process that is geared toward the indiscriminate economic and moral destruction of all members of the Jewish race in Germany." Like most people those days, members of the board understood this as clearly as he did, yet kept quiet and looked the other way. Fortunately Solmssen left Germany in time, before the outbreak of World War II, and lived in Switzerland to the ripe old age of 91.

In 1938, after a member of the board of directors had died and his seat became available, Hermann Josef Abs, then 36 years old, accepted the invitation to join the company's top management. Only shortly before, he had become a partner in the renowned private bank Delbrück Schickler & Co. Why did he leave this well-paid job? One of the official explanations for Abs's behavior is that he wanted to save Deutsche Bank's foreign business for the period after Hitler. What was there to save, except some transitory personal contacts? In later years, Abs made a remark that made more sense. He said that, as an organ player, he had always preferred the instrument with the most registers. In any event, his change to Deutsche Bank came dangerously close to forming a deliberate pact with the devil.

Abs said he was not a Nazi. He really was not the type. But then, many of those who collaborated with National Socialists didn't consider themselves Nazis, either. At Deutsche Bank, the protection of the board of directors made it possible to fend off pressures from Hitler's party. Until 1943, Deutsche Bank was able to keep Nazi extremists out of its top management, though in 1935 it had hired Nazi party member Karl Ritter von Halt as director of human resources and, in 1938, accepted him as a member of the board. But von Halt, a war hero, noted sportsman, and respected banker, was much more loyal to the bank than to the Nazi party. Hermann Abs admitted that he knew about the Nazi extermination camps as early as 1943, since documents exist to prove it, but he never admitted knowing more than that. In any case, among many obscure and forgotten papers from Deutsche Bank's files, historian Pohl found proof positive in early 1999 that the bank gave loans to companies that helped build Auschwitz. The revealing document was a piece of paper from a construction firm, W. Riedel & Sohn, dated March 2, 1943. A worker had noted on an order: "Concrete gas chamber floor."

Breuer responded to these revelations by claiming he was horrified and that he accepted his "ethical-moral responsibility." Without question, he said, Riedel & Sohn had operated on loans from Deutsche Bank. Clearly, the branch that gave the firm the money knew what was going on, as did headquarters in Berlin, because loans above a certain amount required its approval. Was it intentional collaboration? "I'd like to know the company that was not entangled in the web of National Socialism," was the resigned conclusion of the late Ignaz Bubis, then-director of the Central Council of Jews in Germany.

In fact, even U.S. subsidiaries such as the Ford plants in Cologne and Opel (General Motors) were part of the Nazi system, even while they were still clearly under American control. Ford explained its cooperation by stating that until the United States entered the war in December 1941, it had diplomatic relations with the German Reich. Likewise, according to an FBI report, James Mooney, then General Motors' manager of foreign subsidiaries, stated on July 23, 1941, that he would avoid anything that would "upset Hitler." This reasoning is perfectly in line with the explanations of German tycoons.

So Deutsche Bank "went along," though few of its top managers were part of the inner circle of Nazi sympathizers. The bank didn't feather its nest with Jewish accounts or victims' gold. Documents indicate that if the bank did its share of exploiting foreign workers, it did so only indirectly, through its close connections with Daimler-Benz and the chemical conglomerate IG Farben, which produced Zyclon B, the poisonous chemical used in the gas chambers. That foreign slave labor was being used was something every German knew; they were seen at work everywhere in industry and agriculture. Deutsche Bank did take part in confiscating Jewish property, acquiring, for example, the eminent private bank Mendelsohn & Co. in 1938; and from about 1940 on, it opened numerous branches in areas occupied by Germany.

Inevitably, Breuer's takeover deal with Bankers Trust was tainted by these historical events and the discoveries of the bank's involvement with them. But perhaps because of the distance of time and the hope for a better future, it was not so much World War II atrocities that impacted Breuer's takeover plans, but Deutsche Bank's failure following its takeover of London's Morgan Grenfell in 1989. In order to be regarded as a serious player in investment banking, it put more than $3 billion into the London bank, to no avail. Blinded by the glory of having bought a firm with such a distinguished history as Morgan Grenfell, Deutsche Bank let the Brits muddle along without checking on them. It wanted to learn from them; but if the Brits had any wise lessons to teach, they didn't let on. Disappointed, Deutsche Bank changed its strategy in 1995. It reduced Morgan Grenfell to a branch of Deutsche Bank, calling the new institution Deutsche Morgan Grenfell. Not surprisingly, the Brits didn't like this, and many of them quit.

Shortly thereafter, it was discovered that a great deal of money had been systematically embezzled by the London bank's stock managers. Deutsche Bank lost hundreds of millions of dollars, and its managers had to answer embarrassing questions concerning the quality of its control system. Lost in the shuffle was the bank's desire to become a contender in investment banking. Frankfurt's managers sought a way out of this dead end by hiring high-quality experts from high-quality American investment banks and paying them exorbitant salaries. Among them were Edson Mitchell of Merrill Lynch and Frank Quattrone of Morgan Stanley. Some of them turned out to have egos to match those salaries, which impaired communication with headquarters. Quattrone and his entire technology team of 130 people quit in April 1998, most to take positions at the bank's competitor, Credit Suisse First Boston. Carter McClelland, Breuer's head of investment in the United States, left the firm as well.

To be sure, there was rarely any contact, either internally or externally, between British investment bankers and German loan bureaucrats. But whenever the Germans did try to make a perfectly normal loan deal with a customer of the Brits, there was big trouble. The English bankers felt it posed a threat to their commissions. Breuer decided to end the surreal farce simply by incorporating Morgan Grenfell entirely into Deutsche Bank. Thus, after 88 years, the name of the London house disappeared from the world of finance.

This ordeal followed Breuer into negotiations with Bankers Trust. Both in Frankfurt and London, many worried that the Morgan Grenfell disaster might be replicated and bring new trouble, new culture shocks, and, once again, new people. In the United States, criticism was much more subdued in this regard, instead being more focused on Deutsche Bank's past. However, the merger signified for both partners a measurable leap forward. Figures from 1998 put the merged company among the world's leading institutions in all business areas: In project financing, it came in number one; in currency trade, number two; in government bonds, money market securities, and futures, number three; in the securities business, number four; and in real estate financing and syndicate loans, number five.

Statistics like this were certainly encouraging, but they reflected equally on both banks. If only because it is a universal bank, Deutsche

Bank had more to offer the Americans than the other way round—except in investment management, where Bankers Trust had 10 percentage points more than the Germans, and in deposit administration, 80 percent. It is therefore easy to predict how Deutsche Bank will profit from the Americans' know-how in investment banking. On its own, Bankers Trust never managed to capture the really big customers in this area, but instead advised medium-size companies that wanted to grow through mergers. Breuer promised that the new bank wouldn't try to compete with these giants, at least not in the United States—certainly a pragmatic remark, as it was Goldman Sachs and Morgan Stanley who handled the merger between Deutsche and Bankers.

Unlike Deutsche Bank, Bankers Trust had resolved its own problematic history some time before its liaison with Deutsche began. At the beginning of the 1990s, its staff had become conspicuous for its exciting but risky ideas, particularly in regard to new possibilities on the financial market. Furthermore, Bankers Trust was considered a hard sell in the financial world: Subjective preferences took precedence; substance was secondary. Then, in 1994, Bankers Trust introduced a number of financial products on the market, hot futures deals that were not kosher from the get-go. The futures were sold with a promise of high earnings to the standard group of preferred customers interested in making quick money and leaving their losses to those who came later. A major percentage of the new product went to soap manufacturer Procter & Gamble. As it turned out, every single customer had to take a huge loss, and Bankers Trust had to pay $250 million in damages. Its reputation was shattered. The most important action in cases like this—replacing the person at the top—was taken immediately, and Frank Newman took charge of Bankers Trust.

Newman, who formerly had worked for the secretary of finance, curbed his fierce "no-risk, no-fun" staff somewhat and reduced the futures trading significantly. To reestablish his bank's reputation, he bought a consultation firm in 1997, as well as Baltimore's Alex Brown investment bank, which set him back $1.7 billion. In the same year, he made Bankers Trust a presence in Europe's stock trade by purchasing the securities exchange of England's National Westminster Bank. Newman and Bankers Trust were once again regarded with respect. In 1997, the bank boasted an annual profit of $866 million.

The good times didn't last long: The following year Bankers Trust—like Deutsche Bank—was implicated when a major hedge fund went into

Chapter 11. Bankers had to post a $488 million quarterly loss. New York fund manager James K. Schmidt of the Hancock Financial Industries Fund was surprised, therefore, when shortly thereafter, the deal with Deutsche Bank was announced: "It didn't look like Bankers Trust was in a position to negotiate a good price, but they did manage to." Indeed, Deutsche Bank paid no less than 2.1 times Bankers Trust's book value. Travelers Group Inc. had paid only 1.7 times the book value of the distinguished investment bank Salomon Brothers when it took over the company just a little earlier. But Breuer took a different view. He said that after Bankers Trust's stocks fell, he wanted to wait until they were just beginning to rise again and then quickly make his move. Mr. Stockmarket.

Only time will tell whether it was a good deal. Wall Street insiders believe that Newman was pressured by the bank's board to accept Breuer's offer, indicating that it was generous. What will decide the question in the end is how high Bankers Trust's earnings will climb and what Breuer will do with his acquisition. At any rate, Newman was charged with expanding investment banking until the year 2000, together with Josef Ackermann, Deutsche Bank's latest member of the board and in charge of that business area. Ackermann, a Swiss, didn't arrive in Frankfurt until 1996, after he had failed to make it to the top at Credit Suisse. Bringing in an outsider to join its board was a rare break with tradition at Deutsche Bank, but a wise one. Someone like Ackermann is better suited to communicate with Bankers Trust than the typical German banker.

During Deutsche Bank's second attempt to compete in the profitable area of investment banking, Breuer spent at least as much as his predecessors during the bank's first attempt. Hefty sums have been and will continue to be paid. The merger initially increased Frank Newman's net worth to $66 million. The future masters of the investment business, Yves de Balmann and Mayo Shattuck, were courted to the tune of $35 million total. Some 200 Bankers Trust managers were awarded combined bonuses of $400 million. In marked contrast, 5,500 lower-level employees were laid off from Bankers Trust's investment banking department. Surprisingly, Newman quit in the summer of 1999, cashing in about $100 million worth of shares.

In addition, Breuer had to come up with the $9.2 billion purchase price from his bank's reserves. As we have seen, a simple stock trade operation à la DaimlerChrysler isn't possible for Breuer's deal. The money actually had to be earned, and at least in 1997–1998, Deutsche

Bank wasn't doing so great. Between 1995 and 1997, its earnings were cut in half. In 1997, it yielded no more than 6.4 percent interest on capital. Yet by 1998, Deutsche was doing much better, and by 2001 or thereabouts, Breuer plans to arrive at 25 percent for Deutsche Bank.

To shake up his firm, he spent some $1.5 million to start a so-called fitness program, in the course of which the bank was divided into five different business areas. In December 1998, it became clear that Breuer's real purpose was to ensure that all the bank's industrial stocks be handled by a legally separate company, with the power to transfer each of the major portfolios, such as DaimlerChrysler, Allianz, and Münchner Rück, into its own limited partnership. The complex system is to function as a profit center, and above all, to save taxes. Without actually creating a product, it will thus increase Deutsche Bank's profit. What's more, this will keep the bank from being criticized for putting too much of its money into "dead" investments (i.e., those it cannot manage by itself).

This reorganization makes the dead investments look fresh and new again. All of a sudden, Deutsche Bank can show off a huge associated company of international caliber. If that company's portfolio is worth $45 to $50 billion, it would then be number two behind the superstrategist Warren Buffett's associated company Berkshire Hathaway at $70 billion. It would be ahead of the Swedish banking clan Wallenberg's Investor AB, whose posted worth is $30 to $40 million, and ahead of IFI/IFIL, behind which the Fiat family Agnelli is hiding with some $18 to $20 billion. In Germany, the Quandt family is the only competitor to Deutsche Bank's associated company, whose major shares in BMW, the battery company Varta, and the pharmaceuticals company Altena make it worth between 15 to 20 billion deutsche marks.

Separating out this financially powerful area spelled the beginning of the end of the Deutsche Bank system. The financial institution had enjoyed a long, at times painfully long, transition period after the end of the global Soviet empire and the beginning of globalization. Against this backdrop, the bank managers' occasional indecisiveness and sometimes alarming mistakes could probably be attributed to the agonies of separation from a dogma that had served the bank well for decades. Solid and always in the black, it must have been much harder for Deutsche Bank than for, say, Daimler-Benz AG to embrace drastic change.

Deutsche Bank's deal with Bankers Trust is part of its movement into its fifth historical phase. After expansion, defensiveness, consolidation, and establishment of its system, it must return to its beginnings. This means it must expand internally and externally, through numerous mergers and takeovers, and with an increased willingness to take risks. In its "Abs-solutist" phase following World War II, Deutsche Bank had all too often evaluated risks by past standards. It rarely even asked whether companies had new ideas; instead, it inquired about their rating, which was exclusively a product of the past. Innovative ideas and branches of industry were outside its reach and interest.

Since the world has been forming itself anew at a feverish pace post-1990, there are no longer any rules for management to follow, nor are there many viable strategic models. Between 1945 and 1990, Europe had a goal: to restore the status quo and to calmly modernize it, safely protected by the Cold War. Since 1990, even nations at the threshold of economic takeoff can no longer simply follow more-advanced countries, because they, too, are groping for a new concept of the world. The economists are as little help as they have always been—with the exception of Keynes and Friedman. All that can be done in terms of establishing goals is to experiment, and experiments are risky.

That said, no country is as suited for experimentation as the United States of America. Contrary to Europe and Japan, even Corporate America is characterized by many ups and downs, particularly in the relatively new fields of software and microbiology. Failing once is not considered a character defect. The person who founders simply tries something else. Many established companies in America have colorful pasts. Their successes and failures have taken on fantastic proportions. Citibank, General Motors, IBM, Bankers Trust—all have reached both depths and heights not even approached by their German counterparts.

The United States has never had a system such as Deutsche Bank's; that would have smothered its economy. In Germany, on the other hand, it turned economy into an orderly commodity. Such orderliness would equal social suicide in the United States, where chaos inspires and creativity prevails. When a German company reaches across the Atlantic, it may look like it is taking possession of something, but that action really is much more like a didactic play to teach the basics of globalization and whose plot moves along almost subliminally. This is where Daimler-Chrysler and Deutsche Bank/Bankers Trust are very distinct from one another, not only because of the dramatis personae, but also because of the difference in their respective fields.

It is clear where DaimlerChrysler stands in relation to its merger. Compared to Deutsche Bank, its transformation into a Transatlantic World Inc. will take place according to a precise and comprehensive plan—comparable to a military maneuver, about which the American partner knows a thing or two as well. This has nothing to do with the fact that Daimler is from Swabia and Chrysler from Michigan, two places known for good engineering. Rather, the reason is that there are certain intelligible principles behind developments in big industry. Chaos in details is unproductive—in fact, it can have disastrous consequences. The mass-produced automobile is a unique industrial product. This is true in America, in Europe, and on all the other continents. Car manufacture, from concept to distribution, is always most successful when all, or at least most, of those involved think with precision. One might bluntly suggest that the German national character, so grounded in precision, still dominates this branch of industry. Here, German characteristics are accepted, whereas in other contexts they might be considered odd or offensive. If true, Jürgen Schrempp's automotive Transatlantic World Inc. has a real chance of circumventing the culture clash everyone seems to be expecting. In this case, the product, the car, connects the two partners more than their cultural differences separate them. Nothing in the world is as German-American as the automobile.

Deutsche Bank's Hilmar Kopper and Rolf Breuer know all that: otherwise, they wouldn't have acquired major shares in Daimler-Chrysler. However, in regard to their own merged financial conglomerate, things are very different. Financial products are not exactly a German invention, and financial developments in America do not parallel those in Germany. These things have always been done very differently in the two countries. True, the first bankers were European, but this doesn't mean that it was Germany that shaped them. Dealing in financial affairs in Germany meant one was Prussian, exact and precise, more meticulous even than the pioneers of the automobile (who, after all, had great, productive imaginations).

Englishmen and Americans have always been more deft in financial matters than Germans and continental Europeans, with the possible exception of the Dutch. In reaching across the Atlantic to attempt to form a Transatlantic World Inc., Deutsche Bank must combine substantial, not to say brute, financial force and highly flexible Anglo-Saxon know-how—not just inventiveness, but genuine know-how. This combination is very attractive, unless one side insists on winning at any price. In the early days of Deutsche Bank, when superpatience and impatience complemented one another in Wallich and Siemens, this combination was successful. Surely Breuer is aware of that. Can he repeat the founders' success in grand style?

What gives this merger its momentum is not primarily Breuer's attempt to fuse different temperaments, but the dizzying speed at which financial markets around the world keep changing. If one adds the two companies' 1997 statistics, the result clearly confirms the overly cautious aspect of the merged company. This, however, is an academic exercise, suitable for publicity purposes, nothing else. In the new world, the stronger partner must listen to the weaker one rather than the other way around—if only because of a specific strength of the weaker partner: its location in New York City, the international center of the financial world.

Breuer explained his concept succinctly: Europe, he said, is Deutsche Bank's home market. (Alfred Herrhausen had pointed that out, too.) Europeans, Breuer continued, want to improve and compete with the Wall Street elite, but that won't be possible if his Transatlantic World Inc. is seen as an expanded Germany because it is run from the German home base. New York's financial district shouldn't be concerned, either, if Breuer should use his own means to try to put pressure on well-established Wall Street firms via Bankers Trust.

On the other hand, quite a few people would take notice if the new Transatlantic World Inc. were to appear not as a melding of two different parts but as an independent—that is to say, all-new—cultural phenomenon. It has no other choice if it wants to be successful. This will be very visible in our next example.

CHAPTER 4

Case Three: Bertelsmann and Bertelsmen

Mohn from Gütersloh

Ask THOMAS MIDDELHOFF, the young chairman of the board of Bertelsmann, the world's third-largest media conglomerate, about his company's future, and he might start rhapsodizing because he sees unused potential everywhere. The book, magazine, music, and other markets for the company's various products have, altogether, 45 million subscribers, he says. Generate a little more cooperation among the different divisions, Middelhoff believes, and the next growth period is just around the corner.

Middelhoff, who has been in charge since November 1998, thrives on examples like the following: Bertelsmann's music company, BMG, produced the opera *Turandot* in Beijing's Forbidden City. "That was turned into a CD," he told the news magazine *Der Spiegel* (November, 23, 1998, page 34). "Our TV company CLT-UFA produced a film, and our magazine *Der Stern* wrote an article about it. In addition, we can now sell the CD through our clubs and over the Internet."

Everything he wants is at his disposal. Strictly speaking, even the three *Der Spiegel* reporters to whom he told this example in the famous Berlin Adlon Hotel were on his turf. Bertelsmann's subsidiary Gruner + Jahr has a 25 percent share in the 1947-founded Spiegel-Verlag. This does not suffice to force certain decisions, but it does give Bertelsmann the power to block them.

Middelhoff asks loudly and often whether the conglomerate wasn't just a little too democratic in the past, whether its individual governors weren't ruling too independently of the central office. The answer is implicit in the question: He wants to turn Bertelsmann Confederacy into United Bertelsmann. But it isn't all that easy. Shortly before he rose to the top of the company, his predecessor and sponsor Mark Wössner succinctly expressed the company leader's dilemma in public: "You really have a great deal of power, as long as you don't exercise it. When you exercise it, you have trench warfare." Was Wössner, who after 15 years as boss became chairman of the supervisory board, trying to caution his successor not to overbid his hand? If so, why?

Because over everything called Bertelsmann rules the family patriarch and founder's great-grandson, Reinhard Mohn, whose authority is unquestioned. He personally established the company's decentralized structure, a principle pushed to its extreme: Larger divisions work entirely independently and, occasionally, even compete against one another. Leaders must act like entrepreneurs, Mohn insists, attaching to this missive an aura of social responsibility. And though it may be asking too much, everyone at Bertelsmann is supposed to like his or her work. Contradicting Mohn is out of the question. Mohn may be the heir, but he didn't inherit today's well-ordered and profitable company. He is regarded as the true founder of the corporation. Without him there would have been nothing for Middelhoff to take over.

Officially, however, the company was brought into being by Protestant book printer Carl Bertelsmann in 1835, in the town of Gütersloh in the Westphalian flatland, an equal distance from Frankfurt, Amsterdam, and the North Sea, and close enough to the Catholic fortress of Münster—the town where the peace treaty ending the Thirty Years' War was signed—to maintain a sense of the beauty of the diaspora.

For several generations, Carl Bertelsmann's religious publishing house, whose product line focused on the fundamentals of faith, had a strong local customer base before it spread to other Protestant regions in the German-speaking world. It's possible that some of the roots of Reinhard Mohn's social commitment can be found in this past, but they are certainly not what determined his life's work. Mohn's path was shaped by World War II and its consequences.

The Nazi years forced Bertelsmann to a standstill, for not only was the Fascist dictatorship antidemocratic, it was also antireligious. After all, the Nazi movement intended to lead the nation back to its supposedly original Germanic faith. But that's not to say that Bertelsmann's printing capabilities were inactive during the war years. Once World War II started, the government interfered more directly with publishing houses and their products. All of them—even scientific publishers—more or less came under the control of Joseph Goebbels's Reich Ministry of Enlightenment and Propaganda, and informers were everywhere.

During the last two years of the war, the Reich put a stop to the publication of most periodicals. Bertelsmann's turn came in 1944. The publishing house was shut down, and a short while later, Allied bombers destroyed its printing plants. In the meantime, Mohn, while serving in the German army, was captured by the Americans. He spent three years as a POW in Kansas, which ironically became the cradle of the new Bertelsmann conglomerate.

In response to the restrictions imposed on publishing in general during the Nazi era and, specifically, the destruction that had occurred to the family business, Mohn was determined to dramatically expand the company's business base after his return, and even an American POW camp offered ample opportunity to learn something in this regard. By the time Mohn was released, Bertelsmann-Verlag was already operational again; soon afterward, the deutsche mark came into use. Back at home and at work, Mohn introduced his hard-earned American management methods. In addition, he introduced the concept of book clubs.

Book clubs were an idea whose time had come in war-torn Germany. The many air raids on German cities destroyed numerous libraries. The Nazis themselves laid waste to literature in the form of widespread book burnings and subsequent strict censorship. Even intact bookcases were devoid of contemporary foreign literature, of books written by liberal writers during the Weimar Republic, and of titles by Jewish authors. Names such as John Steinbeck, Thomas Mann, Heinrich Heine, and hundreds more had been missing from school syllabi and, obviously, from bookstores for more than a decade.

At the same time, to most Germans books were hardly their primary necessity. They needed to first replace their homes: Beds, chairs, and ovens were surely more important than books. Though independent publisher Ernst Rowohlt tried to fill the gap by putting out inexpensive literature in newspaper format, high school teachers complained that they had to spend most of their meager income on books just so they could do their job. Public libraries—those still standing—were overcrowded and undersupplied. When the first bound books came on the market after the currency reform of 1948, they were priced at 12 marks—the same amount an accountant made in two days.

Into this void came Mohn and his book clubs. They appeased the German thirst for literature, and at half the price of books sold through traditional means. Bookcases in German living rooms filled again, and Bertelsmann grew larger. It was perfect. Even after others, such as Stuttgart's publisher Georg von Holtzbrinck, copied the recipe, Bertelsmann remained number one—not least because under Mohn's direction, the company quickly began to conquer foreign markets. Even many years later, in 1998, when the book club concept had begun to stagnate, Bertelsmann's reading circles still boasted 26 million members worldwide.

Success in hand, Mohn gave his emissaries suitcases full of money to buy companies. In Gütersloh, he built Mohndruck, the giant printing plant, with some 3,200 employees. In Hamburg, Germany's new media capital, Bertelsmann bought more and more shares of the newspaper and magazine publisher Gruner + Jahr, a former family business that published magazines popular with both readers and advertisers, including the politically oriented *Der Stern;* women's magazines, such as *Brigitte;* and how-to periodicals on beautifying, such as *Schöner Wohnen.* Furthermore, Bertelsmann owned other printing plants and indirectly, as mentioned, shares of *Der Spiegel,* Europe's largest news magazine.

Stern and *Der Spiegel* were considered to be critical of the business world, but Mohn didn't care as long as they had a solid customer base. He regarded himself as the German equivalent of Lord Thomsen of Fleet, the British publisher who let his newspapers report whatever they wished, interfering only when the number of subscriptions or ads went down. The Hamburg lawyer, businessman, and ex-senator Gerd Bucerius, who had previously published *Stern,* now was a partner in Mohn's empire, with a 20 percent share. Bucerius used his profits to support his pet creation, Hamburg's liberal-conservative weekly *Die Zeit,* which was often on shaky financial ground. To ensure its survival, Bucerius had established the Zeit Foundation and gained former German chancellor Helmut Schmidt as one of the *Zeit* editors.

After Bucerius's death, Mohn essentially would inherit the ex-senator's clout within the company. It came as a complete surprise, then, that on his 60th birthday in 1981, he announced his resignation as an active member of the board and transferred to the supervisory board. This was clearly meant to set the standard for his successors and all other members of Bertelsmann's board of directors—an idea, by the way, to which Mark Wössner never agreed.

After that, Mohn started property transactions to ensure that Bertelsmann would remain a private company. Today, though the firm is an "AG" (for Aktiengesellschaft, or joint-stock company) according to German law, with stocks, executive board, and annual meetings, its shares are not traded on the stock market because they are in the hands of long-term owners. The major holder is the Bertelsmann Foundation (to which Mohn had given 70 percent of his own shares); the second-largest block is held by the Mohn family; and the third-largest is held by the Zeit Foundation whose shares he would like to buy back. Mohn, who at one time represented all three major shareholders, commented with his Westphalian charm: "I am the general assembly." Only lately has he given away some of his voting power, but not control over the company.

Reinhold Mohn, whom few things disgust as much as a wanton jet-set lifestyle, forced the company into a tight financial-moral girdle. It is allowed to incur debts only up to one and a half times its cash flow; phases of expansion must be strategically warranted and must be financed from the company's own resources; when expansion phases are completed, a new consolidation phase begins during which the company is instructed to focus on making money.

The corporation's headquarters remain firmly grounded in good old Gütersloh. Apart from the central Bertelsmann office, the town of 94,000 has a municipal building, a harmonically developed hotel infrastructure, a theater, four movie houses, an entry road to the autobahn and a small, but not really commercial, airport nearby. The environment offers little to tourists. Those who do want to get to Gütersloh from the big wide world have to fly to Frankfurt or Amsterdam, where they have to board either a train or another plane to Düsseldorf. From there, it is at least another two hours' drive by car. It's easier if one has a company plane.

Nevertheless, Gütersloh has its advantages. The cost of living is lower than in most metropolitan regions, and the standard of living tends to be nicer; the schools are better, customer service is more reliable, and there are few distractions. Basic operating costs for a corporate headquarters are significantly lower than they would be in a glittering metropolis. "You can clear your head there," Middelhoff says simply whenever he is asked about Gütersloh. The sidewalks roll up early, and the closest nightclub is 20 miles away. The closest larger city is Bielefeld, with a population of 330,000, where the grocery giant Oetkers is located, a company that has as much style and is just as inconspicuous as Bertelsmann.

When Mark Wössner took over Bertelsmann in 1983, the company was just entering another phase of consolidation. "Now, let's first make some money," he reportedly commanded. He increased the company's revenue; returns and profit have had an almost parallel growth rate; sales rose from 6 to 25.5 billion marks, and profits rose from 380 million to 1.73 billion. In other words, sales increased by 325 percent and profits by 355 percent: In fact, he managed to keep the increases in returns and profit in balance during his entire 15-year tenure. Not a bad record at all.

In the volatile media industry, it is very difficult to run a company with a consistent degree of competence for one and a half decades, and Wössner's tenure included the unsettling sudden advent of the electronic media revolution, with its pay-TV, digital TV, and the Internet. Wössner, whose background is print media, delegated these fields to others. So, though never quite at ease with the new technologies himself, still Wössner was able to dramatically restructure his company.

When he started at Bertelsmann, there was no electronic media business to speak of, but by 2000, it is expected to account for almost half of Bertelsmann's revenues. Under Wössner, Bertelsmann was the world's largest media giant until the American conglomerates Time Warner (including Turner) and Walt Disney (including ABC) merged. Such a megamerger is not possible within Bertelsmann's corporate structure. True, the company cannot be assailed by Wall Street, but it cannot use it to its advantage either. Nevertheless, using conventional means for strategic acquisitions, Wössner grew Bertelsmann gradually until it became one of the industry giants. By applying the international standard of returns in dollars, during the years of the transition from Wössner to Middelhoff, Bertelsmann, with 58,000 employees and $15.9 billion in revenues, was in third place behind Time Warner ($24.6 billion, 65,500 employees) and Walt Disney ($22.8 billion, 85,200). Behind Bertelsmann came Viacom ($13.2 billion) and Rupert Murdoch's News Corporation ($11.2 billion). Clearly, the Americans are the market leaders, but they also have exorbitant debts and few resources.

When the economy is good, taking out loans to finance business ventures is a perfectly legitimate thing to do, but when the economy begins to stagnate, a firm such as Bertelsmann is much more resistant than other companies. Low returns can be more easily dealt with when there is little interest on debt to pay off, as is the case with Bertelsmann. And, when necessary, there is enough money to make an opportune purchase. Comparisons between Bertelsmann and the Anglo-Saxons usually are faulty because Bertelsmann is a countercyclical type of company. Even so, the corporation has consistently earned 12 to 15 percent interest on capital.

When Wössner's time was up, the corporation's biggest moneymaker was the the Bertelsmann Music Group (BMG), under the direction of Michael Dornemann, who had long been considered Wössner's designated successor. Dornemann's office is in the Bertelsmann high-rise on the corner of 45th Street and Broadway in New York City, close to Times Square. The BMG corporation includes Ariola, RCA, Arista, and Sonopress. It alone contributes 7.9 billion marks to the conglomerate's total revenues of 25.7 billion marks. In Europe, Dornemann is in charge of Bertelsmann's 50 percent share in CLT-UFA, which owns the RTL television stations, including RTL 2, Super RTL, and Vox, plus radio stations with a total revenue of 2.8 billion marks.

In 1997–1998, Dornemann's empire took credit for more than 40 percent of the conglomerate's total revenues, though its 300 million marks represented less than 20 percent of the company's profit. Its momentum in the music business has slowed for the time being, after years of enormous growth, which is why Dornemann's various businesses reported 100 million marks less profit in 1997–1998 than calculated. This enabled Bertelsmann's book group, which recorded a profit of 300 million marks, to draw even with the music business.

The book group is under the direction of Frank Wössner, the younger brother (by three years) of the former company director. His segment brought in $7.3 billion in returns. The book group's most important German publishing houses are C. Bertelsmann, Goldmann, Siedler, and the Bertelsmann Club, a refined version of the earlier Bertelsmann book clubs. Like Dornemann, the younger Wössner, a former insurance manager, is often in the United States on business. There the conglomerate owns, among other companies, major publishers Bantam

Doubleday Dell and Random House, the latter of which includes Knopf and several other well-known imprints. Bertelsmann is now the world's largest trade publisher of English-language books.

Shortly after Mark Wössner resigned, Bertelsmann gained an 80 percent share in Germany's scientific publisher Springer GmbH & Co. KG. The largely international Springer group yielded additional revenues of 615 million marks. Founded in 1842, Springer (not to be confused with Hamburg's Axel Springer Verlag, a conservative newspaper and magazine publisher) is almost as old as Bertelsmann. Its list of authors boasts 70 Nobel laureates, and 60 percent of its line is in English. In the words of Chairman Middelhoff, it is the "Rolls Royce of technical publishing."

Since its additional acquisitions, Bertelsmann moved to third place worldwide in technical information publishing, which according to Middelhoff is ideal for electronic distribution. With a net profit of 8 to 9 percent, Bertelsmann's American publishing houses were above the industry average. Altogether, Bertelsmann's book business makes up 15 percent of the world's book market.

The conglomerate's third-largest company, with revenues of 5.1 billion marks, was Gruner + Jahr AG, headed by Gerd Schulte-Hillen—though still actively monitored by the founding Jahr family. G+J publishes magazines such as *Der Stern, Brigitte, Schöner Wohnen, Geo, Gala,* and *TV Today.* Also the owner of huge printing plants, G+J has increasingly branched out into the newspaper business, publishing such dailies as *Morgenpost, Berliner Zeitung,* and *Sächsische Zeitung.* G+J is considered Bertelsmann's bread-and-butter company. At 780 million marks, it was responsible for almost half the conglomerate's income during Wössner's last year in office.

G+J's Schulte-Hillen, who is also Bertelsmann's vice-chairman, recently had a good deal of trouble with *Stern,* the publisher's best-selling magazine. Founded and led for decades by periodicals genius Henri Nannen, the magazine had become financially independent and—more important—G+J's financial backbone. Then, three strikes in rapid succession damaged its reputation. The first blow was the horrendous affair concerning the fake Hitler diaries. This came at the beginning of Schulte-Hillen's tenure. The second blow was Germany's depoliticization during the Kohl administration. The third blow came when competitor Burda launched the magazine *Focus,* intended to compete with *Der Spiegel* but in fact hurting *Stern,* which has yet to fully recover.

Bertelsmann's technological facilities—in particular its printing plants, including Mohndruck—1997/98 brought in revenues of no less than 3.4 billion marks and a profit of 220 million marks. Mohndruck, which carries the patriarch's name, has invariably been the center of management attention because both Mark Wössner and Thomas Middelhoff ran the plant before climbing higher up on the ladder. The conglomerate's latest industrial branch, Dornemann's multimedia business, posted revenues of 750 million marks at a time when it was still limited to Internet service—via AOL Germany, AOL Great Britain, and AOL France. To modernize its book sales, Bertelsmann acquired holdings in the on-line book service offered by the Barnes & Noble chain.

In total, some 300 individual companies belong to the Bertelsmann group. "We're not a German company," insists Middelhoff, "we're a genuine global conglomerate." Indeed, foreign business accounts for almost 70 percent of the conglomerate's total. In 1998, only 31 percent of its business was conducted in Germany, according to company figures; 30 percent was carried out in the rest of Europe, and 8 percent on all other continents, with the exception of the United States. In the United States, revenues in 1998 equaled those of the unified Germany.

In this phase, CEO Middelhoff isn't quite sure how to define Bertelsmann's future in concrete terms. Even though Europe still accounts for more than 60 percent of its revenues, the conglomerate describes itself as a "European-American company with German roots." Middelhoff sees himself as an "American who by sheer coincidence has a German passport." How far Carl Bertelsmann has been left behind . . .

Thomas Middelhoff

When Thomas Middelhoff leaves his office in Gütersloh to go to his private residence, he passes through the countryside, a ride that brings a welcome distance between him and his job. His home, a recently renovated farmhouse with swimming pool and featuring all the contemporary technological amenities, is a place where he can spread himself out. In the local jargon, it is a "crown domain," a country estate where

Middelhoff lives with his wife, an architect, their two sons and three daughters, and a menagerie of about 70 animals.

Thomas Middelhoff was born in Düsseldorf, the capital of North-Rhine Westphalia, in 1953. The household in which he grew up was headed by an entrepreneur who ran the family-owned Middelhoff GmbH, one of the many textile companies in the region. His upbringing in a business-oriented family helped Middelhoff advance quickly in his own career later on. Middelhoff, born too late to be part of the Adenauer era, is the first CEO to represent Germany's future generation. He studied business administration at the University of Münster from 1975 to 1979. After he graduated, the university hired him as an assistant for its marketing institute. (Marketing and technology are the Bertelsmann chairman's two longtime passions.) He got his first taste of being an entrepreneur when, during semester breaks, he and his father established a branch of the family business in Greece. In 1984, at age 31, Middelhoff was promoted to general manager of the branches of his father's company in the Far East and Greece.

Middelhoff's passion for business and technology earned him a Ph.D. in economics. The subject of his dissertation, which he completed in 1986, was the Internet, a topic that no doubt helped his subsequent meteoric rise more than the degree itself did. That same year he became assistant to the manager at Mohndruck Graphische Betriebe GmbH—that is to say, at Bertelsmann, in Gütersloh.

Before long he was included in the circle of "high potentials," an elitist group at Bertelsmann established by CEO Wössner. His proving ground was Berlin, where he was sent from May 1987 to December 1988 with the task of putting the Bertelsmann subsidiary Elsnerdruck GmbH, a printing company, into the black. Wössner liked to send his chosen on such missions. "You learn leadership, day after day," he said. The job was well worth Middelhoff's while. Immediately following this stint, he became manger of Mohndruck and, simultaneously, of a calendar publisher.

By 1990, after less than four years at Bertelsmann, the 37-year-old was already top manager at Mohndruck and a member of the board of the division of printing and industrial enterprises at Bertelsmann. Following this rocketlike launch, he reached a plateau, and he had to wait another four years for his next promotion. The company's top managers were protecting their wunderkind against premature wear and tear.

At Mohndruck, Middelhoff had to face one of the difficulties of being in upper management. Due to cheap competition in East Germany, Mohndruck temporarily hit a slump, and workers had to be laid off and wages cut. Middelhoff later confessed that it was the most painful experience in his entire professional life. That something could ever go wrong had never occurred to him. He was not, however, held accountable for what had happened. In fact, at the time he was more an observer. He was the man in charge of central planning and of coordinating the company's multimedia business. Hence, his job was really that of a high-level assistant to the general manager. In these areas, Wössner needed a strong man by his side. Wössner felt that Michael Dornemann in New York was becoming too powerful, especially in the area of new media, and had his eye on becoming Wössner's successor. Everything was working in Middelhoff's favor, because, actually, Dornemann was too focused on America and the entertainment business. Furthermore, he was a tad too old to become CEO and hold the office as long as Bertelsmann liked its leaders to before reaching the magic age of 60. At the time of the changing of guards, in November 1998, the New Yorker would already be 53 years old—good for just another seven years. Middelhoff, on the other hand, would have 15 years left, like Wössner had had. Also in Middelhoff's favor was that he was two generations ahead of Dornemann as far as technological developments in the industry were concerned. Plus, he knew enough not to try to push Wössner out prematurely.

While biding his time, Middelhoff's strategic planning advanced the conglomerate's internationalization effort and shifted the company's priorities toward expanding its electronic markets and its Internet activities—considered more forward-reaching than Dornemann's emphasis on entertainment electronics. Middelhoff was fully aware that he was being smoothly pushed ahead of the long-standing crown prince. Whether this bothered him is doubtful, but he certainly recognized that he would have to work with Dornemann for a number of crucial years, so—savvy businessman that he is—he expressed his appreciation for his colleague at every opportunity.

Middelhoff is known for his people skills. Though he tends to be direct, he manages to do so without hurting people's feelings. That character trait serves him well in New York, as it does in Gütersloh. In Manhattan, he is considered the "nice guy from Bertelsmann" by media and beverage magnate Edgar Bronfman. Likewise, in Gütersloh a major part of his job is not to force decisions but to initiate them by being convincing, so that in the end they are made naturally.

This capability was on full display during one of his most daring moves as head of development. Always trying to increase Internet business, in 1995 Middelhoff began seeking a large partner. The largest was Microsoft's Bill Gates, but Middelhoff chose to deal with America Online. He managed to convince Bertelsmann's board of directors—over Wössner's serious reservations—that if it wanted to begin negotiating with AOL, it would have to strengthen its position by buying AOL stock. Even the reluctant Wössner eventually agreed with the decision to purchase AOL stock worth $50 million.

Middelhoff immediately became a member of the AOL board. Later, Bertelsmann sold a portion of its shares for the fantastic price of $225 million (while retaining shares worth $510 million). This one move was enough to earn Middelhoff the respect of Bertelsmann's board of directors, whose fellow members were all a little older than he.

On July 4, 1997, Independence Day, Thomas Middelhoff, the board's youngest member, was elected to succeed Wössner in the fall of 1998. Shortly thereafter, Wössner suggested that his protégé spend the next 12 months in the United States. It was a wise idea, again designed to protect him from premature exhaustion. In the United States, Middelhoff became simply an apprentice. Never again, Wössner impressed upon him, would he be offered such a chance. Aside from the stint at his father's company, Middelhoff had no professional experience abroad whatsoever. He would be able to observe Dornemann's division, then the company's fastest-growing market, "live." As a side benefit he would become more fluent in English.

Middelhoff moved into the Sherry Netherland on New York's Fifth Avenue. The important people he wanted to meet were just a phone call away. And he called them all—from the magnates Michael Eisner (Disney) to Rupert Murdoch (News Corp.), from Gerald Levin (Time Warner) to Bill Clinton's friend Vernon Jordan. He also met Random House's publishing icon S. I. Newhouse in the summer of 1998. It was an opportunity to make history right then and there. It may have looked like a chance encounter with the patriarch at his 70th birthday party, but Newhouse had long since inconspicuously sought to establish contact with Bertelsmann. He was looking to sell Random House, or at least part of it. "Si" had already offered his jewel to Time Warner and Murdoch, but they were stalling; besides, everything had to be done via banks with them. Bertelsmann seemed perfect; if Middelhoff wanted to buy, he could simply write a check.

Needless to say, he didn't write that check at Newhouse's party. But he did explain to Newhouse that Bertelsmann would be willing to purchase either his entire publishing house or nothing at all. That was a more nuts-and-bolts conversation than Newhouse had had with the two other publishers. From a strategic point of view alone, Bertelsmann was more interested in the book business than either Murdoch or Turner & Co.—particularly more interested in Random House, reportedly the industry's best-selling company. Bertelsmann agreed to pay $1.7 billion for the book empire. Bingo.

The deal was characteristic of the Gütersloh-based company. It pursued a strategic goal: to achieve a certain rank and share in a certain market. In no way was this a gamble. That it happened was not a surprise, because the conglomerate's top managers knew which publishing houses and publishing categories would help the company attain its goal. That it happened so quickly was a function of the fact that Bertelsmann didn't first have to ask investment bankers if they could scrape together $1.7 billion. Thomas Middelhoff loves this kind of business culture. He doesn't like to be bothered by analysts and moneylenders. "It's we who have our money," Middelhoff is fond of saying.

For things to remain that way, the young Bertelsmann chief has to keep a trained eye on the company's balance sheet. In 1997–1998 there had been a setback of sorts. Profits did not quite meet the target 15 percent net yield, and the company managers' income in profit-sharing plummeted; employees, who Reinhard Mohn had decided should also share in the company's profit, made 50 million marks less than in the previous year. When such issues come up in discussions, Middelhoff, like Jürgen Schrempp, likes to quote General Electric chief Jack Welch, who favors selling those parts of his company whose revenues are not among the highest in the world. Middelhoff believes this is feasible for Bertelsmann, too.

In contrast, former CEO Mark Wössner, still chairman of the conglomerate's supervisory board and head of the Bertelsmann Foundation, suggests patience. In the company newsletter, *Management News*, he recommended that Middelhoff first "fly" the complex Bertelsmann system for a while before making significant changes. Middelhoff took the hint. He started to reshuffle things very cautiously. The branches of the "past"—books, newspapers, and magazines—bring in the big money; the branches of the "future" still do not. The multimedia business has to be subsidized before it can pay its way. At this point, therefore, Middel-hoff is still pushing *all* divisions of the company to greater achievements. Counting beans and comparing yields is for later. But if Middelhoff was not changing a great many things, he gave them an electrical charge when he took over. He intends for the company to be a noticeable pres-ence on the explosive new markets from the get-go. And so he pushes his people to initiate new developments, to be pioneers. Middelhoff doesn't want to wait for smaller companies to develop great ideas so Bertels-mann can then buy them. He wants the various company divisions and many subdivisions to be creative centers where new concepts emerge. "We are a home for artists and talents," he says.

This momentum is hard to maintain. Because of their size alone, con-glomerates such as Bertelsmann develop a certain inertia. Running them like spin-offs is tricky business and can be a frustrating undertak-ing. Middelhoff, however, is convinced that Internet-related technology will eventually constitute the company's core business and that every-thing will change very quickly. He also acknowledges that America is the Internet's homeland, which gives his American competitors an edge. Middelhoff wants Bertelsmann to have the kind of creative variety that at least makes up for, or at most cancels out, that advantage. Middelhoff, to everybody's surprise, is going to risk a cultural clash in the company.

For Middelhoff, the AOL-TV connection is much more interesting than, say, expensive pay-TV, whose possibilities have largely been exploited already. There is, he says, only a single missing link to the next development: Worldwide on-line services have to be integrated into the cable systems. Middelhoff believes that once this happens, the enter-tainment world will again change radically, and Bertelsmann's company structure will have to be ready for these changes.

Bertelsmann's new boss thinks on a large scale and is ready to risk a cultural clash.

During Middelhoff's reign, the eye for size will open even wider, par-ticularly in the area of electronic media. In contrast to the old Bertels-mann dogma paying every investment out of the company's enormous financial reserves, Middelhoff will bring hot young departments to the stock exchanges to access money. Thus, Wössner and Middelhoff are playing in the same league as Schrempp and Breuer. As another type of Transatlantic World Inc., the company has to combine Germany's oldest industry (printing) and America's youngest (on-line technology)—a feat Middelhoff is confident he'll manage.

The young Bertelsmann chief is reaching for new markets in Asia and Eastern Europe, from where he believes the mass demand of the future will primarily come. Thus the Bertelsmann group is becoming less German and more global. The New York branch of Bertelsmann AG is like a second corporate headquarters. Already, only four of the seven Bertelsmann directors have their offices in Gütersloh. Within the next 10 years, Middelhoff suggests, two non-Germans might even become members of the board. "One has to be more global," stresses Middelhoff, "One has got to grow."

Part III

THE PIVOT
STRATEGY

Case One: Allianz—
The Power Beside You

The Octopus

"AT ALLIANZ, you're always in the shadow of this huge eagle," one of the company's managers said when she quit her job, referring to the insurance giant's company logo, a menacing angular-shaped eagle. "You can't prove yourself doing anything." The bird, while radiating the aura of an empire, is more intimidating than emboldening—a "Prussian Icarus," in the words of German liedersinger Wolf Biermann. But the symbol is appropriate: Allianz, located in Bavaria (Munich, specifically), is the world's largest insurance company—a financial continuation of Prussiandom.

In 1998, the empire's earnings totaled some 107 billion marks in insurance premiums; its profits were about 2.5 billion marks; the balance sheet total was more than 450 billion marks; capital investments were 350 billion marks. Employing approximately 80,000, Allianz has many more holdings in other companies than even Deutsche Bank. But, contrary to the latter, it is not criticized for them. Allianz was behind the merger of Bayerische Hypo-und Vereinsbank, which resulted in Germany's second-largest bank; and it has an almost 25 percent share in Dresdner Bank, Germany's third-largest financial institution. Worldwide, 51 percent of its business is in Germany, 31 percent in the rest of Europe, and the remaining 18 percent mainly in North and South America.

Allianz tallies 44 percent of its premiums from life and health insurance, 56 percent from damage and accidence insurance. Not one to shirk risk, the company was a coinsurer of the German blimp *Hinden-*

burg, which exploded and crashed in 1937 above New Jersey's Lakehurst airfield. Allianz has insured nuclear power plants from day one, assuming a risk that was hard to gauge at first. And since 1985, the company has backed space travel as well. Less palatably, Allianz also covered the risks of Heinrich Himmler's well-guarded concentration camps. Notably, however, the camps weren't considered a risk until 1997, when Allianz's involvement became public.

Like any insurance company, Allianz has good connections with busy, powerful reinsurance conglomerates. The company has a 25 percent share in Münchner Rück (full name: Münchner Rückversicherungsgesellschaft AG), which is also located in Bavaria. Conversely, Münchner Rück has a 26 percent share in Allianz. Both have holdings in Dresdner Bank, and Dresdner in turn owns stock in both of them, although not a lot. Furthermore, Allianz owns more than 90 percent of both Vereinte Versicherung and Hermes Kreditversicherung, more than 36 percent of Karlsruher Lebensversicherung, and 20 percent of Hamburg-Mannheimer.

In short, this is a well-balanced insurance trust. Its spectrum of holdings in other companies is impressive as well: For instance, Allianz has a 37.7 percent share in Hamburg's cosmetics, pharmaceutical, and adhesive tape company Beiersdorf AG (which produces such famous brands as Nivea and Tesa). It owns 10 to 11 percent of Linde (air conditioners), BASF (chemicals), RWE, Veba, and Rheinelektra (power companies), Leifheit (building machines), and Schering (pharmaceuticals). Finally, it has between 1 and 5 percent or more shares in Continental (tires), Bayer (chemicals), Thyssen (steel), Metallgesellschaft (precious metals), Viag (energy), Siemens (electronics), DaimlerChrysler, and Volkswagen.

Among the insurance conglomerate's other holdings are Hochtief AG, MAN AG, Bayer AG, DLW (Deutsche Linoleum Werke) AG, Südzucker AG, Heidelberger Druckmaschinen AG, and Mannesmann AG. Aside from their traditional business areas, some of these companies are also involved in other fields. For example, today Mannesmann is known as a mobile radio transmission and auto supply company, and has almost completely relinquished its past as Germany's largest manufacturer of pipes. Because insurance companies should not speculate in stocks, Allianz's portfolio is extraordinarily well balanced. All German companies in which Allianz has holdings are at the same coin in the Deutsche Bank system's "safe" (that is, low-risk) category.

Allianz also has a wide variety of holdings in other European countries. In the insurance field, it is a major shareholder in England's Gornhill, Switzerland's Elvia group, Italy's RAS SpA, and in Allianz subsidiaries in France, the Netherlands, and Austria. It has a 38.4 percent share in Switzerland's Berner Allgemeine Holding-Gesellschaft AG. Then there are its strategic shares in important European banks; for instance, Allianz owns 10.9 percent of the French Crédit Foncier et Communal d'Alsace et de Lorraine S.A.; 5 percent of Spain's Banco Popular Espanol S.A.; and about 3 percent each of Italy's medium-size banks Banco Italiano SpA, Credito Romagniolo SpA, and Instituto Mobiliare Italiano SPA, companies whose market value is between 60 and 90 million marks each.

Like Deutsche Bank, Allianz conducts personnel politics via its supervisory board. At the annual meeting on July 8, 1998, Klaus Liesen, a fellow student of former Deutsche Bank spokesman Alfred Herrhausen, became chairman of Allianz's supervisory board. It is not an unfamiliar role to him: As we already know, he is also chairman of the supervisory board of Volkswagen (in which Allianz has shares) and of Ruhrgas AG, whose president he was for a number of years. Liesen is also on the boards of Deutsche Bank, Mannesmann, Veba, and Preussag—all companies in which Allianz has stock. On the supervisory boards of Mannesmann and Veba, Liesen serves with Allianz director Henning Schulte-Noelle.

Another current honcho on the Allianz supervisory board is Karl-Hermann Baumann, chairman of the supervisory board of Siemens AG, in which Allianz has holdings. Baumann is also on the supervisory board of other Allianz-connected companies: Deutsche Bank, Linde, Metallgesellschaft, and Schering. At meetings of the supervisory boards of the latter two companies, Baumann regularly runs into Allianz director Schulte-Noelle. Another influential man was Albrecht Schmidt, a member of Allianz's supervisory board, chairman of the board of directors of then-independent Bayerische Vereinsbank AG and one of the powerful at the new Hypovereinsbank. Schmidt was also on the supervisory boards of Lufthansa Commercial Holding GmbH, of Allianz's twin Münchner Rück, and of Siemens and Viag, two companies in which Allianz has stock. At Münchner Rück, he would meet Allianz director Schulte-Noelle, the company's chairman of the board.

Only because Deutsche Bank, as a universal bank, is able to exert a much broader influence on Germany's large joint-stock companies is the Allianz system not considered the bank's equal. That said, there are a number of differences between the two. For one, the right to vote by proxy gives the Frankfurt bank an advantage over the Munich insurance company. And Rolf-Ernst Breuer's incursion into New York in pursuit of Bankers Trust gives Deutsche Bank another advantage over its major competitor in the financial market. Simply put, Schulte-Noelle's Allianz is no global conglomerate, and it's certainly not a transatlantic one. Its firm foundation in Germany (most of the companies in which Allianz has stock are German), where it conducts more than half of its business, gives Allianz a drowsy and provincial air. To date, an increase in activities in other European countries hasn't fundamentally changed that.

Allianz's strong position in the German market has made the company somewhat complacent, its leaders believing it can do almost nothing wrong. The company has formulated a clear picture of insurance risks and of its capital investments, understanding that the more remote its customers and its investments, the more difficult it is to exercise control. Few industries are as dependent on local or regional law as insurance. For Allianz, initially, the simplest and most profitable way of doing business was to try first to completely cover the German market before branching out to other European countries and overseas. To that end, Allianz bought a 51 percent interest in the Deutsche Versicherungs-AG, which was founded on July 1, 1990, to take over the business of the former East German state insurance service, a major coup. (The coup lost some of its glitter, however, when Allianz realized how difficult East German customers were going to be.) The company's next brilliant manuveur came in the fall of 1997, when it acquired a 51 percent share in the French insurance group Assurances Générales de France (AGF).

Since then, in contrast to his usual reticence, Allianz director Schulte-Noelle has justly lauded his corporate behemoth as the world's market leader. It would be more accurate to call it the world's largest insurance company, because apart from the circulation of short-term loans, Allianz does not really deal with the global market. Despite its enormous size, globally, Allianz pursues no more than a harmless, totally risk-free Pivot Strategy. In the United States, Allianz owns only one subsidiary that carries its own name, then the Fireman's Fund, and a 51 percent share in the Hancock group. It acquired the Fireman's Fund

Insurance Company of Novato, California, a property and accident insurer, in 1990 for $3 billion. The acquisition of the Firemen's Fund was the jewel in the foreign crown for Allianz. With this one move, the company almost quadrupled its premium income in the United States. It wasn't until 1995 that Allianz took a step toward a third continent, when it acquired a 14.5 percent share in Australia's property and accident insurance company, MMI Insurance Group. This was followed by the founding, in 1996, of the Allianz Investment Corp. in Munich, with the goal of exploring the Far East.

Its relative reluctance to have a presence on other continents may cause Allianz to obstruct its own emergence as a world player. That reluctance could prove dangerous. If its home market should one day no longer have room for extensive growth, it may be too late. Insurance companies in smaller European countries like Switzerland or the Netherlands long ago successfully dealt with this situation. Today, their main business activities take place outside their national borders. Next to them, Allianz looks like an immovable Goliath.

The Munich company didn't take notice of its ethnocentricity until the Dutch insurance firm Aegon acquired Transamerica Corp. (whose famous pyramid-shaped building towers over San Francisco) in October 1998 for $9.7 billion. Aegon could have been an ideal potential partner in North America for Allianz. As for Aegon, it had come much closer to becoming a Transatlantic World Inc. than had Allianz. Even before the Transamerica deal, the Dutch company had earned more than 50 percent of its pretax profit in the United States, a sum that will no doubt increase dramatically with the acquisition.

So what makes Allianz such a force to be reckoned with? Its tremendous financial power. It can buy any company in the world it wants, and easily if it makes the purchase through the banks with which it is connected. Its insurance reserves alone have reached an astronomical 340 billion marks. For now, though, there are no large U.S. insurance companies available that would be a good match for Allianz. American International Group, which by American criteria is the largest insurance company in the world, is the last company on the continent with which a megamerger à la DaimlerChrysler would be possible. If Allianz wanted to establish itself more modestly in the United States—more like Deutsche Bank, let's say—it would have to make a move on insurers such as Prudential or Metropolitan Life, North America's largest life insurance companies. In the near future, however, there will be no lack of smaller U.S. insurance companies that will be willing to merge with a large company.

In Germany as well as in Europe, Allianz, like France's Axa and Italy's Generali group, is seen as omnipotent. CEO Henning Schulte-Noelle downplays that image, saying that most of the company's holdings are merely capital investments. "We are trying to get maximum returns on investments, not to dominate others," he maintains. And apart from its sheer financial clout, the company also has numerous offices from which to sell Allianz insurance policies. Schulte-Noelle admits that Allianz does carry "some weight" on the market, but he refuses to argue industrial politics. Even without his acknowledgment, it's plain to see that with Münchner Rück, Dresdner Bank, and Hypovereinsbank in tow, Schulte-Noelle can regard himself as a powerful player on the financial markets, powerful enough to give Breuer's Deutsche Bank a headache, even though Deutsche is Allianz's second-largest shareholder.

As far as money and direct, formal influence on companies are concerned, Allianz's status in Germany is unique, and more of an octopus than a cold-eyed Prussian eagle. Prussian, however, were the company's beginnings. On September 17, 1889, Allianz Versicherungs AG was founded by Carl Thieme, director of the Munich Reinsurance Company, and private banker Wilhelm von Finck, when Germany was rising out of economic depression and into the second phase of its industrial revolution. Thieme and Finck wisely took advantage of the spread of mechanization by focusing on accident and liability insurance. On February 5, 1890, Allianz was entered in Berlin's trade register as a joint-stock company (Aktiengesellschaft). Its original capital of 4 million marks was a remarkable sum at the time. Bavaria was involved in the Allianz undertaking from the beginning. Munich bank Merck, Finck & Co., underwrote 1.5 million marks of the original capital, and Bayerische Vereinsbank was good for another 250,000 marks. Deutsche Bank, which was located in Berlin, underwrote 600,000 marks. Smaller amounts came from Dresdner Bank and Haniel & Lueg of the Rhineland.

Ironically, many of the financial institutions that helped Allianz come into being are now dependent on it. As time went by, the need for insurance grew dramatically. Like Deutsche Bank, Allianz was helped along by historic circumstances and opposed by weaker competitors, many of which were later taken over by Allianz. Size was all that mattered. The downside was that the concomitant risks grew dramatically as well. For example, until the middle of the nineteenth century, shipping companies sent wooden boats overseas, but by the end of the century, large companies such as Hapag and Norddeutscher Lloyd were building 20,000-ton express liners; Hapag's director Albert Ballin laid the keels of the 56,000-ton ships of his Vaterland class up until World War I. Unbelievably large insured sums were stipulated in their contracts. "Grow or go" was the trite motto.

As at Deutsche Bank, two men led Allianz for 10 years following its launch: Thieme and Paul von der Nahmer. After 1904, von der Nahmer alone led the company, and he is credited with recognizing the possibilities offered by the growth in German trade volume. Until its 100th birthday in 1990, Allianz had had no more than six different chairmen of the board. Paul von der Nahmer's tenure was the longest, at 27 years; Wolfgang Schieren, who was chairman at the time of the centenary, eventually served 20 years. When Schieren resigned, the median length of tenure of the company's directors was 17 years. Not counting the present chairman, Schulte-Noelle, no Allianz head served fewer than 12 years.

These service records explain Allianz's remarkable continuity on its way to becoming the leader in its industry; its success can also be explained by this continuity. It was such an integral part of the system that general manager Hans Hess not only served during the entire twelve years of Nazi rule, but held the office for another three years after the war. Few employees at Allianz have worked for more than two directors, so from their perspective, perhaps, Allianz resembles a monarchy more than a stock corporation. This also plays to corporate culture: As late as the 1990s there were three different cafeterias in the company's Munich headquarters: one for directors, one for department managers, and one for the rank and file.

Early on, as Deutsche Bank had done, Allianz began to take over other companies in its industry. In 1898, it acquired Dutch Accident Insurance and a few local insurance companies. As it gradually consolidated its holdings, growing very big and extending its sphere of influence, structures still in place today began to emerge. Around 1923, at the height of an inflationary period, Allianz acquired nine large insurance firms. Of the distinguished companies it acquired during this growth period, an even dozen were older than Allianz. Deutsche Lebensversicherungs-Gesellschaft Lübeck had been founded in 1828; Bayerische Hypotheken-und Wechselbank, whose insurance division Allianz took over in 1906, had been founded in 1835; Frankfurter Lebensversicherungs-Gesellschaft, in 1844; Stuttgarter Versicherungs AG (previously Allgemeiner Deutscher Versicherungs-Verein), in 1874. As early as 1919, Allianz started to cover Germany with a web of branches, the first of them in Hamburg. In 1921, it acquired Hermes Kreditversicherung, a national institution of sorts, and it signed the first of its agreements with Münchner Rück.

During the Weimar Republic, between 1919 and 1933, Germany was coping with the demise of its empire, the Versailles Treaty, France's occupation of the Rhineland, hyperinflation, the development of a liberal democracy, and finally, its tentative return to the international stage. These years were wild and difficult, but they also presented many opportunities. Then, just as the vast effort expended during this period was about to come to fruition, the global economic crisis of the early 1930s, leading to the rise of Hitler, destroyed it all.

During most of those years between 1921 and 1933, the Allianz chairman of the board was ex–army captain Kurt Schmitt. He was a talented man who understood what the times offered. To this day, his name is connected with one of the company's most exciting growth periods. He deftly took advantage of the creative financial opportunities that the otherwise brutally destructive hyperinflation—among other factors—generated. It is no coincidence that the year the company grew most, 1923, was the year when inflation was highest. Allianz was not alone in profiting from the crisis. Many new industrial companies, such as that of the Flick clan, were formed for almost no investment.

Allianz established its first contractual connection with Münchner Rück as early as 1921. In 1928, in concert with the young Swabian building and loan association GdF Wüstenrot, it developed a concept of term life insurance that has since become standard for regular agreements with savings and loans; in brief, it meant that every new savings agreement with Wüstenrot was simultaneously a contract with Allianz. With this maneuver, Kurt Schmitt shaped the Allianz identity for the rest of the century.

Schmitt would not fare so well personally, however. In 1933, the vigorous strategist left Allianz to become trade minister during Hitler's second administration. It was a decision that would have near-fatal fallout, but because Schmitt did not work directly for Hitler nearly as long as Reich Bank president Hjalmar Schacht, he was not indicted after the war. Convinced he would be able to lead the National Socialists in the direction he wished, Schmitt realized his mistake in a matter of weeks and withdrew within a year. But there was no denying he had been enthralled by Hitler before the Nazis came to power in 1933. As early as February 3, 1931, the Nazi leader had invited him and the chairman of Allianz's supervisory board, Baron August von Finck, to the Hotel Kaiserhof in Berlin, ostensibly to explain to them the danger of a Communist coup d'état. Because the fear wasn't entirely unfounded, Hitler impressed the bourgeois lords of Allianz. They promised the führer 5 million marks in the event a civil war broke out, to enable him to better equip his SA raiding squads.

But there was a second reason that Allianz sought the Nazi contact. Many SA members were also members of the Nazi party's social-revolutionary wing that wanted to nationalize all substantial private assets. In an attempt to avoid that, Schmitt and his fellow board member Eduard Hilgard contacted Hermann Göring, then-president of parliament and the second-highest-ranking Nazi. He was believed to be favorably inclined toward industry, which is why the two gentlemen from Allianz promised him they would join Hitler's party. They kept that promise, in March 1933, after a prolonged ban on admission had been lifted. They were among the hundreds of thousands of neo-Nazis nicknamed "March victims." In the fall of 1933—by now minister of trade—Schmitt also joined Hitler's SS, an organization considered elitist and favorably inclined toward industry as well. Not much later, Schmitt entered Reich leader of the SS Heinrich Himmler's "circle of friends." Included in Himmler's inner circle were other members of Allianz's supervisory board—Friedrich Flick, Emil Meyer, and Alfred Olscher.

Hitler and Göring soon had Allianz insurance policies, the former for his house on the Obersalzberg and the latter for his gem-studded marshal's baton. The role Allianz played soon turned unsavory. After Kristallnacht, November 9–10, 1938, Allianz, aided by Hans Goudefroy, the company's legal head counsel and later chairman of the board, began to reject all insurance claims by Jews, unless they were living abroad. To be sure, Jews living in Germany would never have received their money anyway. In an example that worse was yet to come, those who had suffered the damage had a "penalty" of 1 billion reichsmarks imposed on *them*.

Allianz suffered no such injustices. During World War II, Allianz expanded its business to the occupied territories, including numerous concentration camps, all run by Himmler's SS. The camp buildings and inventory were insured in many cases by Allianz, which meant that company managers were called on to visit Auschwitz. Business continued as usual in the face of the mass killings.

In 1940, the first full year of the war, the agreement with Münchner Rück was renewed, and Allianz was split into its two characteristic parts: Allianz Versicherungs AG for regular insurance and Allianz Lebensversicherungs AG for life insurance. But the war essentially demolished Allianz, as it had most of the country. Then, the partition of Germany reduced the company's marketing area, and Berlin was ruled out as its headquarters.

Schmitt had been succeeded in 1933 as chairman by Hans Hess, one of the few of his time who was openly opposed to Hitler (he even took part in the resistance movement). On October 20, 1945, some 55 years after the company had been formally founded, the magistrate of the City of Berlin reissued a licence for Allianz. Business started rolling again, but in 1949—the year the Federal Republic of Germany was founded— Allianz Versicherung central management moved to Munich, and Allianz Leben moved to Stuttgart in Swabia.

By this time, Hess had been succeeded by Hans Goudefroy, and under his control, Allianz began to reestablish itself. The company bought shares in Hamburg-Mannheimer Versicherungs AG. In 1953, Allianz Leben and Alllianz Versicherung established a joint advisory board. Beginning in 1954, Allianz hoisted its flag abroad, opening branches in New York, Paris, Vienna, Stockholm, Milan, London, Brussels, Belgrade, Madrid, Amsterdam, Rio de Janeiro, Tehran, Cairo, the Arabian Emirates, Singapore, Santiago de Chile, and Johannesburg. The last nine of those branches were opened during the helmsmanship of the old-fashioned but farsighted Wolfgang Schieren, who took the reigns from Alfred Haase (who had taken over after the premature death of Goudefroy). Under him, the company grew dramatically. Two years into his tenure, Allianz became Europe's largest life and property insurance company.

Then, in 1985, Schieren began a major overhaul of the conglomerate. Allianz Versicherungs AG was renamed Allianz AG Holding, and Schieren

became its director. Allianz Versicherungs AG and Allianz Lebensversicherungs AG became wholly owned subsidiaries under his direction.
Essentially, Schieren now had a real holding conglomerate that served him
as a base from which to pursue what he was truly interested in: new strategies. The two subsidiaries were subordinate to the holding company,
whose part owners were the company's major shareholders: Münchner
Rück had 25 percent of shares; Dresdner, Deutsche Bank, and Bayerische
Vereinsbank owned 10 percent each; and Bayerische Hypothekenbank
had 5 percent.

In 1990, shortly after East Germany was dissolved, Schieren secured
virtually all insurance property in the former German Democratic Republic. As Deutsche Versicherungs-AG (DVAG), the East German insurer
became a direct subsidiary of Allianz AG Holding. This move caused trouble. The East Germans, inexperienced in the insurance business, believed
they had been misled by the Allianz reps. The new insurance policies
offered less protection than they had enjoyed before—though at a loss to
the insurer. Many of these new customers tried to recoup their money by
filing inflated insurance claims.

Schieren did not stay to sort out the mess. He announced he would
retire on October 2, 1991, then transfer to the holding company's supervisory board. In fact, health reasons forced his hand. Henning Schulte-
Noelle became the man on the hot seat. He had to work his way through
not just the Fascist past, but now also the Communist past.

The Man with Verve

Schulte-Noelle is so reserved that even at six-foot-three, people who
don't know him don't notice him. Nothing in his presence indicates that
he presides over world's largest insurance company, let alone enjoys
power. To many, he looks like a lawyer or a CPA. His one distinguishing
mark—a scar on the left side of his face—is a reminder of his university
fencing days. As a student, Henning Schulte-Noelle was a member of
the Corps Borussia, a society whose members, to prove their strength of
character, were required to fight in the fencing loft with ritual sabers at
least three times.

Schulte-Noelle came from a comfortable middle-class background.
The son of an engineer father and a musically inclined mother, his edu-

cation proceeded uninterrupted until he earned his law degree. He subsequently attended the Wharton School in Philadelphia, Pennsylvania, an institution as renowned for its economics curriculum as Harvard Business School. Now fluent in English, he graduated from Wharton in 1974 with an MBA.

After returning from the United States, Schulte-Noelle briefly worked for a law firm. Perhaps he realized early that the law was not for him. In any case, he became assistant to the director in the Allianz North-Rhine Westphalia branch in Cologne in 1975. From 1976 to 1978 he served as director of Allianz's branch in Aachen. Both positions were steps on the ladder of a career reminiscent of Jürgen Schrempp and Rolf-Ernst Breuer. In due course, he was transferred to the company's headquarters in Munich, where he headed Schieren's office from 1979 to 1983. Schieren was a crucial personal contact, and Schulte-Noelle was destined to gain important inside knowledge, even while he learned to walk political fine lines. In 1984, he was once again sent to the "front" for four years, to serve as director of the Cologne branch of Allianz Versicherungs AG.

It became obvious that he was Schieren's heir apparent. In 1988, at the age of 46, Schulte-Noelle became a regular member of the board of directors, as well as director of distribution at Allianz Versicherungs AG and Allianz Lebensversicherungs AG. But when the time came, Schieren changed his mind—to everyone's surprise. Though Schulte-Noelle was promoted to regular member of the board of Allianz AG Holding, Friedrich Schiefer was designated to succeed Schieren as CEO. As a consolation, Schulte-Noelle was also made head of Allianz Lebensversicherungs AG. Then, in mid-1991, before Schieren had left office, Schiefer declined the offer "for entirely personal reasons" and accepted a position at the Bosch corporation, a company more within the Deutsche Bank circle.

Schulte-Noelle finally got the call. Unfortunately, the year Schieren left the company was a fairly miserable one. Precipitous expansion, a growing rate of crimes against property, natural disasters, heavy start-up losses at DVAG, and wild currency fluctuations hopelessly invalidated the company's profit-and-loss projections. For the first time, the company had to take losses in the insurance business proper. Schulte-Noelle was forced to shift gears and focus on consolidation.

He did a good job. The previously spendthrift Allianz bureaucracy was told to cut costs, especially in the area of executive perks. The company shifted to an incentive pay plan. Particularly guilty of frivolous spending was the East German DVAG, so Schulte-Noelle incorporated it as quickly as possible into other parts of Allianz. He was more reticent when it came to downsizing, but he had no such qualms about becoming tighter with customers. The repercussions of this have yet to surface. Being insured by Allianz does not come cheap. Very often, competitors have better offers, but the conglomerate's network and its tightly knit corporate structure protect it from mass cancellations of policies. Also to Allianz's advantage, when it comes to long-term obligations, German customers are archconservative. Competitive offers that are promoted too aggressively—by British companies, for instance—are met with suspicion.

For now, whether Schulte-Noelle wants to or not, he has to content himself with the German market as his base. His overseas activities serve to create and maintain visibility and to start a learning process. Schulte-Noelle is particularly careful in the United States, where the insurance market is huge but the insurance culture radically different. At all costs he wants to avoid getting burned, even if he must forgo some hot opportunities. At this point, it would be difficult to pull off a coup with either his Allianz branch or the Fireman's Fund. And with the rekindling of the American debate over dealing with large German corporations that were involved in the Nazi regime, the possibility for the expansion of Allianz business in the United States is questionable. Allianz knows it is especially vulnerable in this regard, and it doesn't want to elicit negative headlines.

Today, Germans and Europeans in general consider Allianz's dominant role in the insurance business to be a thing of the past. Schulte-Noelle is all too aware of his company's image problem. At Wharton, he learned well how much a company's public image affects its competitive edge. Still, Allianz, the world's largest insurance conglomerate, is something of a sleeping giant—except that it is not really sleeping, merely waiting. By polishing its image and gaining greater financial power, it will be ready.

With the future in mind, Henning Schulte-Noelle continues the policy of expansion abroad begun by his predecessor Wolfgang Schieren.

But he is doing so in a roundabout way. He is trying to reorganize Allianz into a global money machine before he goes on a shopping spree. That seems a safer approach to him than acquiring companies in quick succession, even if it means passing up opportunities. Therefore, he is much more concerned about pure portfolio management than his predecessors were. What he would like best is to combine all Allianz holdings and the various houses of finance it controls into a single entity. Consequently, he keeps his eyes on the company's shares in outside banks. In 1997 he categorized Allianz's shares in Dresdner Bank and two Munich banks as strategic, much like the mutual holdings between Allianz and Münchner Rück. Because they deal with great numbers of customers on a daily basis, Schulte-Noelle says, banks are the perfect place for selling insurance policies, apart from the portfolio value of the policies. Thus, banks are part of the money machine he has turned on. Through this machine, Allianz is already a global player—perhaps not in insurance, but in the area of financial management.

For this reason, in 1997, Schulte-Noelle was thought to be heading for a megamerger of Dresdner, Bayern-Hypo, and Bayerische Vereinsbank. He wasn't—but perhaps simply because he didn't want to go too far. Still, he successfully and with verve engineered the merger between Bayern-Hypo and Bayerische Vereinsbank. This resulted in no less than the second-largest German bank, much to the dismay of the largest one, Deutsche Bank. And not to be overlooked is that Dresdner Bank—now number three—is part of the web of Allianz and Münchner Rück, holding 25 percent of its stocks.

Deutsche Bank's great leader Hermann Josef Abs once said that he liked being in charge of an institution where he could be the organ player pulling all the registers. Henning Schulte-Noelle doesn't talk about things like that. He does, however, play the organ very well.

CHAPTER 6

Case Two: Marriage of Enemies

Krupp and Thyssen

IN THE FALL of 1998, the managers of Düsseldorf-based Thyssen AG steel conglomerate demonstrated to the world where the company was heading: onward and upward. In the first six months of that year revenues had increased by over 24 percent and profit by 37 percent. And there was more: The company's Essen-based subsidiary, Thyssen Industrie AG, a holding company, announced that it had acquired the American elevator manufacturer Dover Elevators, based in Horn Lake, Mississippi, previously a subsidiary of New York's Dover Corporation. In cable elevator production, Dover was number two in America, behind world leader Otis, and in hydraulic elevator production, number one. One year previously, Thyssen had also purchased the British elevator company Hammond & Champness from Dover Corporation. Thyssen's intent was to increase its elevator business through internal growth and additional acquisitions to 6 billion marks (from 3.5 billion in 1998), which would make it number three in the world.

Thyssen used more than elevators to move up. Six months after acquiring Dover, it merged with Essen's Krupp-Hoechst conglomerate (official name: Fried. Krupp AG Hoechst-Krupp). It was the largest company merger ever in Germany's old industrial region, situated between Rhine and Ruhr. Together the two companies, both with rich histories, reported annual sales of 70 million marks—52 percent from abroad—making it fifth place in Germany's industrial hierarchy. Synergistic effects (such as economies of scale), official announcements say, will save the company 550 million marks per year. That remains to be seen.

The new Thyssen-Krupp is separated into five distinct divisions, all with English names. Along with their combined 1998 revenues, they are: Steel (22 billion marks), Automotive (10 billion), Industries (9.5 billion), Engineering (4.3 billion), and Trading (23 billion). Currently, Thyssen-Krupp is Europe's largest and the world's third-largest steel producer. As a supplier to the automobile industry on both sides of the Atlantic, no one could deny it has made it to the top. Its subsidiary Nirosta gives it a 17 percent share of the world market in flat high-grade steel products, which gives it the number one position.

The merger gave a home to a remarkably large number of different subsidiaries and cooperating partners. The Krupp-Hoechst group (which didn't merge until 1993) included such well-known, formerly independent companies as the excavator and escalator manufacturer Ohrenstein & Koppel AG (Berlin, Dortmund), the machine builder Werner & Pfleiderer GmbH (Stuttgart), and the shock absorber manufacturer August Bilstein (Ennepetal). The union with Hoechst resulted in a 50 percent share in MHP Mannesmann-Hoechst Präzisrohr GmbH in Hamm. Krupp already had a 4.6 percent share in Ruhrgas; and since 1994, Krupp's KHA (Krupp-Hoechst-Automotive) has been officially cooperating with sports car manufacturer and engineering firm Porsche AG.

Thyssen's expansion has been international in scope. In the United States alone, the conglomerate owns part of Denver-based TransLogic Corporation, San Diego–based United States Elevator Corp., Troy, Michigan–based Budd Company, and the machine-tool factory Giddings & Lewis. Thyssen has subsidiaries in Austria, France, and Spain, where the company focus is also on elevator manufacturing. Finally, the Dutch steelworks Nedstaal BV and seven former German steel mills from the Ruhr region found protection under the old Thyssen corporation's steel roof. On its own shore, the firm owns 100 percent of the old shipyards Thyssen Nordseewerke GmbH in Emden, as well as 86.84 percent of Blohm & Voss in Hamburg.

In 1998, Thyssen AG, with 122,000 employees, posted revenues of 43.5 billion marks and profits of 2.1 billion marks. Krupp-Hoechst, with some 58,000 employees, recorded 27.6 billion marks in revenue and profits of almost 1 billion marks. The holding company Thyssen Beteiligungsverwaltung GmbH, 50 percent of which is owned by Commerzbank and 50 percent by Allianz-Versicherung, owned 10 percent of the former Thyssen corporation's joint stock, and the Fritz Thyssen Foundation, 9 percent. More on that later. In the Krupp-Hoechst group, Essen's Krupp Foundation held a commanding 51.6 percent; Iran was next with 23.5 percent; and Düsseldorf's Westdeutsche Landesbank owned 7.2 percent. All three share packages carried over to the new firm.

Since the 1950s, Krupp's leader has been the former oil and insurance manager Berthold Beitz, who was born in 1913. Initially, Alfried Krupp von Bohlen und Halbach, the last of the founder's heirs still active in the company, appointed Beitz as the conglomerate's chief executive. When Alfried Krupp died in 1967, his testamentary disposition essentially made Beitz a Krupp: Beitz became head of the newly established Krupp Foundation through which the founder's family, lacking natural offspring, wanted to perpetuate its name. Beitz often showed remarkable chutzpah in that position.

The merger of Thyssen and Krupp brought together the two last great names to emerge from the Ruhr region during Germany's original advance as an industrial nation. The river for which the region was named runs over wide seams of coal, all the way up to the northern German coast and beyond, into the North Sea. During the nineteenth century, coal was as valuable as gold in any developed society, and in the coal-rich Ruhr region large mining companies soon sprang up followed by giant steel mills next to the pithead frames. Steel mills and pitheads were synonymous with the image of the Ruhr region for three quarters of a century, until coal was replaced by crude oil, which powered engines and became a basic component of inexpensive plastics. At the close of the twentieth century, the few remaining mining companies had been incorporated into Ruhrkohle AG; the remaining steel mills became part of the new Thyssen-Krupp conglomerate.

The Thyssen company founder was the diminutive August Thyssen, who in 1871, established a steel plant in Mülheim on the Ruhr. During the 1880s, he expanded the business by buying several large coal mines; he also bought into the Gewerkschaft Deutscher Kaiser coal pits, then took over the company entirely in 1891. In 1889, he acquired large estates around Bruckhausen, where he built a gigantic steelworks— without proper license. When it was half finished, the authorities issued their permit. As in Pennsylvania, Ohio, and Michigan in the United

States, the Ruhr region quickly became its nation's centerpiece. Even during Germany's decline into power politics under Kaiser Wilhelm II and Adolf Hitler, coal and steel maintained their mythological aura.

Their place in history confers on the names Thyssen and Krupp enormous weight. August Thyssen indefatigably and systematically went about establishing steelworks while also acquiring large segments of Germany's mining industry. He was helped in this effort by company veteran Hugo Stinnes, who would eventually hold stock in 4,554 companies, including those acquired through hostile takeovers.

In 1926, long after the World War I arms production boom was over, parts of the Rhineland were still under the protectorate of the victors, and subsequent inflation had led to a decrease in demand. Thyssen was saved only by merging, with four other Ruhr concerns. The consolidated firm was called Vereinigte Stahlwerke.

It was a time of widespread national consolidations in Germany. Large chemical companies had been consolidated under the name of IG (for "Interessengemeinschaft," or community of interests) Farben (dyes). The Krupp conglomerate, however, remained independent. With its 250,000 employees, the Vereinigten Stahlwerke produced some 40 percent of Germany's steel. Nonetheless, the global economic crisis put them in a precarious position, too. Therefore the founder's son and heir Fritz Thyssen joined the ranks of other industrial powerhouses who fell in with Adolf Hitler. Hitler and Göring had been approaching large companies, especially in the Ruhr region, for donations. Fritz Thyssen became one of the Nazi party's first major donors. But he retracted his support even before the war broke out, fleeing Germany in 1939. He was captured in Vichy, France, and incarcerated from 1941 to 1943 in a mental asylum, then in concentration camps until the end of the war. After the war, his break with the Nazis was accepted, and in 1948, he emigrated to Latin America.

After the war, Vereinigte Stahlwerke—like IG Farben—was dismantled per decree of the Allies. The destruction of Thyssen-Hütte was stopped in 1949 with the Petersberg Treaty, signed by the Allies and the new Federal Republic of Germany. In 1951 in Hamborn, Thyssen-Hütte restarted its first blast furnace. Beginning in May 1953, August-Thyssen-Hütte AG was relaunched as a public company. Under its director Hans-Günter Sohl, it began to take control of major segments of the West German steel industry. Sohl's successor, Dieter Spethmann, who retired in 1991, continued the company's rebirth, eventually turning it into Germany's largest steel mill conglomerate. By then, however, members of the Thyssen clan, elevated through marriage to aristocratic status, lived in South America and no longer dealt much in steel. And though in 1995, Thyssen great-grandchildren Claudio and Frederico von Zichy-Thyssen sold their shares to Commerzbank, to this day in Germany nothing says steel like the name Thyssen.

Alfred Krupp was a steel magnate as well, sooner and to a greater degree than August Thyssen. Still, he was regarded only as second to Thyssen. Krupp, instead, became famous as Germany's "cannon king." He started much earlier than Thyssen did. When Krupp was young, capitalism around the Ruhr was on the distant horizon. It was to England that young entrepreneurs made their pilgrimage. Krupp was a very different person from the younger Thyssen. Tall and thin, with a beard like Santa Claus, he took an interest in how his workers lived; he offered them respectable benefits, complete with retirement plan and life insurance, housing, schools, and holiday camps.

Simply put, Krupp never forgot where he came from. He had been forced to start working at such an early age that he remained sensitive to the issues of working and living conditions for the rest of his life. In 1826, at the tender age of 14, he had to take over the leadership of his father Friedrich Krupp's 15-year-old cast-steel factory, which at the time employed six workers. Facing competition from the preferred British products, Krupp personally went to Sheffield's steel centers to copy their recipes. The young Krupp focused on perfecting the manufacture of high-precision rolls and, later, rolling machines and mills. Together with his two brothers, he developed a mill that stamped, rolled, and embossed cutlery in one operation. He also took numerous trips abroad to expand the company's customer base. Around 1850, things began to improve, thanks to Krupp's development of a forged and rolled seamless railway wheel. Then in 1859 came the breakthrough product: cast-steel cannon-barrel ingots. Krupp's first sale was for 300 units to the Prussian government.

Nevertheless, Krupp, who always sought growth, was facing bankruptcy in 1865, and it was not Prime Minister Otto von Bismarck of Prussia and his minister of war Albrecht von Roon who helped him out even though Bismarck and Roon had just brought the war with Denmark to a conclusion and were on the brink of war with Austria. Rather, a French bank came to the rescue. It was not until 1866 that it occurred to Bismarck to order more Krupp cannons and to try to block the shipment of Krupp artillery Austria had ordered. This attempt failed, and ironically, the Prussians and Austrians, who already spoke the same language, now also shot at each other using the same cannons.

It was not until after the Franco-Prussian war of 1870–1871 that Krupp became known as the Cannon King. This title was conferred on him because his cast-steel guns proved so superior to the French bronze models. Krupp became the third point in the "K trinity": Kaiser, Kanzler (chancellor), and Krupp. In the 1880s, Krupp had 20,000 employees, and his company had turned the insignificant town of Essen into one of Germany's leading industrial centers. He resided high above the city's Lake Baldeney in his Villa Hügel ("Villa Hill"), a vast estate with 220 rooms and an entrance hall as overwhelming as the nave of a Romanesque church. (The villa and the surrounding park were not part of the Thyssen-Krupp merger, but remained at the disposal of Berthold Beitz's Krupp Foundation.) As a matter of course now, Alfred Krupp hobnobbed with the aristocracy in his Essen palace. He called on them in return, a tradition continued by his successors, including daughter Bertha, after his death in 1887. In 1902, the company was converted into a stock corporation.

One year after Krupp's death, the brazen Wilhelm II, a member of the Hohenzollern family, ascended the imperial throne he had inherited from his father and grandfather. The German Empire became ever richer under his rule. In the first 15 years of the twentieth century, German industry was considered the world's second-largest economic empire, behind the United States. The kaiser's fleet-building programs necessitated the development of a huge armament industry, which led in an ever straighter line to World War I. As a result, Krupp became the world's largest arms manufacturer. By the second year of the war, his company employed 96,000 people.

Before the war, the company had been in the practice of selling its high-grade arms—among them warships—to many different countries—even to the potential enemy. Until 1914, the year World War I broke out, Krupp was selling half of its arms outside of Germany. In this way, essentially Krupp was helping to build the military strength of countries that were in conflict with each other. By now the German Empire was at loggerheads with many of its neighbors, in particular the world power Great Britain. Krupp's sell-to-anyone policy was about to come to an end. In 1909, Wilhelm II forbade Krupp to make its annual shipment of eight warships to the British Navy.

This edict turned company Krupp into system Krupp. Germany's then–minister of war Joseas von Heeringen explained that when it came to armament, the German Empire was dependent on private industry; in times of war, it offered sufficient production capacities, and in times of peace, it would continue to manufacture its products at full capacity by filling orders abroad. This was considerably less expensive than a government-owned armament industry. Even before the term *military-industrial complex* had been coined, this was one of the concept's earliest definitions. It was the Krupp *system* that established it. The Krupp *myth*, however, wasn't created until Hitler.

No sooner had the Nazis come to power in 1933 than Krupp began to breach the Versailles Treaty by building large destroyers and U-boats (submarines). By now the company director was the former Royal Prussian Legation councillor Gustav Krupp von Bohlen und Halbach. He had married Krupp's daughter Bertha, and was given the right by Wilhelm II to adopt the name Krupp so that subsequent generations could bear the family and company name. The new Krupp became Germany's new cannon king. But during World War II, Krupp was much more dependent on the powers that be than ever before in its history. The name Krupp became an integral part of Hitler's feverish propaganda machine. The Krupp myth was in the making. Even children in Hitler's youth organization "Jungvolk" (young people), which all 10-year-olds were obliged to join from 1941 on, learned on their very first day that they were expected to be fast as grayhounds, tough as leather, and firm as Krupp steel.

No wonder the cannon conglomerate, which was demolished at the end of World War II, later had trouble with its image. Alfried Krupp von Bohlen und Halbach, a shy man who was temporarily incarcerated as a war criminal in lieu of his ill father, bound the company never to produce arms again. Krupp persistently rejected orders of arms and pursued "peaceful" business deals instead. But what was more important for reestablishing the company's reputation was the appointment of Berthold Beitz as chief executive.

During World War II, young Beitz had worked as manager of the Karpathen ÖL AG, an oil company in Poland, whose labor force was made up of prisoners, many of them Jews. Beitz and his wife ignored the Nazis' race-based orders and, like Oskar Schindler, assigned "important" tasks to many Jews, which saved them from certain death. Though Beitz, who otherwise was none too shy, never publicized his humane behavior—and certainly not immediately after the war—insiders were familiar with it. This helped him later to construct a Teflon shield around the company. On the other hand, the cautious Beitz rarely tried to incorporate an American company into the firm. Only the merger with Thyssen made that possible.

Spider in the Web of Steel

Working at Krupp under Berthold Beitz was just as difficult as working a family business in which the founder still interferes. Among the many Krupp bosses after World War II, only a few turned their tenures into a blessing. Certainly this had something to do with the countless limitations the company imposed upon itself or that had been imposed upon it from outside on account of its past. The general opinion whether spoken or not was that if any German company should be prevented from becoming powerful again, it was Krupp. So Krupp operated under three rules: Don't be noticeable, first; don't produce any war materials, second; discontinue manufacturing steel products, third.

The third rule became controversal for Beitz. Per Allied decree, he was obliged to dispose of Krupp's steel mills; but he was determined to preserve Alfried Krupp's legacy to continue steel production, so he performed diplomatic gyrations to try to hold onto them. This made business almost impossible for his top managers. They didn't know whether they were supposed to be running a steel company or not, and so were unable to develop any kind of business plan. Consequently, they were cautious with investments in this area. When Beitz finally managed to have the steel decree annulled, there still was no plan in place. As a result, Krupp lost its distinctive profile. What it had had too much of before, it now no longer had enough of. Furthermore, Alfried Krupp's legacy continued to have a decisive impact. Finally, now that Beitz had won the battle to resume the steel business, he was reluctant to pare it down, despite convincing economic reasons to do so.

Matters worsened. Subsidies for coal and steel proved unable to set the paralyzed company on its legs. In 1963, Beitz and then–Krupp director Ernst-Wolf Mommsen listed the company as a limited-liability firm in the Commercial Register, making it eligible for project funding. Between 1968 and 1990 it was granted some 360 million marks. Next, Beitz and Mommsen sold almost a quarter of the company to the shah of Iran in 1974.

The Iranian money did help Krupp for the time being. Beitz, the master diplomat, even managed to work around the fundamentalist revolution. Mohamad-Mehdi Navab-Motlagh, Iran's deputy minister of economic affairs and longtime ambassador in Bonn, represented his government's interests on Krupp-Hoechst's supervisory board. He had gone to school in Germany, his German was fluent, and he and multi-lingual Beitz got along well. The two trusted one another and therefore factually constituted the most powerful shareholder group on the supervisory board. Not even the new Thyssen-Krupp conglomerate's supervisory committee was able to overrule their objections.

But at some point in the mid-1970s, Beitz recognized that diplomatic maneuvers might be able to keep his company alive, but they could never really put it back on its feet. He also began to see the danger in not establishing a business strategy. He began looking for a vigorous strategist—one young enough not to want Beitz's position. He found that man in Gerhard Cromme from Münster.

Cromme's rise had been lightning-fast. Born in the small northern German town of Vechta in 1943, he was young enough to be unhindered by Germany's past. Tall and thin, almost gaunt, wearing thick glasses, he radiated the aura of a young chemist preoccupied with his experiments and too impatient to answer anything but direct questions. Like Schulte-Noelle, he wasn't the apprehensive kind. To outsiders, it looked as if his every career move had been carefully considered. Cromme had majored in law and economics at universities in Münster, Lausanne, and Paris. Immediately after receiving his law degree, he enrolled at the Harvard Business School.

His on-the-job training began in 1972 at the French glass company Saint-Goubain-Pont-à-Mousson. Three years later, he was head of the pipe department of Halberger Hütte, a Saint-Goubain subsidiary in Germany's Saarland region. In 1984, he moved to Aachen in the Rhineland, where he became director of the French company's sheet-glass firm Vegla Vereinigte Glaswerke GmbH. Then, after 15 years with the company, instead of returning to Saint-Goubain's headquarters as deputy general director, he accepted the board chairmanship of Krupp Stahl AG in Bochum, in the Ruhr region.

At the time, the Ruhr region was again in the throes of a steel crisis. Between 1981 and 1986, the Krupp steel mill in Duisburg-Rheinhausen had accumulated a loss of 1 billion marks—a vast sum at that time. In November 1987, Cromme announced that the plant, which employed 5,300, was going to close. Only then did the three companies—Krupp, Thyssen Stahl, and Mannesmann-Röhrenwerke, all of which were operating at heavy losses—begin to cooperate. Production from the Rheinhausen Krupp mill was transferred to the nearby Mannesmann plant in Duisburg-Huckingen, which saved its staff's jobs for the time being. But the damage had been done; no one at Krupp felt as safe as they had before. To make their fear and anger clear to management, employees in turn tried to scare Cromme and his family by deploying a "steelworkers' guard" in front of his private home. Cromme remained unmoved. Fortunately for all, by 1988 steel was again in demand and, consequently, more expensive. The nightmare faded.

Toward the end of 1988, Gerhard Cromme became a member of the board of the holding company Fried. Krupp GmbH, and only three months later, director of the board. Three months after that, Krupp's chairman of the board, Berthold Beitz, resigned to assume the figurehead post of honorary chairman. Within a short six months Cromme had risen from a subsidiary's beleaguered crisis manager to become the first independent director of the Krupp conglomerate. As main shareholder Beitz still had a say, but Cromme's partner on the supervisory board was now Manfred Lennings, an experienced "Ruhrian."

It didn't take Cromme long in his new post to recognize how desperate Krupp's situation really was. His first order of business was to quickly get it back into the black, but he considered this to be a Band-Aid treatment at best, when in fact major surgery was required. By 1991, he managed to eliminate all negative entries on the balance sheet by generating new profits. He also sold segments of the company that in his opinion created too many problems. These included the departments of armament technology, electronics, and traffic technology. In March 1992, Krupp-Holding was transformed into a public corporation and listed on the stock exchange, which in turn gave it potential money sources.

That Cromme had bought stock in competitor Hoechst AG, a steel manufacturer in Dortmund, on the side, went unnoticed until he owned about one-quarter of Hoechst shares. He coolly announced that he wasn't going to stop there. By mid-1992, Krupp-Holding owned a spectacular 62 percent share of Hoechst. Clearly, that company was ready for a takeover, whether it wanted one or not. And because Hoechst didn't want it, the action became the first truly hostile takeover in the Ruhr region since the days of Hugo Stinnes and Friedrich Flick. Still, by June 1992, most of the stockholders present voted for the merger. Gerhard Cromme was 49 years old at the time. The Ruhr region had a new strategist. It wasn't the banks that had pulled off this deal; it was Gerhard Cromme from Krupp.

He hadn't done it without help from the financial industry, though. To acquire Hoechst, Krupp had borrowed 4.3 billion marks. But it made 2.7 billion marks during the next few years. Between 1989 and 1995, Cromme sold enough subsidiaries to record a total revenue of 4 billion marks; it also acquired companies to the tune of 22 billion marks. Among them were stocks in companies of which Krupp had divested itself prior to Cromme's tenure, such as a 50 percent share of the former trade firm Krupp Handel GmbH. In 1994, Cromme initiated negotiations with Thyssen. They merged their businesses in packing and electronic sheet metal as well as high-grade sheet steel.

Cromme had succeeded in overhauling the entire company. In 1996, he posted a revenue of 24 billion marks, an 80 percent increase since taking office; 59 percent of that business was abroad. Though all this was positive, Cromme, with his eye trained on the future, saw a negative, too: He considered the conglomerate's earning power not strong enough for its size, and he saw its size as insufficient. On the global playing field, Cromme viewed Krupp as an amateur. He had raised the possibility of a merger with Thyssen to that company's director Dieter Vogel. Vogel wasn't interested; his company was more profitable, so he believed it could make it alone. Cromme argued that both firms were basically moving in the same direction, away from steel and into more modern business arenas such as auto industry supply, manufacturing equipment, and trade. Vogel continued to say no.

During all this, Gerhard Cromme had become the new darling of German investment bankers. His membership on the boards of Veba and Allianz—as well those of Bertelsmann, Ruhrgas, and Ruhrkohle— gave him access to the old Deutschland AG's bean counters. Both Dresdner and Deutsche Banks had representatives on Krupp's and Thyssen's supervisory boards. Everyone was well informed, no one more so than Cromme. New York investment bank Goldman Sachs had shared much knowledge of financial markets with him; the banks offered him a loan of 15 billion marks, enabling him to launch "Operation Hammer and Thor," the hostile takeover of the huge Thyssen conglomerate through Krupp-Hoechst, which was half Thyssen's size. Hammer and Thor were like David and Goliath.

Cromme and his staff assumed it would be very expensive to purchase Thyssen—way above market value—but hoped that the merged company would be so strong that it would enable the conglomerate to pay back the billion-dollar loans within just a few years. Krupp and Thyssen, they also figured, had a number of assets that could be turned into cash. Thus, because Thyssen was not only the larger but also the more profitable company, it had to finance its own demise.

That, at least, was the plan discussed and agreed upon with Krupp's director. Eventually, Cromme wanted to tell his colleague Vogel that a hostile takeover was going to take place, prompting talks between Krupp and Thyssen, with the goal of a friendly takeover. Essentially, Cromme was emulating former U.S. president Theodore Roosevelt's motto: "Speak softly and carry a big stick." The big stick was the fact that Krupp could at any time publish its takeover offer of 435 marks per share for Thyssen stock—which was listed at a much lower rate—in the German stock exchange publication. From that moment on it would have been impossible to stop Operation Hammer and Thor.

In early March 1997, all was still quiet on the western front. By the end of the month, however, the media had gotten wind of the deal. The metal workers union rebelled, as their jobs were in jeopardy. Conservative Chancellor Kohl groaned that much was being "destroyed in this republic of ours." North Rhine–Westphalia's minister of economic affairs Wolfgang Clement, who was in charge of the Ruhr region, became indignant over the country's "financial jugglers." Someone dining with State Prime Minister Johannes Rau, now Germany's president, made the analogy to the now-defunct but still memorable American prime-time soap opera *Dallas*. J. R. Ewing, alias Gerhard Cromme, required police protection when he tried to explain to his workers that it was they who were taking over the competition and that the move would *save* their jobs.

The dream had ended. All the while, Thyssen's director Dieter Vogel had been organizing the defense against Krupp, Goldman Sachs, and Deutsche Bank. What under normal circumstances would have been difficult, he now managed to do easily—mobilize workers and unions. Vogel advanced quickly, but there was one stronghold he couldn't breech: Krupp's three major shareholders—the Krupp Foundation, Iran, and Westdeutsche Landesbank, which together owned more than two-thirds of all stock. They stuck together. Thus, Krupp was totally protected against any hostile takeover. Thyssen, on the other hand, was entirely unprotected. Its two largest shareholders owned barely 18 percent. By comparison, at the 1992 annual meeting, Deutsche and Dresdner Banks represented 17 percent with their proxy votes. Vogel was forced to negotiate.

Cromme retreated for the time being. He knew that what Thyssen had always rejected—the formation of a Thyssen-Krupp Stahl AG with the goal of producing high-quality steel—was now within reach. And so it was decided retroactively as of April 1997, with 60 percent voting for Thyssen. Thyssen manager Ekkehard Schulz became the new director.

Cromme had gained time and saved money, but his surprise attack could not be repeated. Gradually, the mood in the Ruhr region changed; perhaps a merger between Krupp and Thyssen wouldn't be so bad after all. Now it was up to the old guard to loosen the knot. The honorary chairmen of both boards, Thyssen's Günter Vogelsang and Krupp's Berthold Beitz—the former age 77, the latter 84—met at Beitz's Villa Hügel. They knew each other well, as much earlier Vogelsang had led the Krupp conglomerate, which made him one of its numerous saviors. Before 1997 drew to a close, the merger was a done deal. What remained an open question was who would lead the new conglomerate. Krupp insisted on Cromme; Thyssen wanted Vogel. The banks, the public, and particularly the investors considered Cromme to be the stronger man; but Krupp was the weaker partner. Consequently, as is so often the case, the merger was in danger of foundering on a decisive personnel issue. Beitz let it be known that without Cromme, there would be no merger.

Salvation came from the East—more precisely, from the chaos in the former Treuhandanstalt in Berlin, a government-founded organization to privatize former East Germany's economic state property. This business went totally out of proportion. Not only that, West German companies grabbed their share simply in order to secure for themselves the new markets and to keep the new local competition at bay—both generously subsidized by taxpayers' money. Treuhandanstalt and its clients also had to deal with the big names in the former East German Communist government and their underhanded dealings and money-laundering schemes. It was a whirlpool in which nobody could stay clean. Certainly not Dieter Vogel.

Vogel, then boss of Thyssen Handelsunion (THU, Thyssen's trade company), had initiated the purchase of AHB Metallurgiehandel (MH) from the Treuhandanstalt against heavy subsidiaries in mid-1990. All of a sudden, in 1992, he was struggling with Treuhandanstalt over how the deal had been pulled off. In 1993, the feds searched the offices of MH and THU. Shortly thereafter, the intricate matter was decided through arbitration, which ended on May 15, 1996. The final agreement obligated Thyssen to pay back 240 million marks to the federal treasury. Ironically, in August 1996, when the whole incident had blown over, Vogel was arrested. At the time, Germany's long arm of the law was reaching out for well-paid managers.

Vogel was released on 2.5 million marks bail, but the prosecutor's office in Berlin wouldn't drop the case, so Vogel was hurt. The threat of a suit and additional questioning by the authorities in Germany's wild East obviously weakened Vogel's position. That wasn't all. The longer the candidates fought over the company's top position, the more the financiers came to back Cromme. Keep in mind that at this time, Rolf-Ernst Breuer's move into the executive suite at Deutsche Bank had strengthened the concept of investment banking in Germany; it held the promise of a great deal of money. Krupp's chairman was considered to be representative of American investment capitalism, whereas Thyssen's boss was regarded as a member of the near-extinct Rhineland clan. In short, Cromme was the man of the future.

Then the inevitable happened: On December 15, 1996, the Berlin prosecutor officially indicted Vogel. Beitz and the bankers won, though it had taken a horse trade. Now the new Thyssen-Krupp AG had coleaders: Cromme moved into the executive suite for Krupp, and Ekkehard Schulz, until then director of the merged Thyssen-Krupp steel company, took the reins for Thyssen. The two instantly harmonized, even granting joint interviews. Time now was working for Krupp and the investment scene. Schulz, an engineer and a talented steel manager two years older than Cromme, has everything required of a solid industrial director. But as a man of finance and a business strategist, Cromme has the advantage.

Thus, after almost 13 tumultuous years at Krupp, Gerhard Cromme is the new man on the Rhine and in the Ruhr. He is expected to provide a stable future for the company. Cromme is doing the same thing with the new Thyssen-Krupp conglomerate that he did with the old Krupp-Hoechst: He is selling company divisions that have small returns and don't seem to fit into the business of the future, and he is acquiring companies with good returns. But a revenue of 70 billion marks is not enough for Cromme. He is well known on the golf courses of the French Côte d'Azur. Soon he'll be seen at Hilton Head as well.

CHAPTER 7

Case Three: Hoechst's Adventure

IG Farben and IG Pharma

J ÜRGEN DORMANN, a professional economist, has been with Frankfurt's chemical company Hoechst AG for a long time. Still, he finds the German tendency to turn a workplace into a "warm and fuzzy" environment distasteful. Expressions such as "Hoechst family" prompt him to retort: "What family? Let's talk of coworkers." In another way, too, Dormann is an anomaly at the company: By 1994, when he had been made chairman of the board of Hoechst, he was one of a very few leaders of the conglomerate who was not a chemist, more specifically, a chemistry professor.

Dormann is an ascetic man, but he is always quick off the mark, and thus often not deterred by other people's feelings. "The entire workforce hates that man," confirms Arnold Weber, the chairman of the Hoechst workers council and the conglomerate's highest-ranking worker representative.

Besides his temperament going against him, Dormann also is held responsible for halting the company's smooth ride and for turning Hoechst topsy-turvy by selling parts of it and acquiring entire business branches. And it wasn't just that he risked the solid footing of what had been at times German industry's most powerful company or that the number of jobs was cut by 25 percent since the beginning of his tenure or that competing companies BASF and Bayer managed to hold onto their traditional values and still make more money. More insulting and infuriating to his detractors was that he decided to discard the conglomerate's distinguished name as if it were an old sock with holes in it. Indeed, as of 1999, the company name became Aventis, with headquarters in Strasbourg, on the French side of the Rhine. To add insult to injury, the French were given a say in the company as well.

How could this happen? Simple. Hoechst AG merged with France's national treasure, Société des Usines Chemiques Rhône-Poulenc, the country's largest chemical company, more than 100 years old and extremely popular. And though it was a bit smaller and less profitable than Hoechst—voilà—it was nevertheless to be a merger among equals. The French also agreed to discard their own company's historic name and become Aventis. The new name is derived from the French *aventure* (adventure).

The fuss over the name change seems a bit hypocritical, since neither Hoechst nor Rhône-Poulenc have kept their original names throughout their histories. Rhône-Poulenc was named in 1928 when the Société Chimique des Usines du Rhône merged with the private medicine manufacturer Etablissements Poulenc Frères. Hoechst AG began (in Hoechst on the Main) in 1863 as the coal-tar dye factory Meister, Lucius & Co. At another time it was called Meister, Lucius & Brüning. Seventeen years later, the factory was called Farbwerke Hoechst. In 1925, shortly after the devastating period of inflation, it became a branch of a new trust of seven corporations, led by the chemical giant company BASF. The organization was called IG (Interessen-Gemeinschaft) Farben.

That same year, 1925, the German chemist Hermann Staudinger (1881–1965) proved that special molecules—macromolecules—formed long, chainlike structures (polymers) by chemical reaction and that they could be synthesized in various processes of so-called polymerization. These discoveries eventually led to the development of plastics and synthetic fibers. (Staudinger would later, in 1953, receive the Nobel Prize in Chemistry for his work in the development of plastics.) Their industrial breakthrough didn't occur, however, until after World War II.

At about the same time, the American chemical company E.I. du Pont de Nemours had also laid the groundwork in the development of these fibers. In DuPont's research laboratories in Wilmington, Delaware, a team led by Wallace Hume Carothers discovered that polyamides could be melt-spun into fibers or made into transparent film. One, called Fiber 66, would become nylon. DuPont obtained 130 individual patents for its development. Subsequently, IG Farben chemist

Paul Schlack, who was familiar with Carothers's work, found another way of achieving the same result. He called his product Polyamid 6, which later became Perlon fiber. These developments would be responsible for the explosive growth in the chemical industry for several postwar decades.

In the 1930s, IG Farben, mainly composed of the big three chemical corporations BASF, Bayer, and Hoechst, had grown as big as DuPont. Though already founded during the heyday of the Weimar Republic, the IG Farben cartel became very close to the Nazi regime and its economic program. Similar to the insurance giant Allianz, IG Farben developed its own attachment to the Nazi party NSPAP early in 1931. Like the Allianz management, the IG Farben executives were concerned that leftists would come to power in Germany's unstable political climate and that the company might be nationalized, and they supported Adolf Hitler, making secret contributions to the Nazi Party as early as 1931. During the war, IG Farben experienced unparalleled growth; it had an interest in 379 German firms and 400 foreign companies. But near the end of the war, its facilities, in particular those of BASF, were bombed extensively; and that was just the beginning of the end of its boom perod.

After Germany surrendered, the Allies argued over what to do with the chemical giant. It wasn't until 1952 that they agreed to redivide the company into its original parts after World War II, Farbenfabriken Bayer in Leverkusen, Badische Anilin und Soda Fabriken (BASF) in Ludwigshafen, and Farbwerke Hoechst (previously Meister Lucius & Brüning). Under the IG Farben umbrella, they all had to specialize; now they seemed handicapped by a lack of balance. To regain their balance, each tried to cross into the markets of the other two. In the end, all of them made a great deal of money on chemical fibers, synthetic materials, drugs, and fertilizers.

During this period, though there were debates about costs, no one really suggested paring down, so all of them erected majestic new headquarters for themselves. The seemingly never-ending economic boom in the new mass-product business resulted in huge revenues. In 1960, Hoechst's revenues were 2.7 billion marks. In 1977—when Hoechst was the German chemical industry's number one company—revenues reached 10.1 billion; and in 1990, they climbed to around 45.9 billion. The number of employees between 1960 and 1990 increased from 50,000 to 173,000.

In 1961 Hoechst established American Hoechst Corporation in New York City. Since then, the chemical company has had a presence in most geographical and product markets in the world. And the resegmentation of IG Farben in the mid-1970s meant that Germany no longer had one chemical company the size of DuPont, but three, all headed by former chemistry professors. But all good things must come to an end, and the boom brought about by the discovery of synthetic fibers was no different. Labor costs in Germany gradually climbed so high that production at home was no longer profitable. And there were no major secrets left to be revealed about the production of synthetic materials and chemical fibers, meaning they soon could be produced anywhere and, in most other countries, more inexpensively.

Nevertheless, as late as 1982, one of those countries where production would have been cheaper, Kuwait, acquired a 24.5 percent share in the Hoechst conglomerate through its Kuwait Petroleum Corporation. Hoechst, in turn, acquired the American chemical company Celenese in order to centralize the mass production of its materials there. This did not interfere with "family" life at Hoechst. Since its re-formation, it had not gone through a serious crisis—that is, until Dormann knocked on the door. As a member of the board of directors, this gaunt man with shadows around his eyes had initiated few reforms—not that he was expected to, because such actions could have jeopardized his career, as it had for his predecessor Wolfgang Hilger, the "Soldier King."

Dormann may not have been assertive, but he had been very observant. He had noted that high-volume business could no longer be counted on to bring in big money. "Synthetic materials," he would later say, "is something you can buy at any street corner." But that was only one of the problems that he took note of. Worse, he thought, was that Hoechst—and Bayer—had started to lose their positions as the world's leading pharmaceutical companies. Worse yet was that the Federal Republic of Germany had instituted a prohibition on genetics research.

Hoechst had tried to make inroads in the high-tech fortresses along the U.S. East Coast, but not very effectively. In contrast, while everything in Germany seemed to be paralyzed, the young Southern Californian biotech company Amgen, which had been financed through venture capital in the 1970s, became the world's market leader. When, in 1994, Dormann moved into Hoechst's executive suite, the conglomerate's return on fibers and synthetic materials was almost twice as high

(20.9 billion marks) as for its pharmaceutical business (11.6 billion), but yielded a net loss of 320 million marks. By comparison, the pharmaceuticals department had made an operating profit of 1.5 billion marks, far more than any of the company's other branches. Dormann knew immediately what to do—get rid of polymeres and fibers, period.

The new director didn't believe that gradually shifting the company's focus was going to resolve such a serious structural dilemma. Dormann decided that the solution was to sell what generated low returns and purchase what promised high returns—and all at a ratio that would yield a record revenue. To launch his Pivot Strategy, he began looking for a strong, a very strong, company in the United States, because that's where modern pharmacological research was being done. On the other hand, competition there was much tougher, too. All of these were drastic measures, which, according to Anglo-Saxon doctrine, were necessary to shake up, modernize, and pare down the company, then take it to the top of contemporary industrial chemistry—while not excluding the possibility of eventually marrying a partner of equal value. Dormann's strategy was personally risky because he had no guarantee that he would still be in office to take the credit for the positive results of his upside-down strategy. After all, he would turn 60 at the turn of the century.

Dormann on Tigerback

At first everything went very fast. "Derust and defrost," Dormann ordered. The analysts and investment bankers cheered, as they are wont to do when someone starts selling, purchasing, and merging. They first cashed in on Dormann as early as 1995. Hoechst purchased the pharmaceutical company Marion Merell Dow (MMD) from America's Dow Chemical for 10 billion marks, which earned it a 2 percent share of the huge U.S. pharmaceuticals market. This acquisition was perfectly in line with Dormann's strategy. Already dominating the French pharmaceutical company Roussel-Uclaf, Hoechst's business became part of the new Hoechst Marion Roussel organization (HMR), which advanced the Frankfurt conglomerate from eighth to fifth place on the list of international pharmaceutical companies.

While German companies were losing their lead in the world league of pharmaceutical production in the 1980s, elsewhere dramatic events were taking place. The big Anglo-Saxon and Swiss manufacturers with their manifold connections had become virtually unchallenged. The Swiss companies Ciba Geigy and Sandoz had merged into a new company called Novartis. The family firm of Boehringer in Mannheim had been acquired by Switzerland's Roche conglomerate.

In 1996, in first place in the international pharmaceutical industry was the American company Merck, with revenues of $13.3 billion. Behind it was British conglomerate Glaxo Wellcome—the result of a merger the previous year—with $13 billion. With $9.9 billion, Novartis was in third place; the American Bristol Myers Squibb was number four with revenues of $8.7 billion. Next came Hoechst Marion Roussel. Before HMR was founded, the strategists of the old Deutschland AG had thought about establishing a German IG Pharma à la the former IG Farben. But Manfred Schneider, head of Leverkusen's Bayer conglomerate, didn't think much of major mergers, nor did Jürgen Strube, his colleague at BASF.

Dormann, who was a fan of mergers, quipped, "Where's Leverkusen?" and then began to look around abroad. He spent another 5.3 billion marks to buy out the independent shareholders of the French firm Roussel Uclaf, which manufactured the abortion pill RU 486. Dormann spent nearly another billion on the acquisition of the American genetics company Copley. For the time being, Dormann believed this gave him a strong enough axis in the United States.

Initially, things went well. Thanks to HMR, the company's U.S. market share climbed to around 4 percent. But then HMR sales slumped again. Backpedaling, the analysts and investment bankers now said the takeover of MMD had not been a good idea after all; furthermore, they claimed they had warned the Germans early on of the risk. Clearly, they said, Dow Chemical had its reasons for selling the company to a foreign firm. But Europeans tend to look at such deals differently. Usually, their primary purpose is not to make big money right away; they prefer to take their time, integrating and, if necessary, putting the merged companies back on their feet. In point of fact, soon after the takeover Dormann had to recall two drugs that had been developed by MMD prior to the merger. Still, Hoechst's boss was counting on at least four promising drugs appearing on shelves in medicine cabinets all across America.

In the pharmaceutical industry, the development, release, and sale of a drug are usually a gamble and always subject to probability theory. In short, they're always long shots. From the time drugs are introduced to the market until their sales peak takes seven to twelve years. On the other hand, German pharmaceutical companies that regularly introduce new drugs average at least a 20 percent rate of return. American, British, and Swiss companies do better, at a rate of 25 to 30 percent. Dormann had just reached 16 percent. If the company he forcefully turned in the direction of pharmaceuticals is to yield the results he is aiming for, Dormann has to establish as much continuity as his Swiss and Anglo-Saxon counterparts have achieved.

Dormann is well aware of all this, but that didn't make it easier to bear during the transition period (which he called a "somewhat bumpy stretch"). Hoechst's figures were not as good as those of its competitors. Nor were the company's stocks doing well. Benchmarking and shareholder values forced Dormann to cut the research budgets, which prompted a minor rebellion at Hoechst. To quell it, he agreed to a contract with the company's workers council that assured no layoffs but regular investments until 2002. At the same time, Dormann sold still more parts of the company.

He also ordered the conglomerate's French subsidiary Roussel Uclaf (RU) to return rights to the controversial abortion pill RU 486 to Edouard Sakiz, the drug's coinventor and former chairman of the company's supervisory board. (Sakiz subsequently began to manufacture the pill independently on a not-for-profit basis.) Dormann also got rid of Hoechst's age-old penicillin production, which was no longer very profitable. During the first four years of his tenure, the number of employees dropped from 180,000 to 40,000.

Dormann also reduced the size of the company's board of directors from eleven to seven, and they now function as holding company directors, concentrating much more on strategy and corporate policies than did the previous board. Business operations are now forged and held accountable at this level—similar, Dormann notes, to procedures in the company's foreign subsidiaries. And in keeping with modern management theories, he dismantled corporate management's tribunal power structure. Furthermore, he added the former directors of the Brazilian and American branches to give him two experienced managers among the company's directors. Their inclusion, in particular, was regarded as innovative. In the classic Deutschland AG—and most notably in the chemical industry—anyone heading a branch was categorically regarded as unfit to be a member of the board of directors at headquarters. In the past, being delegated to outpost service had been considered a kind of exile that effectively signified the peak of one's career. Therefore, being a branch manager had been of no interest to the really talented and/or ambitious people. In the course of globalizing Hoechst, Dormann turned that tradition upside down. "Being German and *gemütlich* alone aren't sufficient qualities for running a global business," Dormann used to point out.

So far, he had reached only one stop along the way toward his goal of transforming the former chemical company into a "life science conglomerate" that would focus on pharmaceuticals, biotechnology, and veterinary medicine. He needed still more pharmaceuticals business, and he had to further pare down old and less-profitable business areas. To those ends, he sold the equipment manufacturer Uhde—a foundling really—to Krupp. He also offered such well-known Hoechst brands as Revira and Ticona on the market. Herberts, a varnish manufacturer of paints with a long tradition, was sold to the DuPont conglomerate for 3.1 billion marks. Dormann's most drastic measure of this kind was the sale of plastics manufacturer Celanese. In fact, it was more like firing the company; he simply turned it into a separate public corporation.

Dormann was, in effect, emulating the British chemical conglomerate ICI, which five years previously had unloaded its pharmaceuticals branch by splitting off the firm Zenica. Dormann combined most of his classic chemicals business—in other words, chemicals and technical synthetic materials—under the new umbrella of Celanese AG. With 15,000 employees and revenues (in 1997) of 9.6 billion marks, he bragged that the new big enterprise would be among the world's leading industrial-chemical companies. Indeed, the new public corporation could claim the number one position for such tongue-twister products as acetic acid, vinyl acetate, acid anhyride, cellulose acetate for cigarette filters, and polyacetal.

Legally, Celanese was a thoroughly German company, subject to German corporate law. Economically, more than half the company's returns came from the United States, the home of four-fifths of its fixed assets and nine-tenths of its sales. Hoechst originally had acquired the company for its low American production costs. The German public corporation had been superimposed on it only so that Celanese could remain tax-free for its shareholders in accordance with Germany's conversion tax law. Celanese's new stocks were listed on exchanges in Frankfurt and New York, but initially were distributed among Hoechst's old shareholders. For 10 Hoechst shares, an investor received one Celanese share. The pertinent deposits on Celanese's equity account were not made from the issuance of stocks but from Hoechst's profit reserves. Dormann, however, wouldn't be Dormann if he hadn't transferred 3.2 billion marks of Hoechst's debts to Celanese.

By splitting off Celanese, Hoechst AG shrank by some 20 percent. Though management tried very hard to maintain the same value for Hoechst stocks on the German DAX index, by focusing on its more modern business areas, Hoechst—formerly the leader among the IG Farben's successor companies—had become the caboose. In addition, Dormann was forced to accept losses and lower profits from current operations. Still, he was undeterred from carrying out his strategy. The complaints of anxious HMR employees didn't faze him. When some of them, in an open letter, criticized "management's activities, which are hurting business," the supervisory board continued to back management.

The reorganization Dormann engineered during his first four years in office is considered the most radical ever of a German company. Not even the audacious architects at the new Mannesmann, who had turned that company in the direction of telecommunications, or the revolutionaries who had turned the Rust Belt company Preussag into an all-around transportation firm were seen as quite so radical. Dormann had taken a great risk. But every step he took changed the company in a way that made it impossible for the supervisory board to disapprove. If the deal went wrong, Dormann would graciously resign, never mind that the shareholders would have paid for his venture with their stocks' devaluation, and the company's employees with their jobs. If, on the other hand, it went well, he would remain in office and the shareholders would profit—at least in the long run.

Among those stockholders, doubtless the one most concerned by the reorganization was Kuwait Petroleum Corporation, whose holdings are administrated by the interpolated portfolio management firm Gallus. That means it's neither bank boards nor investment managers that are most nervous about Dormann's actions, but the emirate's emissaries.

When Hoechst and Rhône-Poulenc were about to merge, they asked a great many questions, and most of them for good reason, considering they had had an actual blocking minority of almost 25 percent in a completely German blue-chip company. Dormann's maneuver would leave them with only 12 percent, in a company governed by French law and with an unfamiliar name.

The great finale to the Dormann show is about to begin. Measured by an old patrician saying, "Anyone can sell cheap and marry poor," not even the first part of Dormann's strategy has worked out as planned. His company's revenue—the part of the Hoechst conglomerate that is measurable—has fallen even further behind that of Bayer and BASF. In 1977, Hoechst led the industry with a revenue of 10.1 billion marks. In 1990, the company had reached 45.9 billion marks, and subsequently, close to 52 billion. After the sale of Celanese, revenues declined to about two-thirds that amount.

Jürgen Dormann next proceeded pursuant to American management laws and Wall Street's criteria and risked entering into a marriage with a French native. According to popular opinion, that meant straddling the fence—a dangerous enterprise. Though the French were willing to accept Dormann as their boss, they wouldn't accept the German company's name, and vice versa. The name game proved highly sensitive, as did the choice of the new conglomerate's capital in the Alsatian city of Strasbourg. Assigning the holding company located there the name Aventis was a maneuver that could have been nullified if both national subsidiaries hadn't accepted the name. To be specific, the conglomerate's Rhône-Poulenc branch, located in Lyon, is called Aventis Agro, and the Hoechst part, located in Frankfurt, is called Aventis Pharma.

Jürgen Dormann has no trouble explaining his decisions; he is prepared for everything. Aventis Pharma, he says, is the second-largest company of its kind in the world, at least for the time being. That, he emphasizes, is what he brought to Frankfurt, former location of Hoechst headquarters, once the world's largest pharmaceutical company. The Hoechst name appears only at an intermediate level, and only as one-third of a name at that, of sub-subsidiary Hoechst Marion Roussel. It also appears in the name of the Lyon Veterinary branch, Hoechst Roussel Vet. Otherwise, there is no more Hoechst.

Other sub-subsidiaries to Frankfurt's Aventis Pharma are Centeon, Rhône-Poulenc Rorer, Pasteur Mérieux, Connaught, and Dade Behring. Sub-subsidiaries to Aventis Agro in Lyon are AgrEvo, Rhône-Poulenc Agro, Rhône-Poulenc Animal Nutrition, and Merial. This deal can be said to have no equal; there is no example after which it is modeled. Immediately following the merger, many denied that it was *setting* an example. Perhaps Dormann can take comfort in believing that being ahead of one's time is sometimes not known until much later. But it was, in his own judgment, a ride on the tiger's back.

As far as revenue is concerned, Hoechst has "married poor" for the time being. In 1998, both partners' combined returns added up to no more than 35.8 billion marks. Dormann appears to be turning the Schrempp, Breuer, and Cromme systems upside down. He puts quality and profitability above size. In other words, in the new core business, a company's new optimum size is smaller than in auto manufacturing or installations. This way of thinking does make sense. Aventis is no longer a huge chemical company the way BASF and Bayer still are. But Dormann isn't interested in a dinosaur with gigantic revenues and in need of subsidies. That Bayer and BASF have returns of 60 billion marks leaves him cold. He is no longer one of them. IG Farben is dead.

If he had not split Celanese off but incorporated it into his holding company, he would only have reached the 1990 return rate, and in that case, Hoechst would have been too big for a marriage with Rhône-Poulenc, which was interested in a deal between equals. Celanese had to go before Rhône-Poulenc could arrive. This way, the company is a great deal more international than it would otherwise have been. No less than 90 percent of Aventis's return (Hoechst's 1990 revenue: 73 percent) is made outside of Germany, and more than 87 percent of all employees work outside German borders. Dormann calls the company a "non-national conglomerate," number one in agricultural products and number two in pharmaceuticals. After the Celanese deal, Dormann said, "We've made it through, thank God. I'm happy." At the time, he had been with Hoechst for almost four decades.

With the finalizing of the merger, Aventis had to get started on the detail work. Dormann's plan is to become a global counterconglomerate in competition with Merck, Bristol Myers, Pfizer, American Home Products, Johnson & Johnson, and Ely Lilly—all of them American and all of them among the pharmaceutical industry's 10 largest companies. He hasn't quite reached his goal yet. In terms of revenue, Aventis Pharma is number two. Its range of products and earning power, however, don't compare with most of the competition's. Dormann's Aventis is still a borderline company; its strategy is to become a global counterconglomerate. But in real life, it started out as a nonnational company, with its headquarters in Europe and an axis in the United States, so the Pivot Strategy describes it best at present. We will see.

Part IV

THE GLOBAL COUNTER-CONGLOMERATE

Case One: Siemens—
Shocks in the Power Net

Leviathan

I N EARLY 1998, Siemens AG, Munich's electronics company, shipped 11 diesel locomotives to the Norway state railroad system. Their design featured a nice chassis built of good material, resulting in a smooth drive capability. That all went to waste, however, in the rough north, for the railroads there were uneven, the tracks bumpy. Again and again, noted a *Spiegel* reporter, oil pipes had broken or a one-time fire had started in the cabin.

These locomotives were symbolic of the entire conglomerate. In 1997, the company, being run from a distinguished royal palace in Munich, had 380,000 people on its payroll. With an annual revenue of 107 billion marks, the firm was Germany's third-largest industrial company and Europe's largest electronics firm. After 150 years in business, it seemed there was hardly an electronic product that Siemens hadn't manufactured at some point in its history. On its 150th anniversary, the conglomerate was still active in some 200 different business areas.

It would be difficult to name another electronics conglomerate with such extensive know-how as Siemens. Generation after generation, it continues to be administered as if it were the international museum of electricity. The less flattering view of those knowledgeable in the corporate culture of the electronics industry is that the conglomerate's structure is museumlike—that is to say, outdated—in its core areas of business. While always attempting to keep pace with current developments, in the end Siemens has often been a few steps behind. For exam-

ple, though it owns countless technical patents, this kingly house of electricity has had trouble marketing them properly. Still, director Heinrich
von Pierer is floating on vast liquid resources, which give Siemens solid
financial power. Financial power, that is, not profit-making strength. A
2.7 percent rate of return won't earn it any laurels. For that kind of yield,
Peter von Siemens pointed out to his fellow members on the conglomerate's supervisory board, "The greengrocer around the corner wouldn't
even open his store."

Von Siemens is one of the many great-great-grandsons of Ernst
Werner Siemens, a former Prussian artillery officer and the firm's
founder. Some 7 percent of Siemens capital stock is still owned by the
family, which is descended from the Prussian aristocracy. Considering
that in 1998 there were 585.63 million Siemens shares valued at about
$130 each, this is no trifle, but somewhat less impressive considering
that it is spread among some 270 members of the clan.

For decades, the common investor regarded Siemens stock as a safe
bet, which is why innumerable portfolios included it. General opinion
holds that the founding family is, however, still the conglomerate's major
shareholder. This fact alone makes the company unique. Also notewor-
thy is that Siemens may be the only company of international stature
whose founder was personally responsible for the essential technical
inventions of the day and who built a company that firmly held its
ground for 150 years, still carries his name, and is, at least in part, still
controlled by his family. Naturally, such an institution is bound to have
its rituals. Until recently, a technician always headed the company and a
member of the founding clan was chairman of the supervisory board. In
a break with that tradition, Siemens's present director, is a lawyer, and
the family member on the supervisory board is no longer its chairman.

But that is not to say that Siemens is not still a technicians' company,
and a patriarchy as well—though a modern version. There always has
been and still is a great deal of money to be made in electricity. No
form of energy since the beginning of the Industrial Revolution has
been in such constant demand as electricity, in all its various imple-
mentations. Unlike coal, oil, and gas, it is a secondary carrier of energy,
a user and processor rather than a producer. For this reason, those
working with electricity have always been involved in the processing
industries. This fact has fundamentally determined the thinking in that
field. And except for wartime, Siemens employees have always been
relatively fortunate. To this day the company supports its retired work-

force by way of a pension fund, health insurance, cultural events, and short-term leisure activities.

The company traditions date back to the genius Ernst Werner Siemens, later von Siemens (1816–1892), who was born on an estate in Lenthe, Prussia, near Hanover, but one that was cash poor. Full of technological ideas and almost obsessed with inventing, he joined the Prussian artillery to gain the engineering training he needed but that his father could not afford. Chemical experiments he conducted in prison (where he was incarcerated for acting as a second in a duel) led, in 1842, to his first invention: an electroplating process. But before that, in 1841, his service in artillery workshops set him on his life's work. There he saw an early implementation of an electric telegraph (invented by Sir Charles Wheatstone in 1837). He recognized its possibilities and went to work improving it. In 1847, he directed the laying of an underground line for the army, and more significant, persuaded a young mechanic, Johann Georg Halske, to start a telegraph factory with him in Berlin. Telegraphenbauanstalt Siemens & Halske, which remained the company's name for more than a century, grew rapidly.

Werner von Siemens's technological brilliance and creativity made him tantamount to Prussia-Germany's Thomas Alva Edison. With his technological vision and economic sense, he might even be compared to Bill Gates of Microsoft today. Like the Rothschilds did in the financial sector, Siemens expanded his business beyond German borders through family members. One of his inventions, an engine-room telegraph, was rejected by his own country, so he sold it to Great Britain via his brother Wilhelm and to Russia through his brother Karl. Thus, Siemens was a multinational company from the start.

Von Siemens and Edison can be said to have transformed electricity into the nucleus of the industrial world. Not surprisingly, this made them direct competitors. Germany's Edison company AEG (Allgemeine Deutsche Electricitätsgesellschaft, or General German Electrical Company), which was founded by Emil Rathenau, became Siemens-Halske's major competitor during the era of both Kaiser Wilhelms. But where Siemens was the product of factories, AEG was the product of banks. That was the difference between the two until the demise of AEG in the 1980s.

The Siemens corporation's occasional financial needs were met by Deutsche Bank, where, conveniently, Georg von Siemens was at the bank's helm. The former AEG, on the other hand, was a customer of

Disconto-Gesellschaft. With both Siemens and AEG based in Berlin, Germany's capital city evolved into a metropolis of the international electronics industry, the most modern industrial branch of its day. An entire district in Berlin was called Siemensstadt, and a number of AEG and Siemens factories were featured in architecture textbooks.

Despite the vastly growing demand for electrical devices, Siemens never quite established itself as Germany's largest industrial enterprise. Around 1907, the number one position was held by Krupp, followed by Siemens, Gelsenkirchener Bergwerke AG, and AEG. This didn't change much over the next turbulent decades. During the Third Reich, Siemens, as one of Hitler's largest armament factories, expanded, as did numerous other companies. After the war, Siemens—with its three main companies, Siemens & Halske, Siemens-Schuckert, and Siemens-Reiniger—moved from Berlin to the Bavarian cities of Erlangen and Munich in Bavaria. In the mid-1960s the conglomerate merged into today's Siemens AG. But that was already the era of rapid advancement in the automobile industry, so by 1984, VW, and Daimler-Benz were larger than Siemens, while Veba led the pack; and at the dawn of the new millennium, DaimlerChrysler and Volkswagen are ahead.

That it has never been the country's largest company does not diminish its founder's accomplishment in securing for his company decades of an almost carefree future. To repeat, Siemens was Germany's first multinational corporation. And because the business of electrical engineering essentially advanced on its own—propelled by such developments as electric locomotives, power plants, telephone installations, electric lightbulbs (Osram), and household electronics—all the company had to do was keep moving along already laid tracks. By selling many of its products to state monopolies, such as the railroad, post office, and military, Siemens continued to grow, whereas AEG, innovative no longer, went into decline.

As recently as 1998, the Siemens structure still reflected its technological history and loyalty to the state. Listed by number of employees, its eight major divisions were industry (98,300), communications (66,100), energy (39,500), information (34,100), traffic (28,600), construction parts (35,100), medicine (22,400), and light (26,200). Revenue rates essentially corresponded to these figures: for example, 24.7 billion marks for industry and 5.7 billion for light. Arranged by profits, however, the order was markedly different: Communications was easily number one at 920 million marks, with medicine far behind at 30 million. But surprisingly, the real lagger, was information, with 52 million marks in profit and revenue of 13.6 billion marks, it had the lowest rate of return.

Siemens' relationship to the state was apparent through its participation in government-funded projects on land, sea, and in the air. A leviathan such as Siemens follows its own laws, even when it comes to profit and loss. The company managers covered many losses by using internal "crisscross subsidies"; others it covered with hidden reserves. The company's organization was further skewed because of its public subsidies. Siemens had long been linked with a covert, sometimes even overt, international cartel of huge electronics companies, which, like Siemens, were well connected politically and worked together on various major projects around the world.

One of the largest of the cartel projects was to develop a gigantic nuclear power system around the fast-breeder technology. The project was considered a failure, though some of the research later proved to be valuable to the standardization of today's nuclear power plants.

Today at Siemens, Heinrich von Pierer laments that nuclear energy accounts for "2 percent of business but 90 percent of our headaches." At the beginning of the nuclear age, Siemens and Kraftwerks Union (KWU), its power plant subsidiary, experienced a major boom. Siemens alone built seven of the world's ten largest power plants, which began generating power between 1978 and 1989. Then everything came to a standstill as both government and industry were finally forced to face the overwhelming problems of waste removal and the concomitant risks. Hence, the company's hope for thriving business abroad did not bear out. Siemens in fact ranked fourth in the world in the number of nuclear power plants produced, behind America's Westinghouse with 76 units, France's Franatome with 63, and America's General Electric with 54. Siemens had less than half of third-place GE, only 23.

Ironically, the precursor to nuclear energy, nuclear fission, was a process discovered in 1938 by two Germans, Otto Hahn and Fritz Strassmann. Germany's leading physicist of the time, Werner Heisenberg, blocked the development of an atomic bomb and tried to lead nuclear research in the direction of energy production, for which he didn't get much money (see: Thomas Powers: *Heisenberg's War,* Alfred A. Knopf, 1993). So the real development of nuclear energy from fission reactions began with the program to produce atomic weapons in the

United States, called the Manhattan Project at Los Alamos, New Mexico, toward the end of World War II.

The Munich company turned to other areas in hopes of again becoming a technological leader. It took part in aviation and aerospace projects, including participation in the airbus consortium as partner in the Messerschmitt-Bölkow-Blohm (MBB) technology conglomerate. Siemens also received funding to develop solar cells; it acquired Arco's (Atlantic Richfield) entire solar-industrial production; it received subsidies to build the express train ICE (Intercontinental Express); finally, the company accepted large amounts to advance the computer industry. Unfortunately, Siemens tended to attack these projects halfheartedly. Remarkably, its insouciance has not tarnished its reputation as a reliable manufacturer of quality products. Whenever something has gone wrong, the entire company is there to repair the damage.

In the end, somehow, Siemens always makes things work out. Above all else, it is a house of engineering, and as such, still number one. Siemens didn't have to become a Global Counterconglomerate vis-à-vis Westinghouse and General Electric, because that's what it has been for many years. The Siemens world comprises more than 300 firms that are either part of the holding company, affiliated with it, or otherwise a part of the conglomerate that is included on its balance sheet. Siemens has major subsidiaries bearing the company's name in 32 countries. New York's Siemens Corporation alone has 11 subsidiaries in various industrial branches and seven states. Another 450 firms are considered to be within headquarter's sphere of power, but have not been consolidated. Siemens shares its profitable, though not particularly sophisticated, household appliances business with that of the large electronics corporation Bosch as Bosch-Siemens-Hausgeräte GmbH. Each conglomerate owns 50 percent of shares. Increasingly, Bosch-Siemens is targeting the American mass market, exemplified by its takeover of Amana in 1999.

Year after year, the company's international financial management alone has contributed between one-third and one-half of the annual profits. Insiders joke that if Siemens sold itself and simply let its money accumulate, it would rake in more profits than the 1997–1998 posttax profit of 2.66 billion marks. The Siemens legacy has empowered the conglomerate throughout its long life, and its "partnership" with the public sector has only strengthened its reserves. That Siemens has remained relatively independent of the Deutsche Bank system also has given it some flexibility, even when things have gone wrong.

In the past 10 years, however, though hardly noticeable at first, cracks have been appearing in the giant's walls. Numerous new electronics products have not responded well to the traditional way of doing business. Plus, privatization has enabled the competition to satisfy public demand to such a degree that Siemens has difficulty protecting its markets. For the first time since 1901, the company is exhibiting signs of weakness.

According to a bank analysis made for private customers in late 1998, "Since the early 1990s, efforts toward successfully restructuring the company are being made. To no avail so far." Repeatedly, the gains made from downsizing were lost to extraordinary expenditures and better-prepared competitors. Heinrich von Pierer, chairman of the board since 1992, has been branded a weak man. This judgment may be premature, for it is a very lengthy process to turn around a dinosaur such as Siemens—especially if it isn't suffering any losses. On the other hand, in such situations, weakness will make itself known.

The Man in the Palace

Heinrich von Pierer, a man of diplomatic demeanor, is clearly the product of the long-standing Siemens culture, perhaps its final product. If he wants to make history, he will have to attack that culture, because it no longer expresses the ethos of the company's founder, but rather the detritus of bureaucracy and rigidity.

Von Pierer was born in 1941 in Erlangen, the future home of Siemens. The family nobility (Austrian) was bestowed in 1900 on grandfather Eduard Pierer von Esch, an Austro-Hungarian major general. At the University of Erlangen, von Pierer earned his undergraduate degree in economics and, later, a law degree. In 1969, he became a corporate counsel at Siemens headquarters, where he met CFO Heribald Närger, who eventually was to become chairman of the board and von Pierer's most important patron.

Eight years later, he was transferred to the subsidiary KWU, producer of electrical power stations, including many nuclear power plants, where he distinguished himself as someone who could take care of a

commercial business and manage large projects. In 1987, shortly before
the last great Siemens nuclear power plant was completed, KWU, Trans-
formatoren Union AG (TU), and parts of Energie-und Automation-
stechnik (the company's energy and automatization technology) lost
their independent status within the conglomerate, though collectively
they still went by the name of KWU. Pierer advanced to commercial
director of that division, and later, to director. Once identified as a high-
flier, things happened quickly for him: In 1990, Pierer joined the company's board of directors; in 1991, he became deputy chairman of the
board, which was essentially a ticket for the chairmanship.

When the current director, Karlheinz Kraske, a technician, retired in
the fall of 1992, he expressed relief that he would henceforth be spared
the tiresome but necessary visits to Bonn to maintain the company's
political contacts. Pierer felt just the opposite: Between 1972 and 1990,
he had been active in local politics as a city councilman and member of
the archconservative Christian-Social Union in his native Erlangen. In
the early 1970s, he almost became a member of parliament, with hopes
of perhaps being appointed federal minister later on. In the end, he
decided on a doubtless more comfortable career as manager. Now at
Siemens, he could have both, business and politics.

Pierer's leadership style reflects his political personality. His speech-
writer is Stephan Heinrich, former ghostwriter for Chancellor Helmut
Kohl. While Kohl was still in office, Pierer, recipient of huge govern-
mental subsidies for Siemens, would hire 1,000 apprentices just to do
Kohl a favor. During the heyday of their friendship, a sort of job-
exchange program was instituted. Civil servants in Bonn worked at
Siemens for a year, while Siemens employees worked for the administration.

Then his presidential management style began to lead the company
astray. Heinrich von Pierer had never been a fan of shareholder values,
insisting, "We're not a company that would maximize its profits in the
short run." But when long-term maximization went further and further
off keel, the analysts took notice. Unfazed, von Pierer refused to let the
banks' young firebrands dictate how he ran his company.

The risks have grown, however, and radical decisions have become
necessary, decisions that Siemens's director has shifted abroad for the
time being. When he assumed office, Pierer promised a 4 percent rate of
return after taxes. When that didn't bear out, in early 1994 he started the

company's first major productivity program. The program was called Top Siemens (for time-optimized processes). Then–top supervisor Franz Ende called it "pure actionism that consisted merely of obligatory exercises." It proved inadequate; its workshops and seminars lulled reluctant industrial officers into bored sleep.

Matters became more serious, forcing Pierer to change tactics. This he has attempted in a number of ways. In 1997–1998, for example, Pierer earned money by selling the Security and Dental Technology division, his 40 percent share of the British GPT Holdings Ltd., and the wholesale organization called I-Center. Then he had to turn around and spend 400 million marks to fold the computer chip factory in England's North Tynside, which he had launched to great fanfare only a few years earlier. These moves were not enough. The balance sheet for the year still indicated grave problems.

Pierer's next decision was to institute a tough 10-point plan for improving productivity. Part of that included a major divestiture program, during which the semiconductor, passive construction elements, pipes, and electromagnetic components divisions were transformed into independent companies, some of them with their own stocks. The copper news cable division, a technologically obsolete branch, was put up for sale to the highest bidder. Likewise, Starkstromkabel-Technik (power cable technology) was sold to the Italian tire manufacturer Pirelli, and Siemens Schienentechnik GmbH (track technology) was sold to Vossloh. ICE-Technik, for which Siemens was the leading underwriter, was threatened with deep cuts. KWU and the cellular telephone division have become sluggish.

All those sales enabled Siemens to buy something that year, too: Westinghouse's power station department. But Pierer's back was still against the wall, so the otherwise easygoing boss had to get tough on his employees as well. The conglomerate's 16 department heads were told they had to report on and justify developments in their areas on a quarterly basis. Pierer's intent was to increase the rate of return on net worth from a measly 10 percent to 15 percent.

Hope appeared on the horizon. Siemens-Nixdorf Informationssysteme AG (SNI), which had been ailing for years, began to show improvement. And in early 1999, former Motorola manager Gerhard Schulmeyer took SNI under his wing. He merged the company's computer, software, and telecommunications departments to form a new core area of Siemens, called IuK (for Informatik und Kommunikation, computer science and communication). The original SNI sells only cash registers, but the new division, with 40 percent of the total revenue, promises to grow into the largest block in the Siemens empire. To facilitate this growth, Siemens plans to acquire sizable U.S. companies. Rumors even mention Motorola. But it came out that Siemens cooperated with the second-rate Japanese computer company Fujitsu.

Heinrich von Pierer has not been easy on himself through all this upheaval. He has defied his own nature and confronted shareholder values. He recognizes that without a decent rate of return, he cannot expect a decent value for Siemens stock, which is something he must have if he is to carry out his plans. Pierer's goal is to have Siemens listed on the New York Stock Exchange by mid-2002. To achieve it, a great deal of preliminary work has to be done—in accounting, among other areas. At the annual meetings in 1998 and 1999, 500 million marks in common stock had been approved—an enormous capital increase, and without offering options. If the stock price were to remain at the mark it was at the end of 1998, this capital increase would translate into some 12 million marks in cash. As soon as the stock is traded on Wall Street, the financially strong company can go on a shopping spree, mainly in the United States. And when Pierer goes shopping, he wants to use the currency stocks to proceed in a way comparable to his shrewd countryman Jürgen Schrempp.

CHAPTER 9

Case Two: Cabinet of Beetles

Hitler and Porsche

WITH THE NEW millennium approaching, *Business Week* magazine devoted its January 1999 issue to the most outstanding managers of the decade. Among numerous Americans were two Germans, from the same industrial arena: Jürgen Schrempp of DaimlerChrysler and Ferdinand Piech from Volkswagen (dubbed "Baron von Bug" by the editors).

According to the piece on Piech, since assuming office in 1993, he has turned a $1.1 billion loss into a $1.3 billion profit, to put his company close on the heels of Toyota, the world's third-largest automaker in terms of number of vehicles sold. At the time, the new Beetle had been declared an undisputed hit on the American market and had increased VW's U.S. sales by 63 percent. Piech, the article continued, was obsessed with turning VW, the company his father had once led, into a global powerstation.

Piech, an Austrian, is in fact the third in his family to direct VW (a conglomerate established by the state), though not in consecutive tenures. Years, sometimes decades, separated the leadership of his grandfather Ferdinand Porsche, and his father, Anton Piech. Now it's Ferdinand Piech's turn to make history, and some think he may be regarded as VW's most successful director since the era of the conglomerate's original leader, Heinrich Nordhoff (who, incidentally, was also related to the VW clan: His daughter Barbara married Ferdinand Piech's brother Ernst).

It was not, however, Piech's Austrian grandfather who was the initiator of the liaison between German state and Austrian family interests. It was another Austrian native, one Adolf Hitler. While serving as Reich chancellor and Germany's führer, Hitler still thought himself an artist manqué, and in the spring of 1934, reportedly he met with Porsche in Berlin's Hotel Kaiserhof, where they enthusiastically produced sketches for a car for the German people (*Volkswagen* is German for "people's car").

Porsche's diaries suggest that Hitler invited him, a well-known engineer, into the Reich Chancellery through the offices of Daimler-Benz director Werlin as early as the winter of 1933–1934. The chancellor told Porsche that he was investigating the feasibility of a mass-produced car for the general public, to be priced at less than 1,000 marks (about $250 US at that time). At the time, even simple two-seaters like a Hanomag, nicknamed "Army Bread," still cost twice that amount. Hitler had been inspired by Henry Ford, whose Model T sold for just under $250. Porsche wrote Hitler a letter on January 17, 1934, telling him he had come to the conclusion that the national economy wouldn't be served by the introduction of an inexpensive, no-frills car, but he did have an alternative to suggest.

Porsche maintained that a "standard utility car" could not be developed into a high-quality car at the stipulated price. Therefore, an entirely new concept was called for. He suggested a vehicle with a 1,250-ccm opposing-piston rear-mounted engine, a 2.5-m wheelbase, a 1.2-m track, an unloaded weight of 650 kilograms, a speed capability of 100 kph (62 mph), and average gas usage of 8 liters per 100 kilometers which means 30 mpg. (Remarkably, these remained the parameters for the VW for more than 20 years after World War II.) According to Porsche's calculations, such a vehicle would have to be priced at 1,550 marks. On June 22, 1934, Porsche's office and the Reich Association of the German Automobile Industry (Reichsverband der deutschen Automobilindustrie, RDA) signed a contract heralding the development of a German people's car. The most important clause in the contract read, "Calculations should be based on production costs of 900 marks per car and a quantity of 50,000 units."

The contract also stipulated that the first test cars be built within 10 months, financed by the association with the ridiculously small sum of 20,000 reichsmarks ($5,000) per month. The entire project construct was so utopian that it looked like a conspiracy on the part of the competition—Opel, Auto Union, Ford, Adler—to ensure it would never get off the ground. But Porsche was no ordinary engineer. When he was still at Daimler-Benz he had submitted an idea to develop a version of a people's car, but company management had rejected it. Nevertheless, Porsche's office had done some preliminary work on such a vehicle, as evidenced by a document titled "Exposé Concerning the Manufacturing of a German People's Car," written for Hitler. Now, fortunately for Porsche, he had three ready-made prototypes.

Subsequently, Porsche reworked his concept and produced three more prototypes in his private garage. These became known as the "VW 3-series." But because the RDA continued to limit its financial support, the three cars weren't tested until 1936, when testing took place on sections of the autobahn in southwestern Germany. After 50,000 kilometers (30,000 miles) the RDA agreed that further development seemed appropriate. In 1937, Porsche had another 30 of his people's car, called VW 30-series, built at the Daimler-Benz plant, which was not interested in manufacturing compact cars itself, so there was no conflict of interest.

The test drives were a big secret. The cars from the new series were relentlessly driven over the streets, for a total of almost 1.5 million miles. Some withstood the grilling for more than 60,000 miles, an astounding achievement at the time. SS members were randomly picked as drivers and given strict instructions not to talk about the tests. They were also expected to drive the vehicles the way actual customers would later use the final products.

Thus, the Society for the Preparation of the Volkswagen (Gesellschaft zur Vorbereitung des Volkswagens, or Gezuvor) was founded with Porsche, Werlin, and the Strength-through-Joy director Bodo Lafferentz as managers. In 1938, Porsche's office decided on the final Beetle design and produced a new prototype series, the VW 38, whose motor had been shrunk to 996 cubic centimeters of capacity. (The 1,134-ccm engine that would be used in the postwar Volkswagens was developed later, during World War II, for military use.) At the rear axle Porsche attached the torsion-bar spring suspension he had invented—one of the last great inventions in car mechanics.

Originally, the vehicle was supposed to be called KdF car (for Kraft durch Freude, or "strength through joy"). And customers whose interest in it had been piqued had to pay for the car by collecting 5-mark stick-on coupons every week for a number of years. They were given no choice of colors, either; the car was offered only in a dreary, uniform blue-gray.

Soon, the German Workers' Front, among whose subgroups was the organization Strength through Joy (KdF), published a professionally designed KdF car brochure. It offered the car in two models: as a pure sedan for 990 reichsmarks and with a soft sunroof for 1,050 marks.

No one, however, had the chance to buy the car at those prices. Though the KdF staff had announced that the first vehicles would be shipped in 1940 upon completion of the Midland Canal plant, the war interfered. The KdF cars went to the Wehrmacht in the form of amphibious vehicles and jeeps, and they created a sensation. Thanks to their innovative air-cooling system, VW engines wouldn't freeze at the polar circle or overheat in northern Africa.

But in 1938, Porsche did not know that war would interrupt his plans. In September of that year, Volkswagenwerk GmbH was founded in Berlin, with 50 million marks' worth of common stock. Porsche not only was in charge of general planning at the plant, he also ran it, making him, de facto, VW's first president. In May 1938, the plant's cornerstone was laid in the Lower Saxon town of Fallersleben, and 30,000 workers were hired to manufacture 1 million KdF cars annually. Situated near the canal between the Elbe and Weser rivers, the plant became a prime example of a mono-model factory, following the mass-production principles of the American Scientific Management guru Frederick "Speedy" Taylor. Sixty years later, to Porsche's grandson Ferdinand Piech, the behemoth is a white elephant. "You no longer build such large factories nowadays," he remarked in a 1999 interview with the weekly *Der Spiegel,* "where more than three thousand cars roll off the assembly line. We have five miles of chain conveyors alone. . . . If they break . . . it's going to be like an earthquake" (*Der Spiegel* 6/99 pages 91ff). Piech's plan to separate the monster he inherited from his father and grandfather into five different factories capable of efficiently manufacturing different models will take years to implement.

At the time the plant was built, however, the KdF monoculture was intended to dominate the entire geographic area. In July 1938, the neighboring rural communities were consolidated under the name "City of the KdF Car," indicative of the Nazi party's Socialist component. In April 1939, the big machine tools arrived.

By that time, however, Porsche, who had a short attention span, was already busy working on the next big Nazi project, the so-called people's tractor. Consequently, his son-in-law, lawyer Anton Piech, was put in charge of the City of the KdF Car as general manager of Volkswagen-werk. More of an administrative job than a creative one, Piech's role relegated him to the background.

When Ferdinand Porsche died in 1951, his son Ferry expanded the Porsche engineering office in Stuttgart, turning it into a technological center and a sports car factory—today's Porsche AG. Porsche's daughter, Louise, Ferdinand Piech's mother, built a network of car dealerships and holding companies—today's Porsche-Holding, Austria's fourth-largest conglomerate. Both Porsche companies remained in the family, while initially Volkswagenwerk remained a property of the state. After the fall of the Nazi regime, for years no one knew who the actual owner of VW-Werk was.

Nordhoff, Hahn, and the Four Rings

As it turned out, the Austrians were succeeded by the Anglo-Saxons. On May 25, 1945, the Fallersleben assembly, appointed by the British occupation force, renamed the town Wolfsburg, after a nearby castle. Consequently, Volkswagenwerk's ruins were called Wolfsburg Motor Works. As for the cars built there, in general, the British and Americans viewed Porsche's Volkswagen as a dreadful jalopy that not one of their automakers would have any interest in it. The auto establishment intended to let the project quietly expire. The 17,000 people still living in Wolfsburg had other ideas.

On January 1, 1948, a new director was appointed to run the still ownerless company. Former Opel manager Heinrich Nordhoff—in other words, a General Motors man—who was in his prime, immediately took advantage of the situation. "When I started out here," Nordhoff related in the 1960s, "the car had as many flaws as a dog has fleas." Nordhoff quickly accelerated the production of the "people's car" using a one-model policy; he also standardized customer service and instituted the export of the automobile. A little over a year and a half after the currency reform that introduced the deutsche mark, the 100,000th VW rolled off the line; two years later, the 500,000th; and another two years

later, in 1955, the one-millionth vehicle left the assembly line. Nordhoff's autocratic rule lasted until 1961. By then, the owners had been
identified: 40 percent of the plant now belonged to the Federal Republic of Germany and the state of Lower Saxony. They had the crucial right
to vote, too. Though 60 percent of the stock was distributed as "people's
shares," these were nonvoting shares.

During Nordhoff's tenure, Volkswagens became almost more popular in the United States than in Germany. On the home front, it was popular because it was so robust and easy to maintain; in the United States,
owners loved it because it was so practical and so distinctive. Ad cam-
paigns featuring such tag lines as "The Volkswagen keeps running and
running and running . . ." were started in Germany. And in the United
States, the New York advertising agency Doyle Dane Bernbach
launched a series of now-classic print and TV commercials that elevated
the Beetle to the status of a cult symbol. The American-born nickname
Beetle was eventually so widely used that it became the Volkswagen's
official name.

By the mid-1960s, the American VW branch, headquartered in
Englewood Cliffs, New Jersey, established standard service centers all
over the country, at which point it became official: More Beetles were
sold in the United States than in Germany; ultimately, more than half of
all cars manufactured in Wolfsburg were exported to the United States.
Dating from the late 1950s, Volkswagen of North America had been
headed by the young economist Carl Horst Hahn, son of one of the cofounders of Auto Union and Nordhoff's chosen successor in Wolfsburg.
Highly sensitive to markets and consumers, Hahn was credited with
much of VW's success in the United States. In the mid-1960s he was
made sales director in Wolfsburg, but not president.

Toward the end of his tenure, Heinrich Nordhoff had become too
entrenched in the Beetle monoculture. In terms of production technology, this had turned into an almost inescapable trap. The monstrous factory on the Midland Canal required that a single model be
manufactured in huge quantities, so when Nordhoff tried to produce
Volkswagens that were a little bigger and more modern on the same platform with the same motor, it failed. More trouble came in the guise of
consumer advocacy. Ralph Nader criticized the VW as unsafe because
the windshield was too close to the driver's forehead. VW responded by
making the windshield round. When the car was declared too slow in the

United States, the old VW engine was given a larger bore. And so forth. Soon VW had spent as much money adapting the Beetle to U.S. safety standards as it would have cost to develop a brand-new model.

In the late 1960s Nordhoff gained some maneuvering room for his company after purchasing Auto Union from Daimler-Benz. Essentially resurrected by Carl Hahn senior, the modern version of Auto Union's two-stroke DKW, which had been completed in 1939, took off. Subsequent Auto Union models had some success, too, but the practical and simple engine began to get a bad rap as a "stinker." Under VW's control, it was finally abandoned.

Ironically, Auto Union staged a comeback with what had been its weakest brand, the Audi. It combined a four-stroke engine and front-wheel drive, a combination, as it soon turned out, with a future. The first Audi 100 was released in later days of Nordhoff's regime. Having developed it clandestinely, an Auto Union team led by the former Daimler-Benz engineer Ludwig Krauss nervously presented it to Nordhoff. Legend has it that he walked around the vehicle a few times, both surprised and annoyed, before leaving with the words, "That car will be built."

The production of the Beetle, in contrast, was beginning to decline, and Nordhoff had lost his hold over the supervisory board. He was unable to have his favorite candidate, Carl Hahn, approved. The top supervisors decided on Brown-Boveri manager Kurt Lotz, a former member of the general staff. Nordhoff died in 1968 while still in office, and so never had to pass the baton to someone he didn't support.

Nordhoff's successors—Lotz, then Rudolf Leiding and Toni Schmücker—were all enmeshed in the company's lengthy transition period punctuated by internal intrigues and external struggles. Throughout, the company had to focus on its two weak spots. First, it was helpless against the unions. On the supervisory board, where, following Germany laws, the labor force and the shareholders are equally represented, the unions typically had one of the major shareholders on their side—either the federal government or the state government of Lower Saxony, sometimes both: The Social Democrats, who were close to the unions, almost always happened to lead one of the two governments.

The second major problem was model policies. Nordhoff's successor Lotz wanted to increase his options using an approach that would become popular three decades later: acquiring companies that were in a different league from VW. He purchased the ailing NSU AG, whose technical accomplishment was the Wankel engine Ro 80; it had also developed a medium-range car of the later Passat class, the K 70. Lotz built an entirely new plant just to manufacture that car. But his new subsidiary, called Audi NSU Auto Union AG, never really got off the ground. It did, however, exemplify the new technology that was diametrically opposed to VW's old technology: front-wheel drive and front-mounted engine.

As part of this option expansion, Lotz even made an appearance at BMW's headquarters, where he dropped remarks to the effect that the Munich company would never make it by itself; that one day it would have to merge with VW if it didn't want to surrender to Daimler, so why not do it now. People at the BMW citadel, beleaguered by Lotz and his people, sneered, "Lotz of troubles," and "He who laughs Lotz, laughs best."

Lotz's efforts failed. With VW deep in the red, the members of the board, aided by the unions, toppled Lotz. His successor was the robust production manager and former governor in Brazil, Rudolf Leiding, formerly of Audi. Leiding was exactly what the company needed. He had the courage to transform the Audi 80 into the VW Passat and to replace the Beetle with the VW Rabbit. Though this process that had begun under Lotz, the company had been hemming and hawing for 10 years. Now Leiding came along 1973 and just did it—and it worked. In the beginning, few noticed—or admitted—that the new cars were clunkers compared to the Beetle. People were impressed by the Rabbit's accomplishments as a vehicle and approved of its spacious design. The Rabbit became the forerunner of a standard formula for high-quality compacts that was to hold for three decades. More important for VW was that the Rabbit, like the Beetle, turned out to be classless; people from all walks of life were driving Rabbits.

A worthy successor to the Beetle had been born, and Leiding became a hero, though not to everyone in northern Germany. When the company wanted to open a U.S. branch to manufacture the Rabbit there, the German unions balked. They feared jobs would be cut in Wolfsburg, as well as at other VW plants such as Emden, Kassel, and Hanover. Relations between the unions and Leiding cooled. Again, insiders began seeking allies among the workforce and the major media. Leiding, they claimed, was "untenable"; they needed someone who was able to deal with the unions.

That someone seemed to be Rheinstahl director Toni Schmücker, who had spent a significant part of his career at Ford. Initially, everything looked bright for Schmücker. The company and its products were ideally positioned on the market and were generating good profits. When earnings climbed high enough, Schmücker and his CFO Friedrich Thomée went shopping. At the time, diversification was temporarily in vogue, and VW followed the trend; it acquired Triumph-Adler, an office machine store lacking in imagination. Next Schmücker managed to do what Leiding had been unable to accomplish: establish a VW factory in the United States, in the Pennsylvania town of Westmoreland. Unfortunately, it was not a success, and temporarily at least, VW fell out of favor in America.

With business going downhill in general, Schmücker also faced a personal challenge when he suffered a serious heart attack. He believed the handwriting was on the wall and resigned. Yet again, Carl Hahn's name was put forth. By this time he had left VW to serve as chairman of the board of tire manufacturer Continental, in Hanover, the capital of Lower Saxony. Continental was one of VW's suppliers. More important was that, through his position there, Hahn was now part of the Deutsche Bank system, and a protégé of Alfred Herrhausen, one its rising stars. Furthermore, the political situation in Hanover and Bonn, where VW's major shareholders were located, had shifted in Hahn's favor: Lower Saxony was governed by the Christian Democrats; and though the Social Democrats were still ruling in Bonn, their economic expert, pragmatic Helmut Schmidt, was at the helm.

Finally, Carl Horst Hahn's hour had come. But he was walking into a tougher situation than any he had faced at Continental: He had to introduce a new Rabbit model. Despite Audi and VW Passat, the company was still far too dependent on one type of car—now the Rabbit. Luck was on his side. The new model was a hit with the audience. He decided to put his stakes on expansion, even though he was hardly sitting on a big money cushion.

By the time Schmücker left VW in 1981, the company had sold 2,333,700 vehicles, of which 334,300 were Audis. Hahn's goal was to double that figure. Fortunately for him, the political climate favored his style. As a conservative, he felt increasingly comfortable with the company's policy of codetermination, especially after the Christian Democrats (CDU) won the national election shortly after he assumed office. It didn't hurt that he was a good friend of the then–northern German CDU luminary and longtime VW board member Walter Leisler-Kiep; Hahn felt he never need worry about his contract being renewed.

Hahn also adopted Chancellor Kohl's culture of consensus and made compromises with the VW unions, though some on the board thought he went too far. At that time, VW was the only large company in Germany's entire metal industry that was able to gracefully circumvent the national debate on wages raging between IG Metall, the union, and Gesamtmetall, the employers' association. VW's board used its independence to avoid disruptive strikes; conversely, the unions got the company to concede to above-average wage increases (because it was represented on the supervisory board, with the right to vote, the union knew the company's figures). It was agreed that the company's stability must not suffer on account of the general wage policy, but there was no consensus regarding how high the company's profits should be allowed to climb. For that reason, VW stocks had not been a good investment for decades.

Carl Hahn always had a deep affection for the four rings of Auto Union, since his father was one of its cofounders. Though the symbol was now used only on the Audi brand, he was eager to develop the VW corporation into a greater version of Auto Union.

In 1986, VW took over Seat, the Spanish carmaker, which had belonged to a number of European car companies over the years. After Germany's reunification, Hahn had a supermodern plant built in Saxony, the former East German state, and another one in Slovakia. Then he took over the Czech car manufacturer Skoda, which had been a quality brand during the 1930s and 1940s, hoping to make it successful on the East European markets. With the brands VW, Audi, Seat, and Skoda, he in fact was back to the symbolic four rings.

The VW conglomerate continued to participate vigorously in what seemed a surreal German-unification boom. But when it petered out, VW found itself facing existential problems: Even when production was running at full capacity, the bottom line showed no profit. In 1992, which turned out to be Carl Hahn's last year, VW sold 3,498,800 cars, a full 70 percent more than during Schmücker's last year, including 472,500 Audis, 358,000 Seats, and 186,200 Skodas. Still, discounting the manipulations of creative accounting, the "profit" on return was minus 2 percent.

In the wings was Daniel Goudevert, a French linguist who had joined the board of directors in Wolfsburg via Citroën, Renault, and Ford. He had long been considered Hahn's successor because he fit into both Bonn's and Wolfsburg's model of consensus. But things had changed: He no longer did. Hahn, who had recognized the conglomerate's problems without being able to solve them, ended up supporting Ferdinand Piech, a man who, some said, had gasoline running in his veins.

Full Throttle with Ferdinand Piech

Ferdinand Piech is regarded as the modern edition of his namesake, his grandfather Ferdinand Porsche, the Beetle engineer. They both belong in a special technological class, and they also are remarkable for their powerful wills. Both have proven repeatedly that will find a way to get their way no matter how strong the opposition. The *Financial Times* once called Piech the "Rottweiler of the motor world." Where they part company is in style. Porsche preferred to wait for things to happen, and he felt most comfortable as the owner of a design bureau, whereas Piech has always had a plan for his life that he has pursued purposefully. His goal was to extend the tracks his grandfather had laid—either in Stuttgart at Porsche, or at VW, his grandfather's most famous child. To Ferdinand Piech, the new Beetle is a matter of genetics.

Born in Vienna on April 17, 1937, Porsche's grandson didn't really witness firsthand much of what his father and grandfather accomplished in KdF City. When the war was over, the French put his grandfather in jail, and the rest of the clan moved to the family estate at Zell-on-the-Lake in Austria. Piech attended school there and in Salzburg, until his father died in 1952, only one year after his grandfather. His mother Louise had secured the post of Volkswagen's general agent in Austria to augment the family's income. She also inherited half of her late father's engineering company in Stuttgart. Led now by her brother Ferry, in 1948, that company additionally manufactured what would become the legendary model 356, a two-seater sports coupé with a larger bore VW engine.

As befitted his social status, Ferdinand Piech was sent to Zuoz, a Swiss boarding school. After earning his high school diploma, he remained in Switzerland where, in 1962, he became a licensed engineer at Zurich's famous technical university, Eidgenössische Technische Hochschule (ETH). In 1963, he started working in the family business, the Porsche company, in Stuttgart. He was put in charge of engine testing. (Today, as one of Porsche's 10 grandchildren, he still owns one-tenth of the company, which alone adds up to a 10-figure deutsche mark amount.)

Piech got along well with his more reticent but highly competent Uncle Ferry Porsche, who quickly recognized his nephew's abilities while acknowledging the problems Piech's hot temper could cause. He quickly advanced Piech into the company's test management and shortly thereafter into development management. On April 1, 1971, at barely 34 years of age, Piech was promoted to technical manager of the company. And there he stayed for a while: The other Porsche heirs and the Porsche workers council didn't want him as head of Porsche AG. Nor did Ferry Porsche want that—not yet. Porsche knew that Piech eventually would be the right successor, but that it was still too early.

When Piech realized that he wasn't going to be president of Porsche for a long time, he left the company and briefly became a freelance engineer. During that time he developed the basics for a five-cylinder diesel engine for Daimler-Benz. But by August 1, 1972, he had started working for VW's subsidiary Audi NSU Auto Union AG, later Audi AG. The company had a department devoted to "special tasks of technical development." Piech was put in charge of it. Under his leadership, the special tasks soon became primary tasks. One year later, Piech was general manager of testing; one and a half years after that, he became head of development. At the same time, he took charge of power unit development at big mama VW. On August 1, 1975, he joined Audi's board of directors as head of technical development.

In 1983, Piech became deputy chairman of the board. Never before had he waited for a job so long—eight years; he was 46 years old. At that age his grandfather was already general director of Austro-Daimler. But VW director Hahn made him wait five more years for the top spot. Piech felt he had no choice but to wait; he certainly couldn't return to the family business, whose partners had decided that in the future, family members would no longer be allowed to advance into the company's top management. Finally, on January 1, 1988, Piech, now 50 years old, became chairman of the board of VW's subsidiary. But in a break with tradition, he was not simultaneously made a member of VW's board. Hahn, too, was leery of Piech's renowned temper.

Piech set to work on Audi's cost problems in a way typical of him: He went on instinct. The parent company in Wolfsburg, in fact, should have been doing the same thing, tackling cost issues, because whereas Audi had a 6 percent profit on return in 1991, its best result ever, VW's figures were not anywhere near that. And Hahn, who would have liked to run the conglomerate for a few years past the standard retirement age of 65, was given the thumbs-down. In April 1992, Piech was appointed Hahn's successor. Daniel Goudevert, who only six months prior had been considered a shoo-in for the post, became his deputy. (Goudevert would resign soon afterward and, later, launch a management foundation.)

It didn't take Piech long to get rid of all the top managers he didn't like. Then, to resolve VW's cost issues, in the fall of 1993 he lured the Spaniard José Ignacio López de Arriortúa away from General Motors because López was known for his ability to organize cost-lowering plants. Later, GM accused Lopez, who previously had worked at VW's competitor Opel, of giving Piech confidential files from Opel's vault. The suspicion cast on Piech and López thrust VW into a serious image crisis—precisely the purpose of the General Motors assault.

For years, Piech and López didn't dare show their faces in the United States. The affair ended in 1995 with a settlement that did not absolve Piech and López. VW agreed to pay General Motors, or Opel, $100 million and to purchase auto parts worth $1 billion over several years. During all the legal skirmishing, López had done at VW what he had been hired to do: radically revamp the purchase structure to lower costs. López then left VW at the end of 1996 to work in his native Basque provinces. For his part, Piech emerged largely unscathed, and he moved on to his next challenge.

In addition to cost problems, Hahn had left Piech with all four brands substantially damaged. Through technology, design, cost reduction, and a revolutionary personnel policy, Piech managed to resurrect all four of them. Crucial to his success was his platform strategy. He reduced 16 different silos into four platforms that fit the different models of all four brands—Audi, Seat, Skoda, and VW. By the end of 1998, Piech had put 47 percent of his products onto these platforms. This resulted in a cost reduction that was so spectacular that the entire auto industry now speaks of platform strategies. VW's posttax profit climbed from 1.36 to 2.45 billion marks in 1998. By the end of 2000, 90 percent of VW's products are expected to be on the four platforms.

In this way Piech established equal quality standards for all its car brands. Thus, someone who purchases a Skoda doesn't have a car that's inferior to an Audi with the same platform; he or she has only a different image. Piech was also persistent in positioning the Audi brand to compete against Mercedes and BMW, at almost any cost. And in 1998, Audi surpassed BMW in Germany and Europe.

Still, despite all his success, Piech has not been able to advance to the league of auto industry's big moneymakers Ford or DaimlerChrysler. Furthermore, VW still hasn't been able to develop a more profitable medium-range car. In Germany, the company's core market, upper-medium-range and upper-range automobiles amounted to less than 8 percent of all newly licensed Wolfsburg cars in 1998, in contrast to DaimlerChrysler's 30 percent and BMW's 35 percent. Another class of cars that rakes in big bucks is barely represented at VW: minivans, small trucks, and jeeps. In the United States, these will represent half of all new licenses at the turn of the century—and in the Chrysler division of Jürgen Schrempp's company, 70 percent of production. At VW, it's 4 percent. Not until 2002 is a jeep jointly developed by VW and Porsche slated to roll off the production line. Conquering that market will be difficult for Johnny-come-latelies. Moreover, new competition might lower profits, exacerbated by threatened tougher environmental standards for that class of vehicles.

Likewise, heavy trucks are not part of Piech's business yet, either. If he wants to make serious money with them, he'll have to cooperate with a really big company, such as MAN or even Volvo. Piech openly admits that he is waiting for the next economic crisis so he can buy a truck manufacturer cheaper. He has incorporated these plans in his long-term projections extending to 2010, called Vision 2010. Apart from the Audi A-8, the situation is similar with regard to the VW luxury class.

Vision 2010 makes it clear that Piech is counting on the six passenger car brands: Skoda, Seat, Volkswagen, Audi, and the brands acquired in 1998—Bentley, and Rolls Royce—though BMW also has a stake in Rolls Royce. He anticipates that the sports car brands Lamborghini and, probably, Bugatti, as well as the special engine factory Cosworth, will be part of Audi. By then, he expects the 3-liter (consumer) car and the 18-cylinder supersports car to be available from the company. The 1998–1999 upheavals in the world of mergers demonstrated to Piech that buying a brand during an economic boom is twice as expensive as expanding an existing brand. Just look at BMW. Thus Piech is putting himself under pressure to succeed, stressing, "We're always at full throttle."

In 1998, the full-throttle company with its almost 300,000 employees posted revenues of more than 130 billion marks. It is Europe's largest passenger-car automaker, Germany's second-largest industrial company, and—together with Toyota—the third-largest car company in the world. Of some 4,257,400 cars sold in 1997, 2,971,900 were VWs, 546,400 Audis, 402,800 Seats, and 336,300 Skodas. One year later, the percentage of sales was 65 percent for VW, 14 percent for Audi, 12 percent for Skoda, and 9 percent for Seat. Presently, the conglomerate has plants in Spain, Portugal, Belgium, Poland, the Czech Republic, and Slovakia. Outside of Europe it has factories in Argentina, Brazil, Mexico, South Africa, China, and Taiwan. In Brazil, Mexico, and China, where VW got involved early and in a big way, the company is the market leader.

Piech wouldn't be Piech if he didn't systematically safeguard his conglomerate while implementing his long-term strategy. And though he won't be around to ensure the realization of his Vision 2010 (his contract with VW expires in 2003), he intends to hand over to his successor a company that produces 6 million cars per year and has a 6.5 percent rate of return—which is very ambitious. In the United States, Piech plans to pick up where the "golden sixties" left off, with the Beetle becoming America's cult car. Whether the New Beetle will manage to achieve that is not yet clear, but that VW needs a new plant in North America is obvious.

VW runs a sales and marketing subsidiary in Auburn Hills, Michigan, with 242.4 million marks' worth of common stock. That company can be expanded, and Piech wants to use it as a basis for advancing on the U.S. market à la Toyota and Honda. The two Japanese firms manufacture their popular medium-range cars Camry and Accord in the United States, both of which are market leaders in the passenger-car business there. Piech is off to a good start: The new Passat model received the same superb grades from car critics in 1998 as its Japanese competitors, and consumer magazines even put it in first place. But superb ratings do not necessarily translate into superb sales.

Piech wants to turn his company into a classic Global Counterconglomerate, not into a Transatlantic World Inc. à la DaimlerChrysler, Deutsche Bank, or Bertelsmann. During his first five years in office, he assembled all the necessary ingredients. He plans to spend the next five mixing them together. If he does realize what could be called his Vision 2003, he will be among the Big Five in the business, perhaps even in fourth place depending on the criteria and the dollar exchange rate. The company once set in motion by Hitler now meets the requirements of a Global Counterconglomerate like few others. Piech has taken aim at Ford, General Motors, and DaimlerChrysler, and as far as they're concerned, he has opened the throttle all the way.

CHAPTER 10

Case Three: Being German with Lufthansa

Stars and Skies

THE WORLD OF Lufthansa is a big wide world. Stretched across advertisements all over the globe is a multicolored airplane that is three times as long as the standard passenger aircraft and as slender as a sharpened pencil. Six familiar names are written on it: Varig, Lufthansa, SAS, Air Canada, Thai, and United Airlines. "Star Alliance—The airline network for Earth," the ads read.

Together, in 1997, the alliance of these six transported 180 million passengers on 1,347 planes. That is approximately the number of adults in America. Four additional airlines are affiliated with the alliance: All Nippon, Singapore, Ansett, and Air New Zealand—which have 381 airplanes that transported 73 million passengers in 1997. Thus, that year, the alliance's 1,728 airplanes carried some 253 million people, more than the total U.S. population. Then British Midland joined the group.

But what does "alliance" mean in this context? First of all, it is Deutsche Lufthansa's response to globalization. "We complement one another like DaimlerChrysler," Lufthansa's president Jürgen Weber insisted after the latest airline joined the alliance, "virtually without any overlaps. The same is not true to that extent for the others." By the others, he means the large alliances of British Airways/American Airlines and Swissair/Delta Airlines. Like Star Alliance, whose main members are Lufthansa and United Airlines, the other two are structured as European-American cooperations, unions that typically don't mean much more than joint frequent-flyer programs and travel routes. Alliances like that can be easily dissolved.

Lufthansa/United is meant to last. The Star Alliance was designed as an integral part of Jürgen Weber's corporate policy. Its members dispatch flights jointly, consolidate routes, and use joint flight numbers for their passengers (code sharing). This system enables them to offer their customers immediate connecting flights within their own network on any continent. Because neither Lufthansa nor United offers short- or medium-range flights on continents other than their own, the alliance increases considerably the rate of return and constitutes a global offer that is unparalleled.

This has put Star Alliance in the powerful position of being able to select its members as it pleases. But it also means it has to fend off attempts by the competition to lure its partners away. The managers of British Airways, for instance, who have a reputation of being ruthless, have tried to "steal" Thai Airlines from the Star Alliance by acquiring Thai shares.

The concept of the Star Alliance was not invented by Lufthansa, but the German airline has been the constant driving force behind it. From the start, Jürgen Weber, who helped his company overcome a serious crisis in the early 1990s, was determined to build a strong global alliance with other airlines. He has continued on this course, even though Lufthansa is already the market leader in airfreight and number two in passenger traffic. Its market shares, however—2.9 percent in freight and 6.5 percent in passengers—were not nearly enough to enable the airline to exercise price control; therefore it could not guarantee high rates of return. The competition has remained so tough that only alliances can secure adequate profits.

For a long time, European airlines found transatlantic alliances difficult to realize, because almost inevitably they would have led to an American partner becoming dominant. Not only were U.S. carriers considerably larger than European airlines, they also enjoyed more liberal traffic rights in Europe than the Europeans did in the United States. But things were about to change. Politically informed U.S. airline managers, such as then–United Airlines boss Stephen Wolff, predicted that the end of the Cold War would also put an end to American privileges in the Old World. Furthermore, Wolff was convinced that it would be easier for him to book his network of domestic routes at full capacity if a renowned European airline brought in additional passengers.

Weber and Wolff were about to make history in the airline industry. They signed a cooperation agreement in October 1993. Its contents created a sensation. From the start, the deal between Lufthansa and United went beyond simple code sharing. The Germans would use United's terminals at such busy airports as New York's John F. Kennedy and Los Angeles International, which would significantly cut down on clearance time for its customers, especially through immigration and customs. There were also to be airplane exchanges. For instance, Boeing's long-time customer United has ordered more and more European planes for its short-range flights. Since 1996, United has ordered 111 airbuses of types A-319 and A-320.

In addition to its traffic alliance, Deutsche Lufthansa AG has also established a travel alliance. There is probably no country in the world where the holiday travel business is as brisk as in Germany. Two-thirds of Germany's population of 80 million can afford to travel. They also have the time to do so. German wage earners have more leisure time than the average American worker. The majority enjoy six calendar weeks off per year. That alone stimulates the tourism industry. In 1997, 62.2 million holiday trips lasting at least five days were booked by Germans, totaling 80.1 billion marks. The highest per capita returns come from vacations involving airfares and package deals. To secure that aspect of the industry, Lufthansa joined Karstadt, a department store chain largely owned by the mail-order giant Quelle, owner of travel agencies offering package deals. Moreover, Karstadt, via its subsidiary Neckermann-Versand, was in control of Germany's second-largest tour-package company, NUR (Neckermann und Reisen). Lufthansa also owns the charter airline Condor, under whose umbrella are the tour companies Fischer, Kreutzer, and Öger.

Lufthansa and Quelle took this huge hodgepodge and transformed it into the travel conglomerate C (for Condor) & N (for Neckermann) Touristik AG. The new company is Germany's second-largest travel trust. The largest one by far is the Touristik group established by Preussag AG, the former power company. Today Preussag controls the largest European tour company, TUI (for Touristik Union International), plus the shipping group Hapag-Lloyd, including its charter planes and travel agencies. This division became final when Lufthansa profitably sold its 18 percent share of Hapag-Lloyd to Preussag. The shipping companies Hapag and Norddeutscher Lloyd had been the airline's partner since the founding of Lufthansa, almost without interruption.

Internal operations at Lufthansa are decentralized, as are its external operations. For the sake of cutting wages and taxes, it was turned into a holding company (and pared down in the process). This holding company combines the independent firms Lufthansa Passage Airline (for passenger transportation), Lufthansa Cargo AG, Lufthansa Technik AG (for maintenance, overhaul, and repair), LSG Lufthansa Service Holding AG (catering), Lufthansa Systems GmbH (computer science), and Lufthansa Commercial Holding GmbH for all remaining affiliations.

At 15 billion marks, Passage had by far the highest revenues in 1997, followed by Cargo (3.9 billion), Technik (3 billion), Condor (1.9 billion), and Service (1.5 billion). The computer science division brought in some 600 million marks that year. Lufthansa's total revenue in 1997 was about 26 billion marks. The profit ratios were similar, adding up to almost 2 billion marks. And between 1988 and 1998, the company became debt-free. Now it only has to work for the interest on its capital, which significantly increases its operating options.

Lufthansa's bottom line has looked especially good in recent years, owing to many fortunate, if unrelated, events. For instance, Commercial Holding recorded an impressive profit of 270 million marks in 1997, mainly because it sold its 33 percent share of the travel agency chain Deutsches Reisebüro GmbH and a share of Amadeus Data Processing GmbH. In 1998, Weber's balance sheets were bolstered by 377 million marks from the sale of the shares in Hapag-Lloyd. Most significant, however, were the lower gasoline prices and the higher dollar exchange rate. In the airline business, most income is made in U.S. dollars, while most expenditures are in other currencies. Of course, in the future, Lufthansa could just as easily be on the wrong end of gas prices and exchange rates.

In spite of its now-international image, Lufthansa still stirs up people's emotions. "Lufthansa German Airlines," it is called around the world. This is due in part to the many decades when it was state-owned. As in most other countries, this made it the national carrier. This status also gave Lufthansa employees the security common to public servants. After only 15 years of service, for example, essentially, they could no longer be fired. As it was, the company's real partner wasn't its customers, but the public transportation union Öffentliche Dienste, Transport und Verkehr (ÖTV). On occasion, the union went so far as to ensure that certain Lufthansa employees held jobs that had long since ceased to have a purpose. Those in a positions of authority who turned out to be ineffective could be transferred only by way of a promotion—with its accompanying wage increase. All Lufthansa employees were protected by the federal and state pension offices. The salary of a senior pilot was the same as that of a—in Germany well-paid—federal undersecretary, and it came with a corresponding pension. And because there were at least eight complete crews for each large plane, flight personnel costs were exorbitant.

On one hand, Lufthansa had to put up with state authorities interfering in its business. On the other hand, it also depended on them, for without the international air traffic agreements negotiated by the Ministry of Traffic and Transportation, there would have been no international business. Despite its hindrances, however, Deutsche Lufthansa moved way ahead of most other carriers in terms of technology, safety, and quality. Firmly reestablished in 1955 after a 10-year hiatus, it has been able to reconquer its U.S. market, particularly in New York, thanks in part to highly qualified U.S.-based employees. But make no mistake, this is a thoroughly German company. In the same way that Daimler-Benz and Volkswagen came to embody "Germanness," so, too, has Lufthansa, with its state-of-the-art technology, spacious cabins, on-time arrivals and departures, and high-quality customer service. In short, the crane—its symbol—can always be relied upon.

Strictly speaking, Germany's commercial aviation can be traced to before World War I. On November 16, 1909, Deutsche Luftschiffahrts AG (DELAG, German Aviation Inc.) was founded in Frankfurt am Main, which again today is the center of Lufthansa's operations. Initially, the DELAG fleet was composed of the blimps invented by Count Ferdinand von Zeppelin, which were produced in Friedrichshafen. Between 1910 and 1914, seven of those dirigibles were scheduled to land in Baden-Baden, Frankfurt, Düsseldorf, Hamburg, Berlin, and Leipzig. World War I, however, put an end to this prelude of nonmilitary-related German aviation. Pursuant to the Versailles Treaty, even commercial blimps manufactured after the truce had to be handed over to the Allies.

In the late 1920s and early 1930s, Zeppelin (as blimps are called in Germany) manager Hugo Eckener developed a new airline service, whose huge airships the *Graf Zeppelin* and *Hindenburg* crossed the South and North Atlantic 163 times after 1930. They could fly 7,000 miles nonstop. The flight from Berlin to Rio, which lasted four days, was the first regular, nonmilitary transatlantic route. The *Graf Zeppelin* had five 550-SAE-horsepower Maybach engines; the *Hindenburg* had four 1,300-horsepower Daimler power units. Their top speed was 72 to 90 miles per hour, and they were kept aloft by helium. But again, war interfered. Only the United States could supply helium, which, after Hitler came to power, it refused to ship to Nazi Germany. The switch to highly flammable coal gas brought an end to long-distance dirigible travel when the *Hindenburg* caught fire while attempting to land on the Lakehurst airfield in New Jersey on May 6, 1937. More accurately, however, Lufthansa's commercial history can be said to have begun in the 1920s, though not as an individual entity. Following World War I, the German government decided to build a national airline system, using regional companies as its foundation. Two of those came to dominate German aviation at the time: Deutscher Aero Lloyd, incorporated in 1923 and based in Berlin, and Junkers Luftverkehr, which was founded in 1924 by the airplane producer Junkers and authorized to operate an airline.

On January 6, 1926, those two companies merged—along with all other German aeronautic concerns—to become Deutsche Luft Hansa Aktiengesellschaft (Hansa referred to the old north-European Hanseatic trading league). The company's logo—a crane—was taken from Aero Lloyd, and its colors—blue and yellow—were taken from Junkers. Luft Hansa quickly became the airline of choice for all German air services, and by May 1926, it was serving 57 domestic and 15 international airports.

But Luft Hansa was a government-private monopoly, and eventually the German Reich controlled 26 percent of the new Luft Hansa's shares; German cities and provinces held 19 percent; and private organizations and regional airlines had 27.5 percent each. Chairman of the board was Emil Georg von Stauss, the Deutsche Bank board director, indicating that at least on paper the private sector was still in control. The mayor of Cologne (later to become West German chancellor Konrad Adenauer) was also a member of the board. Aero Lloyd pioneers Otto Julius Merkel and Martin Wronsky became top managers; and from Junkers came Carl August von Gablenz, an inspired pilot, and Erhard Milch, whose future was in Hitler's air force.

That same year, 1926, Luft Hansa became a member of the International Air Traffic Association (IATA). The traffic limitations the Versailles Treaty imposed on Germany had been lifted in the spring through the Paris Air Traffic Agreement, and the airline wasted no time in expanding its reach. A Luft Hansa expedition corps led by Robert Knauss flew from Berlin via Moscow to Beijing on two three-engine G 24 Junkers planes, each with a capacity for nine passengers. The seven-leg 6,000-mile adventure lasted from July 23, to August 30, 1926. Between 1931 and 1941, the airline flew from Beijing to Shanghai, but on different airplanes and via another route. Between August 18 and 26, 1930, a Luft Hansa crew under Wolfgang von Gronau flew from List on the island of Sylt to New York on the water plane *Dornier Wal.* This flight was repeated in 1931 and 1932 via different routes.

The aviation world was daredevil in those days, exemplified by the motley fleet with which Luft Hansa started out. Its 162 planes were constructed from 19 different patterns—which today would be a technician's nightmare but was standard practice at the time. Technological advances in the industry seemed to occur in spurts. In 1919, a single-engine two-seater was state of the art; 10 years later, Luft Hansa was flying a four-engine G 38 Junkers. The plane seated thirty-four, six in the glass-enclosed wings between the engine and cabin. Shortly thereafter, the company boasted of its 12-engine superairship Do X by Dornier that was even more spacious. Both the G 38 and the Do X had been commissioned by the German Ministry of Traffic and Transportation. Already government and industry as well were showing an interest in exploring the construction of oversized airplanes.

While these federally subsidized planes didn't exactly conquer the market, they didn't lose Luft Hansa money, either. But the first financially successful plane for the airline was the Junkers Ju 52, which first took flight in 1932. That three-engine, 17-passenger airship became the counterpart to the McDonnell Douglas DC-3. Records show that a total of 4,825 Ju 52s were built in Germany, half, as it turned out, earmarked for the German air force.

With the war in progress, some 200 Ju 52s were in service, only 80 of them for the airline. The others were leased to the newly established Reich Ministry of Aviation, headed by Hitler's second-in-command Hermann Göring. As air minister, Göring made it clear that Lufthansa was an instrument of the state, that is, part of the air force.

But Lufthansa had much earlier blurred the lines between nonmilitary and military service. In 1934, now sporting its new name, Lufthansa, the airline served as an instrument of state commerce and diplomacy. Military pilots were trained at Lufthansa even before Hitler came to power.

The airline became more involved with the Reich when in 1940, protected by the Hitler-Stalin Pact of 1939, it began flying to destinations in the Soviet Union. This service provided the German air force with strategic information, which Hitler used in his surprise attack of the Soviet Union in 1941.

Lufthansa's fleet during the war years included Junkers's 40-seat Ju 90, a giant four-engine aircraft whose military version was called Ju 290; and the Bremen airplane maker Focke-Wulf supplied Lufthansa with its four-engine Fw 200 Condor. (Developed by the renowned engineer Kurt Tank, the Condor had astounded the world in 1938 when it made two nonstop flights from Berlin to New York—a sensational achievement at the time.) So while Hitler's armies were controlling much of Europe on the ground, Lufthansa was dominating the commercial air traffic. Before the end of the war brought a temporary end to Deutsche Lufthansa, its formerly impressive fleet comprised one Fw 200 Condor, one Douglas DC-2 and one DC-3, one Ju-88, and several Junkers Ju 52s.

As the war drew to a close, many Lufthansa employees were drafted into the air force they had heretofore served only as suppliers. Many of them were killed. Another casualty was Lufthansa pioneer Martin Wronsky, whom the American occupation force appointed as Lufthansa's "executor." On December 12, 1946, he committed suicide.

Though the Allies forbade both East and West Germany from establishing their own airlines, in 1950, Hans M. Bongers, Lufthansa's former traffic director, proposed the establishment of an aviation agency with the hope of gaining enough experience to enable him to eventually resurrect the disbanded airline. When the British force denied him a license, Bongers instead founded a private consulting firm, the Bongers Office, in Bitburg.

This office would become the new Lufthansa. On May 29, 1951, then–head of the Ministry of Traffic and Transportation Hans-Christoph Seebohm ("Airbohm") appointed Bongers as adviser to the federal government in aviation matters. After he had furnished the recently formed Preparation Committee Air Traffic (VAL, for Vorbereitungsausschuss Luftverkehr) with pertinent facts, the pieces were in place to form a preparatory airline corporation in Bonn. In 1953, the public corporation Luftverkehrsbedarf (Luftag) was founded, and Bongers was reinstated as director. The company was subsidized by the Federal Republic of Germany, the German Railroad, and the State of North Rhine–Westphalia.

In the summer of 1953, Luftag ordered four four-engine Lockheed 1049 Super Constellations with seating for 85, four two-engine Convair 340s with seating for 44, and three DC-3s. The airplanes were flown by foreign pilots while Lufthansa pilots were being retrained in the United States.

At the end of that year, Hamburg became the site of the new company headquarters. On August 6, 1954, Luftag was renamed Deutsche Lufthansa Aktiengesellschaft. Under the new moniker, a Convair began its first domestic flight on April 1, 1955; and on May 15, a Super-Conny took off on its first international flight. Regular air traffic to North America began for the first time in Lufthansa's history in April 1956; and the first nonstop flight from Frankfurt to New York took place on February 13, 1958, in the last of the Super Constellations, the L1649a Starliner, signaling the end of the superluxury flying days.

Lufthansa rang in the era of the jet plane in 1961 with a Boeing 707, following in Pan Am's footsteps. This marked the reentry of Lufthansa on the market as a premier air carrier. It was widely known at that time that Boeing was set to launch within the year its next and much more revolutionary jet, the medium-range Boeing 727, featuring three rear-mounted jet engines. When Lufthansa upgraded to the new plane, it so dramatically increased the number of passengers per plane that Lufthansa was forced to transfer its operative center from remote Hamburg to centrally located Frankfurt am Main. The company now owned a fleet of Boeing's Intercontinental Jets for long-range flights and of Boeing 727s, which were called Europe Jets, for medium-range flights. All that was missing was a spacious "city hopper."

Lufthansa's head of technology, Gerhard Höltje, traveled to Boeing's Seattle, Washington, headquarters to talk expansion. At the instigation and with the aid of Lufthansa, the Boeing 737 was developed for short-distance shuttle routes. When it was released in 1968, Lufthansa was its first customer (it is still being manufactured in the year 2000). Lufthansa baptized the plane "City-Jet." Thus the company had a trio of Boeing jet planes, which made life easy for technicians and comfortable for salespeople.

As Boeing corporation's largest overseas customer, Lufthansa reigned supreme. Only 10 years earlier, Pan Am's legendary director Juan Trippe, the first to order the Boeing 707, had so tight a lock on the new jets that competitors, including Lufthansa, had to wait years for the plane. But by the time Boeing was ready to crown its success with the Boeing 747 Jumbo Jet, the tables had turned. Pan Am launched its transatlantic flights with the Jumbo Jet on January 22, 1970, and Lufthansa did so only three months later, on April 26.

Soon thereafter, two managers who were to put their stamp on an entire era rose within the company: Herbert Culmann, who began his 10-year tenure as the new Lufthansa's first chairman of the board in 1972, and his head technician Reinhardt Abraham. Culmann, a financial expert, worked to ensure that the quickly expanding company would become economically stable. Abraham, for his part, took advantage of Boeing's (at the time) financial weakness to buy cheap through discounts and with cash.

Ultimately, Abraham put an end to the Boeing monoculture. He ordered an intermediate-size plane, the 270-seater McDonnell Douglas DC-10-30, to fill out the fleet. In addition, when the European aviation industry, for the most part united in the Airbus consortium, offered the giant aircraft Airbus A-300, a short-range plane, he ordered that, too. In short, Abraham changed the company's philosophy: Rather than dealing with one aircraft maker and several engine manufacturers, he now began to work with only one engine manufacturer (General Electric) and several aircraft makers.

Abraham introduced variety to the wide-body class: the Boeing 747 had four jets and was very wide; the McDonnell Douglas DC-10 had three jets and was used on long medium-range and short long-range flights; the Airbus A-300 and later the A-310 each had two jets and were used on short-range and medium- to-short-range flights. General Electric supplied the engines for all of them. The maintenance crews cheered, and the profits climbed. With an eye on the market for smaller jets, which was still controlled by Boeing and McDonnell Douglas, Abraham urged the airbus industry to design an entire aircraft family, not just variations of its giant aircraft.

The Culmann/Abraham years were for Lufthansa a period of relative comfort and prosperity, but one that clearly contained the virus of change. IATA's cushy rules about widely regulated air traffic and tariffs with their contractually stipulated profits were still entirely intact. There continued to be clear distinctions between scheduled flights and chartered flights. But Boeing and many big airlines had overextended themselves with the Jumbo Jet and were showing signs of weakness. Pan Am had started to spin out of control and soon crashed altogether. National carrier Lufthansa, however, protected mainly by the closed market system in Germany and Europe, stayed on course.

Then in 1982, dramatic changes took place in the company's executive suite: Herbert Culmann's contract as chairman of the board was not renewed. Hermann Josef Abs had been replaced as the man in control of the supervisory board by Walter Hesselbach from the Bank für Gemeinwirtschaft, which was owned by the German unions at the time. The Social Democrat Helmut Schmidt was chancellor of the Federal Republic of Germany, Lufthansa's major shareholder. He was not inclined to put fellow party members into leading industry positions simply because they were fellow party members. As far as Schmidt was concerned, Reinhardt Abraham would have been a worthy successor to Culmann. But Abraham was a nobody in the world of politics—nor was he interested becoming a somebody. Thus, Heinz Ruhnau, who had for a long time served as undersecretary at the federal Ministry of Traffic and Transportation and on Lufthansa's supervisory board, became the new chairman of the board.

Ruhnau was a Social Democrat and a trained locksmith. He had created a stir as a forceful union boss when he was still young. Like Helmut Schmidt before him, he became an equally dynamic senator in the city-state of Hamburg and, subsequently, had an inconsequential tenure as a manager. Then he moved on to serve an eight-year term in the country's Social Democrat–ruled capital as federal undersecretary of transportation.

The 1980s were not a time of unadulterated bliss for traditional airlines. President Jimmy Carter had signed the airline deregulation bill, which eliminated any restrictions on competition among air carriers. What American airlines were lacking in revenues and profits from domestic flights, they now tried to make up for in international flights, preferably on the North Atlantic route. Consequently, it turned into a money-losing route for most airlines, Lufthansa included. The European Commission threatened to make things even worse when it, too, began to gradually deregulate air traffic. As a politician, Ruhnau was able to slow down that process, but he soon realized that he had to prepare Lufthansa for what looked inevitable.

Caught between the economic boom, politics, social politics, and the task of running the corporation, Ruhnau became overextended. Nevertheless, he managed to impress the supervisory board—enough, at any rate, to convince its members renew his contract for another five years. In the face of much criticism, Ruhnau managed to steer Lufthansa in the right direction through two risky decisions: He persistently invested in the air cargo business and in the expansion and modernization of the fleet. By the time Ruhnau left, only Singapore Airlines' average age of planes was younger than Lufthansa's. Unfortunately, this two-pronged strategy put a serious financial strain on the company.

Toward the end of Ruhnau's tenure, Lufthansa was flying to 176 destinations in 84 different countries—from Anchorage to Helsinki, Tokyo, Melbourne, Buenos Aires, Lima, San Francisco, and Vancouver, including such exotic places as Addis Ababa, Luxor, Mauritius, and Rönne. Abraham's call for a varied Airbus fleet had been heeded. Lufthansa had acquired all Airbus models from the first A-300 Bs to the smaller short-range jets A-320 and A-319. Furthermore, Lufthansa sponsored the development of the four-jet, long-range Airbus A-340 to replace the slightly obsolete DC-10 (later MD-11).

Though Ruhnau wasn't always as adept at hiring personnel as he was at keeping the fleet competitive, by the time he resigned as chairman of the board in 1991—seven months before his contract expired—he had personally seen to it that one Jürgen Weber had risen quickly within the company.

Weber's Web

Jürgen Weber is a man any mother would be proud of. He's smart, respectable, easygoing, and nice-looking; in short, he's middle-of-the road, even though sometimes, understandably, he talks and behaves like a bureaucrat. Given his moderate nature, his accomplishments at Lufthansa seem even more impressive. Barring the unforeseen, he stands to become the least controversial and most successful of all Lufthansa's presidents.

Jürgen Weber grew up in surroundings similar to those of Jürgen Schrempp. He was born on October 17, 1941, in Lahr, a town just north of Freiburg, close to the border of Alsace, France. Lahr is a place difficult to leave; the cuisine, the wine, and often even the weather are good there. Like Schrempp, Weber didn't descend from the financial aristocracy. If he wanted to buy something special during his college days, he had to work for it, which he usually did as a ski instructor.

Weber majored in aeronautics at the renowned university of technology in Stuttgart. After receiving his diploma in 1965, he stayed on to work as a research associate until 1967. Lufthansa discovered his talents right there and recruited him, offering him a job as one of its engineering managers in Hamburg, a department soon to be headed by company legend Reinhardt Abraham. Weber's association with Abraham determined the course of his career. In 1974, Abraham sent him to Frankfurt to head Lufthansa's department of domestic and international maintenance. Four years later, he took over the main department of flying equipment. Though this was a promotion, it was not an earth-shattering career move. When Weber celebrated his 45th birthday, he still held that position, and his chances for further advancement were looking slim. Then, after more than eight years in the same job, he began to advance again—and quickly.

In early 1987, Weber was promoted to Lufthansa's general manager of technology. In that position, which was somewhat outside the mainstream company hierarchy, he was able to demonstrate fully his capabilities, thus moving to the head of the line of those who were hoping to succeed Reinhardt Abraham. Formally, he was accountable to the Federal Office of Aviation for maintaining the Lufthansa fleet. The company's top management wanted him to pay particular attention to the technology department's bottom line. This job was to be his final training ground within an ossified administration. Two years later, on April 1, 1989, Jürgen Weber was appointed as deputy member of the board.

From this point on, he advanced quickly. On January 1, 1990, Weber took over Abraham's seat as a regular member of the board. Less than a year later, in October 1990, he became vice chairman of the board, to the surprise of many. In May of the following year, the supervisory board designated him Heinz Ruhnau's successor. (Ruhnau had announced he was going to retire as of September 1.) Never before had a Lufthansan advanced so quickly from the ranks to the top.

In his new position, Weber was confronted with many immediate challenges. The company's productivity was low. Aside from its bureaucracy, personnel expenses were straining the bottom line. Then, part of the fleet had to be withdrawn as a result of the Gulf War. By falling back on reserves and selling some older jets, Lufthansa had still been able to make an—albeit slim—profit in 1990. Still, immediately after assuming office, Weber was facing huge losses, amounting to 444 million marks in 1991, and to 735 million marks in 1992. Compared to its equity of 1,526 million marks, it was clear that the situation was becoming critical.

Seemingly imperturbable, Weber managed to turn the entire company around. Though Lufthansa was still controlled largely by the government, Weber wanted to restructure it as a private service company. The two unions involved had to live with a 12-month wage freeze. And entire business areas were split off, making it possible for the company to renege on long-term wage agreements. In sharp contrast to Ruhnau, who had defied the overwhelming cost and increased personnel to 50,000, Weber quickly cut the workforce to under 47,000. These moves enabled Weber, after less than three years in office, to increase Lufthansa's productivity by 31 percent. As a result, Lufthansa stock climbed so high that the company could be privatized.

Weber was able to dislodge Lufthansa from the tight grip of the government only by cutting the company loose from the federal and state funds that provided the pensions for all of its retired employees. Once the claims of the company's workforce had been transferred to a pension insurance association, the government could begin to cash in. In September 1994, the federal minister of finance sold much of the government's Lufthansa stocks, holding onto a share of around 37.5 percent. In the second-largest stock auction in the history of German business, that package was dispersed among many different buyers.

Since then, no one has had a blocking minority at Lufthansa. Instead, sources indicate that the company has only two major shareholders: MGL Münchner Gesellschaft für Luftfahrtwerte mbH, with 10.05 percent of Lufthansa stocks, and the State of North Rhine–Westphalia with 1.77 percent. MGL is owned primarily by Dresdner Bank and Bayerische Landesbank (44.5 percent each) and Bayerische Landesanstalt für Aufbaufinanzierung (Bavarian State Organization for Financing Reconstruction, 11 percent). With the exception of a minor setback in 1996, Weber has been able to boast steadily climbing profits since 1993, although danger looms on the horizon as the price of crude oil increases.

In 1997, Lufthansa and United Airlines, in cooperation with SAS (Scandinavia), Thai Airways, Air Canada, and Varig (Brazil), established the Star Alliance. Later members—Air New Zealand, Ansett (Australia), Singapore Airlines, and Air Nippon Airways (Japan)—have turned this network into a web with virtually no gaps. "To complete the whole thing," Jürgen Weber says, all he needs is an ally in China. But what China? Then the Star Alliance will be "represented everywhere, with one strong partner in every part of the world." According to Weber, the alliance is already years ahead of all the others.

Its advantages are obvious: Star Alliance is not an organization with equity participation, but its members increasingly coordinate routes and programs. At the same time, it allows a global exchange of technical know-how from which each member profits. They all utilize electronic systems, from purchasing to check-in, from travel agencies to ticket windows and the Internet. Checking baggage, reservations, and bonus systems have been standardized, meaning that the customers of one alliance member can use the frequent-flyer lounge of any other member. Thus, Jürgen Weber, who started out in a defensive position, has built the largest coalition of airlines worldwide—the industry's first global conglomerate, not merely a counterconglomerate.

Lufthansa's shareholders have reason to rejoice. To keep up with the current 5 to 6 percent growth of the worldwide passenger flight market, the German airline plans to acquire at least 18 new airplanes per year. And to ensure that his company earns profits of more than 2 billion marks, Weber has started to offer Lufthansa's technology and electronic services to so-called third customers. During the first six months of 1998 alone, Lufthansa-Technik AG signed 60 new contracts with international airlines. The company's computer center, currently the largest one in Europe, is ideal for outside customers.

Internally, Lufthansa's president has launched Program 15, with the goal of lowering the cost of carrying one person for 1 kilometer to 15 pfennigs. To that end, his sales organization must be prepared to make last-minute decisions in order to fill every plane to capacity, if possible. That gives prebooked economy passengers the chance to advance to business class so that their coach seats can be sold to late arrivals. Jürgen Weber likes that.

Perhaps Weber's most impressive characteristic is that he's a hands-on administrator. He doesn't learn what's happening at the front only through hearsay or from official reports. He travels 300 days a year—not always with Lufthansa—and sometimes joins the crew in the cockpit. At airports, he remains inconspicuous. What is not inconspicuous is what he has done with Deutsche Lufthansa.

CHAPTER 11

Case Four: Airbus Four XX

Boeing's Nightmare

STEPHEN WOLFF WALKED out of the United Airlines administrative "cockpit" and into the one at US Airways. True to form, he started digging to find ways to improve the company. As soon as he hit upon the company's cost calculation, he made two big decisions: Fuel and maintenance expenditures had to be cut and new airplanes had to be ordered.

The orders for the new planes were awarded to the four-nation Airbus Industrie. The top managers of this group of European (French, German, British, Spanish) companies, whose sales offices are in a glass building near the airport in Toulouse, France, popped the champagne corks. US Airways ordered 109 Airbus jets of type A-319, with 124 seats, and 15 of the related model A-320, with 150 seats. On October 16, 1998, the first plane, an A-319, was ready for delivery at the Airbus plant near Hamburg harbor in Germany. Gradually, the American airline wants to acquire up to 400 Airbuses of each model.

Today's Airbus Industrie program comprises three complete series of models:

- The giant aircraft A-300 and A-310 of the first Airbus generation, with two engines and 220 to 266 seats, for short- and medium-range flights
- The more slender giant models A-330 and A-340 of the second Airbus generation, with 263 to 400 seats and four and two engines,

respectively, the former for extremely long-range flights, and the latter, for medium-range distances

- The narrower A-318 to A-321 models, with 100 to 182 seats and two engines each, for short- and medium-range flights

All three series are in direct competition with those of Boeing: The giant aircraft of the first generation competes with the Boeing 757; the more slender giant aircraft competes with the Boeing models 767 and 777; and the smaller Airbuses compete with the Boeing 717 and all derivatives of the popular 737. The only Boeing model the Europeans have so far been unable to compete with is the 747 Jumbo Jet, a superb plane on which Boeing has a monopoly. But Airbus has not given up its efforts to come up with a winner against the 747. A 555-seat Super Jumbo is already in the computer design stage and has been given the project name Airbus A-3XX. Four nations, one formula: Airbus Four XX.

The Boeing 747 is not only the largest, but also is perhaps the best commercial airplane in the world. Its demand for long flights from America and Europe to the Far East and Antarctica has put the Jumbo Jet, which came on the market around 1969 (and since then has been thoroughly overhauled), in an enviable and unique position: On the one hand, the demand for the Jumbo Jet is large enough to guarantee its manufacturer a large profit; on the other, it has such limited, specific use that developing a product to compete with it has to date been considered not really worth the effort. If the Airbus A-3XX were put on the market, so goes the thinking, neither Airbus nor Boeing would make money. Instead of one big winner, there would be two big losers.

But as logical as this sounds, Boeing hasn't been able to discourage the Europeans from going ahead with their project. They hope that their more state-of-the-art product will also be more in tune with the market, and perhaps one day will become unrivaled, in which case, the balance of power would shift 180 degrees.

Even half a victory would help the Europeans. They haven't failed to notice that Boeing always gives its Jumbo customers large discounts when they simultaneously place orders for other Boeing products. In this way, the American company subsidizes its less successful models with the profits from its Jumbo monopoly. Without that monopoly, Airbus believes, Boeing would no longer be able to offer such generous discounts, thus enabling Airbus and Boeing to operate in identical markets with similar products. For Airbus, this would be a win-win situation.

Boeing president Phil Condit is fully aware of this threat. In many ways, it looks like a worst-case scenario from his point of view. Boeing is standing against the low evening sun with the light to its face; it recognizes the outline of the danger but can't make it out clearly. Though the cost of developing an A-3XX seems prohibitive—$12 billion—if it were completed, Airbus would have the most up-to-date aircraft on the market. Condit takes some solace in that Airbus hasn't set the launch date or a tentative rollout date for the "threat."

The market for the Jumbo is entirely dependent on the demand from the Far East, which of late has become sluggish in the wake of crises in Japan and some neighboring nations. Therefore, Airbus is holding back on the launch of the A-3XX project, even though the aircraft's construction will have a very long development and marketing time. This gives Phil Condit perhaps another two years. The Boeing 747 monopoly will probably last until far into the new millennium's first decade.

This doesn't, however, solve Condit's problem with Airbus. Boeing's top two moneymakers, the Jumbo and the Boeing 737, are aging. Their basic design was created back in the 1960s. The 757 and 767 models, which were developed 15 years later, never became really popular enough to finance expensive new developments. Thus the company still depends on the Jumbo and the 737. The giant two-jet Boeing 777 (Triple Seven), the only model in Boeing's program that is considered revolutionary and unique, isn't bringing in much either, though it is still too early to tell.

With the exception of the Triple Seven, none of Boeing's products meets the technological standard or has the long-term economical advantages of its respective European counterpart. The Airbus consortium's French technology experts especially have seen to that. Airbus was the first company to introduce the supercritical wing, the two-person cockpit, and the fly-by-wire system. Long before the Americans met a similar standard with their Triple Seven, Airbus had computer-assembled its jets. The Europeans have also surpassed Boeing in terms of product development, production technology, and the product itself. To repeat: Boeing leads only with the Jumbo—and in terms of corporate structure.

The Boeing Company, founded in 1916 by William Boeing, son of a German immigrant, has always been a private firm. In the 1930s and during World War II, it earned its stripes with some top-notch products: the two-engine Boeing B-247, introduced in 1933, is considered the mother of American passenger aircraft; and the 1942 four-engine B-29 Superfortress, with its pressure cabin and 4,500-mile range, was the weapon that ultimately won the war for America. Altogether 3,970 of these 60-ton mammoths were built. They became the terror of Europe as well as the Pacific. Two of them carried the atom bombs dropped on Japan in 1945.

After World War II, Boeing began producing the frightening B-52 Stratofortress, a superbomber with eight jet engines and a 12,000-mile range. Meant to threaten the Soviet Union, it failed to decide the Vietnam War. The company began manufacturing 744 B-52s, then discontinued the series in 1962. Still, four decades later, this aircraft is a backbone of the American air force. Military experts believe it has another four decades left. If they're right, then the B-52 essentially will have a life span of about 80 years, a unique milestone in the history of aviation.

On the experimental front, the earliest flights of this enormous jet took place as early as 1952. This did not make Boeing the unqualified leader in its field at that time, but the company went on to fully exploit its sophisticated jet technology for commercial business. In 1954, it launched the 707/720, known to aviation buffs as program number 367-80, or Dash Eighty. In quick succession, the company introduced the 727 (1960), the 737 (1967), and finally, the 747 Jumbo in 1969. Originally, the Dash Eighty and the Jumbo had been designed as military aircraft, whereas the 727 and 737 were always intended to be purely commercial planes. This double-track strategy gave Boeing the advantage that only now, after more than three decades, is in jeopardy on account of Airbus.

All the other jet manufacturers in the world—De Havilland, Vickers, and British Aircraft Corporation in England, Aérospatiale in France, Fokker in Holland, and General Dynamics (Convair) and Lockheed in the United States—have dropped out of the race. Only McDonnell Douglas (MDD) remained, though it never invested as much in the non-military business. Its market share crumbled however, and in 1997 it was taken over by Boeing. Thus, the Seattle-based company has captured all markets and all manufacturers of American airliners.

Something similar happened in Europe—albeit in a very different and complicated way. There, Airbus united the entire industry. Unlike Boeing, the European company has never been a hierarchically structured firm, but rather a composite of political interests and technological ambition. It isn't a company, but a consortium, heavily sponsored by France, which was counting on Airbus to salvage the French aircraft industry. The disaster with the Concorde in the early 1970s only underscored this resolve.

The Concorde project was launched on November 29, 1962, as part of an agreement between the French and English governments. The supersonic aircraft was to be built for a hefty sum to be forked over by the taxpayers. The plan was to recapture the lead in commercial aeronautics from the Americans. Though the Concorde was a technological work of art and is likely to remain a unique achievement, it never had a chance of becoming a commercial success. "Too small, too loud, too expensive," as then–Lufthansa president Herbert Culmann summed it up. True, the airplane could reach New York from Paris or London in two and a half hours, but that was its maximum range. It couldn't fly to the Far East, to Australia, or even to the Cape of Good Hope without time-consuming stopovers. And on shorter overland flights, the Concorde wasn't allowed to fly at supersonic speed. Consequently, the U.S. airlines reneged on their numerous buying options, as did the European and Asian airlines; in the end, Air France and British Airways were the only carriers left in the project. Ultimately, a mere 20 Concordes were built.

Subsequently, France put its entire aeronautic focus on the Airbus consortium, which had been established in 1970. (In the 1960s, the commercial jet market was controlled by Boeing, McDonnell Douglas, and Lockheed, all American companies. To be able to compete effectively, West Germany and France agreed to form a consortium to produce commercial jets.) Its first product, the giant jet A-300 B, designed for short- and medium-range flights, was released in 1974. Initially, the British, along with French, Germans, Dutch, and Spanish, were to comprise the consortium, but the British pulled out because its Labour government did not have faith it would succeed. The British stayed involved in Airbus, however, limiting their cooperation to building aircraft wings. The consortium, a form of unlimited partnership, thus became primarily controlled by Germany and France. Then, in 1979, Britain became an official member, and the Netherlands' Fokker-VFW was joined by Belgium's Belairbus as associated production members.

For a long time France and Germany each had a 37.9 percent share in Airbus; England had 20 percent, and Spain, 4.2 percent. France is represented by Aérospatiale, Germany by DaimlerChrysler Aerospace Airbus (DASA), England by British Aerospace (BA), and Spain by Construcciones Aeronauticas (CASA). While DASA and BA are private companies, the state has some control over Aérospatiale and CASA. In 1999, DASA took over CASA, which technically gave the Germans the lead in the consortium with 42.1 percent. To be fair, the Airbus system is not a holding company that heads a number of individual manufacturers; it constitutes the joint subsidiary of the individual producers. Money, power, and profit are theirs, while Airbus Industrie is in charge of sales, marketing, service—and losses.

Though this complicated structure is rooted in politics, it has worked surprisingly well. Shortly after Airbus was launched on the global market, there was an Atlantic divide of sorts. Previously, as mentioned, Boeing and McDonnell Douglas had almost total control of the market; today, Airbus and Boeing are increasingly controlling their respective home markets as well as competing for customers in the Pacific—though thanks to the Jumbo, the Americans are still in the lead in the Far East.

Boeing management in Seattle is understandably concerned that Airbus is gaining customers in the United States while Boeing is losing clients in Europe. In 1998, the Europeans received 556 firm orders, a number that approached Boeing's 656 orders. In the first eight months of 1999, Airbus had won 288 firm orders, compared to 134 for Boeing. Airbus hasn't won, but it's becoming a closer race. That said, it's worth noting that the cyclical jet business has gone through similar periods before. In 1994, Boeing's condition was much more serious, and the two rivals went head to head, but Boeing managed to disentangle itself from the clinch and move far ahead.

In fact, in 1998, Boeing's lead was wider than the number of units sold indicates. In terms of units produced, the American company was ahead of Airbus by only 18 percent, but its revenues were almost three times as high. But Boeing has other problems. Boeing's new president Phil Condit tried to solve those problems à la Rockefeller senior: After taking over competitor McDonnell Douglas in 1997 in a spectacular move—thus gaining a huge share in armament commissions—he wanted to blitz Airbus in a merciless price war. His goal was for Boeing to win three-quarters of all purchase orders, leaving Airbus with the remaining fourth.

If he had succeeded, Airbus would probably have had to shelve its $12 billion Super Jumbo project, for who but the respective governments could have financed it? The old suspicion that the entire Airbus consortium was highly subsidized would then not have been refutable. (In fact it was not true, as the United States and Europe had agreed in 1995 that a 30 percent government involvement in the development costs of such projects didn't violate the spirit of free competition.)

In any case, the threat of a trade war never materialized, though the competition is hotter than ever. In 1999, Boeing's attempt to regain control of the market failed mainly because Airbus had made inroads with former Boeing-only customers such as American Airlines, United, All Nippon Airways, and Korean Air Lines. Worse for Boeing was that its perennial customer, British Airways, ordered the Airbus product as well, even though it had been offered a comparable product at a lower price. The British believed that the more modern Airbus jets would be less expensive in the long run because of lower maintenance costs.

Problems and competition aside, the truth is, no modern airline wants to be at the mercy of a single company that has total market control. Perhaps even if Airbus had been in serious trouble, the airlines would have turned to the consortium more readily, because especially after Boeing's takeover of MDD, the market would otherwise have become monopolistic. For that reason alone, Condit's attempt to defeat the consortium turned out to be a serious strategic mistake. As an aviation expert, he should have been able to predict the customer response.

A field of two is not, however, a dream come true for the airlines. They're aware it would be all too easy for the Big Two to one day agree on minimum prices. Therefore, the airlines would like to see a third company emerge to compete with Boeing and Airbus. A reputable manufacturer of business jets such as the Canadian Bombardier would have a real chance with a good 80- to 100-seater.

Until that competitor appears, the industry remains a world of two. Airbus—unlike Boeing—supplies only the nonmilitary sector, and so is considerably smaller than Boeing. In 1998, the consortium had a revenue of $13.3 billion. The American conglomerate, with its larger jets and sizable military and aerospace business, posted $55 billion. By the end of that year, the Europeans had sold a total of 3,200 Airbus jets, 2,000 of which are operated by 160 airlines. Boeing boasts that kind of business with just one of its models, the 737. Nevertheless, Airbus Industrie has grown into the classic Global Counterconglomerate more clearly than any other company. So the American giant must be on the alert. Europeans have a reputation of being tenacious. As few as 15 years ago, no one would have thought them capable of seriously challenging America's aircraft industry. At that time, Boeing's hotshots brushed news of Airbus's successes off like gray hair on a black suit. Today they're paying attention.

Frankenstein's Games

During the first 10 postwar years, Allied restrictions prevented the German aircraft industry from reestablishing itself. When at last, in 1951, the aircraft industrialists were allowed to reenter their—often severely damaged—factories, they realized that they had to look for other business opportunities. Willy Messerschmitt, who had launched the world's first fighter jet, built a futuristic cabin scooter on three wheels, with two seats and a plastic roof. Ernst Heinkel, arguably the German aircraft industry's most innovative entrepreneur, began building crankshafts and transmissions, then moved on to motor and cabin scooters. Kurt Tank, the ingenious engineer from Bremen, went to South America.

The British, though war-torn, too, had managed to preserve part of their highly efficient aircraft factories, but they had grown much too big as a result of wartime armament production. Fortunately, for them, the technology developed during the war helped them to quickly recover with such revolutionary airplanes as the jet clipper De Havilland Comet 1 (maiden flight: 1949) and the Vickers VC 10. But after two Comets disappeared without a trace during flight, no airline would buy it, even in its improved form. Then when the BAC 1-11 failed to become a hit, the British could take no comfort in their role as aviation pioneers, because the business was going to the Americans.

The French fared similarly. During the German occupation in World War II, France's technology came to a virtual standstill. Though the French did manage to design the two-jet, medium-range Caravelle, it flopped in the key U.S. market, though it was offered there before the Boeing 727. The Caravelle sold better in Europe, but not enough better. The pragmatic French next developed a Super-Caravelle, but no satisfactorily larger model. Under the auspices of the future Airbus Industrie, the French hoped to realize an entirely new design. The French also wanted to include the supersonic Concorde in their plans. Ultimately, the plan was for a Super-Caravelle to roll off the assembly lines as a French product, accompanied by an Airbus as a European product, and the Concorde as a Franco-British product. Metaphorically speaking, the Super-Caravelle never took off and the Concorde crashed altogether. Only the Airbus remained.

France aligned the front. The American superpower, went the Airbus credo, had to be met by a pan-European counterforce. In December 1970, Airbus Industrie was officially formed and incorporated in France as a *groupement d'intérêt économique* (GIE). The Airbus members, with their different backgrounds, now agreed to focus all their experience on a single model series. The rich multiculture of Europe's aircraft factories led into a more profitable monoculture. Though, as mentioned, the British went through a defeatist phase, neither the French nor the German enthusiasm waned. In a sense, Germany was in the best position of the four: It was looking for salvation not at home, but in Europe, and so it had nothing to lose. England and France, on the other hand, could win only after recouping their losses. Furthermore, no matter how much the respective governments assured one another of their friendship, cooperating with Germany was not exactly the French's first choice. Ironically, it turned out to be their best choice.

It was also the Germans' best choice. When German federal finances later went through a difficult period in the wake of the two oil crises in the 1970s, the Airbus project, which was receiving large amounts of start-up money, was at risk on several fronts. But because the French had put their prestige on the line, they salvaged it again and again. In short, without the French, Airbus would not exist.

In Germany, it was the southern German political legend Franz-Josef Straus who stood firmly behind the project. Strauss, longtime prime minister of Bavaria, became Airbus Industrie's chairman of the board, a position to which he brought great honor. He and the French agreed that, for security, the consortium shouldn't restrict itself to a single Airbus model. They were backed by Air France and, as mentioned, by Lufthansa (at the time, government-owned).

This was the origin of the Airbus "family" strategy. It was the only aspect of the group that seemed clear and simple. In other regards, Airbus Industrie resembled an artificial product from Frankenstein's lab. For example, after many mergers, France's aircraft industry had turned into Aérospatiale; England's Bristol Aeroplane Company had been incorporated into the British Aircraft Corporation, which later turned into British Aerospace; and in Germany, things had become really complicated. Only Spain's CASA celebrated its first three-quarters of a century under its original name in 1999.

The German story started with Ernst Udet, who as a fighter pilot in World War I came second to the Red Baron in downing enemy planes (62). He had founded his Udet Flugzeugbau GmbH in 1922. In 1926, the company was incorporated into the newly established Bayerische Flugzeugwerke AG. That company was swallowed by the highly successful Messerschmitt AG in 1938. (The first Messerschmitt plants had been built in 1923.) The engineer Ernst Heinkel founded a firm in Warnemünde the same year as Udet, grandiosely called Ernst Heinkel Flugzeugwerke GmbH. Heinkel built numerous commercial and military planes, watercraft and land vehicles, and fighter jets and rocket aircraft, all while setting new records in the air. In 1943, the company, which meanwhile had merged with other aircraft factories, was transformed into Ernst Heinkel AG.

Hugo Junkers, an inventive professor at the Technical University in Aachen, began building airplanes in Dessau in 1913, when he was 54 years old. He put together the world's first all-metal airplane, and later he built the legendary Ju 52 ("Aunt Ju"). The feared dive bomber (Stuka, short for the German *Sturzkampfbomber*) Ju 87 carried his name, though before it went into the testing phase, in 1934, Hugo Junkers was pushed out of his company by the Nazis. In 1935, his heirs were forced to transfer the aircraft factories to the government for 9 million marks. By 1942, Junkers Flugzeug- und Motorenwerke AG was nothing more than an armament factory with 140,000 employees.

Thirteen years after the war, the Junkers plants were acquired by the newly founded Flugzeug-Union-Süd, which was run by the companies Heinkel and Messerschmitt. Junkers was maintained as the independent company Junkers Flugmotoren AG. Thus the first significant postwar partnership of the old aircraft companies came about.

A second major partnership is associated with the name of Ludwig Bölkow, who was the engineer in charge of the last and most sophisticated version of the German fighter plane Me 109. A short three years after World War II, Bölkow established his own engineering business in Stuttgart, which became Bölkow Entwicklungen KG (Bölkow Developments Ltd.) in 1956, and Bölkow GmbH in Ottobrunn (near Munich) in

1965. The firm was a think-tank-cum-technological-center as well as an armament and aerospace company—a unique combination at the time. In 1959, the firms Bölkow, Heinkel, and Messerschmitt joined forces as the Entwicklungsring Süd (Development Trust South).

Soon the two partnerships were joined by Hamburg's shipbuilding family, Blohm. It represented Hamburger Flugzeugbau GmbH, which had been founded in 1933 as a division of the family's large shipyard Blohm & Voss. It had designed a business jet that was later released as Hansa-Jet, which wasn't very successful. Other northern German companies were gathered around the legendary Focke-Wulff-Werke by the Weser river. They came together as Vereinigte Flugtechnische Werke Bremen GmbH (VFW), where the noted engeneer Rolf Stüssel developed the grass-runway jet VFW-614. Initially called VFW-Fokker, that tie was subsequently severed, and Hamburg's and Bremen's aircraft factories never joined forces again until they became Airbus members.

In the late 1960s, out of these developments came two additional partnerships, one really a merger. In southern Germany, the groups Heinkel/Messerschmitt and Bölkow GmbH united in 1968. They were joined in 1969 by the Blohms' Hamburger Flugzeugwerke. Thus the names Messerschmitt, Bölkow, and Blohm became MBB GmbH, which under Ludwig Bölkow as president quickly became a large, internationally respected, enterprise. Along with Bremen's VFW-Fokker and France's Société Nationale Industrielle Aérospatiale (SNIAS), Bölkow's company developed the Airbus A-300B from definition to testing. This proved to be the decisive partnership.

The Blohm plants in Hamburg-Finkenwerder served as Germany's factory. Like the Bremen plants, Spain's CASA, and England's British Aircraft, they had to ship their finished parts to Toulouse, where they were assembled by SNIAS technicians. This aspect of the consortium has remained virtually unchanged in two and a half decades; the only exception is that Germany was eventually permitted to assemble some of the smaller Airbus models in Hamburg and ship them to customers.

The division of labor works like this: Germany supplies the less complicated parts of the fuselage, the rudder assembly, and the smaller Airbus model fittings. Electronically advanced France contributes the complex cockpit and other parts of the fuselage; it assembles all the Airbuses except for the smaller jets manufactured at the Hamburg plant. The wings come from England, and Spain's CASA is responsible for the Airbus's remaining fuselage parts, the landing gear doors, side doors, and elevator units.

To ensure that all these parts are at the right place at the right time, the Airbus companies developed their own tracking system unlike any other in the world. Enormous jumbo airplanes with small wings and fat bellies constantly shuttle back and forth between Airbus factories. They have to be able to accommodate entire wings and airframe sections for full-size airliners. During the first 10 years, this was done by the monstrous propeller plane Super-Guppy, then by the mammoth jet Beluga, an Airbus A300-600 shaped like a bratwurst. Completely assembled Airbuses are routinely flown to another plant, where they are equipped with seats, kitchens, and toilets, whereupon they are flown back from whence they came. The reasoning for the return flight is that before an airplane can be turned over to a customer, test flights must be performed anyway, and this would serve the purpose.

Airbus has a workforce of about 32,000, supplemented by more than 1,500 suppliers in 19 different countries—500 of them in the United States. American suppliers include aero-engine manufacturers Pratt & Whitney and General Electric, AlliedSignal, Goodrich, Honeywell, Rockwell, Collins, Rohr, Sundstrand, and Westinghouse.

It is virtually impossible to compare the profitability of the geographically dispersed and electronically controlled Airbus production to Boeing's traditional, more centralized production procedures. An American consulting firm calculated that Airbus Industrie's productivity would increase by at least 20 percent if the consortium were structured as a typical industrial enterprise. The Airbus top managers do not set strategic targets; instead, the individual partners figure out the company's strategy among themselves—and no one can override the French and Germans when they are in agreement. The Airbus president essentially takes his orders from the powers that be in the consortium's different companies, but is accountable when the group doesn't sell enough aircraft. Imagine if DaimlerChrysler's main shareholders manufactured their own cars and then told the board members what to do. This unorthodox structure can be traced to the political parentage of Airbus; it was never a private enterprise. Many find it puzzling that Airbus, given its unusual organization, has developed into the sole genuine Global Counterconglomerate in its industry. Consequently, the lingering suspicion that somewhere there must be undetected subsidies will no doubt remain as long as the aircraft empire continues in its current form. Suspicion aside, this unique conglomerate is working because it has been controlled by special people.

The Lothringian Cross

Not far from Chamboilet Les Deux Eglises, former French president Charles de Gaulle's last residence, stands a huge double cross, with the short crossbeam on top and the longer one underneath. It is called the Lothringian Cross, and de Gaulle saw something mythical in it. To him, it stood for France, the Grand Nation. It was under that cross that de Gaulle had prevented England's membership in the European Economic Community (EEC) and deterred that country's partnership in the original Airbus program. France wanted to determine the partnership's direction. England's absence at the time made Germany an equal partner to France, though it never had equal weight—until now.

Lothringia, for centuries the embattled border region between the two countries, would have been a logical location for the new Airbus holding company, just as the Alsatian Strasbourg is a good location for the Aventis headquarters. But Germany wanted to make Holland the seat of the holding company because of its lower taxes. It was overruled by France, whose Ministry of Finance in Paris then offered the future holding company lower taxes equal to those in the Netherlands for setting up headquarters in Toulouse.

From the beginning, and to this day, the partners squabble, and France usually prevails. The most important positions have always been filled by Frenchmen, and so the French have consistently determined the company culture. And with headquarters in Toulouse, the Airbus personnel, too, is predominantly French. The problem this creates is that the other partners can easily become outsiders. Though Airbus management counters by pointing out that there are 33 different nationalities represented among its 2,700 employees, the consortium is at heart French. The only concession is language, which is not French but English.

Still, remarkably, the predicted clash of cultures has never really materialized. Amazingly, this joint organization of diverse nations, which is complicated, sensitive, and acutely prone to personality problems, couldn't have worked better or more effectively. The reason for this is twofold: Airbus has always had a common enemy; and from the beginning it was shaped by strong personalities. During the early years, these tended to be people who preferred to spend their time in the cockpit rather than at the office. They were united not by the idea of a nation or of social status, but by the phenomenon of flying. This had the same intoxicating effect on its participants as racing had at Daimler-Benz. This, above all, has led to the Airbus success.

The first architects of this success hailed from France. They included, most notably, Henri Ziegler and Roger Beteille. Ziegler, a prominent member of the French Resistance and therefore close to Charles de Gaulle, was as qualified a technician as he was a politician. He was dubbed a "statesman of industry." Unquestionably, expertise in engineering coupled with political skills are still the right mix for a top manager at Airbus. No one could explain the partnership's concerns and represent it as unconditionally as Henri Ziegler.

In 1973, Roger Beteille succeeded Ziegler. The difference was barely discernible. Both were graduates of the elite French Ecole Polytechnique. Both were considered to have well-rounded, easygoing natures. While Ziegler's guffaw instantly evaporated tension, Beteille had a knack for amusing double entendres. Former astronaut Frank Borman praised him effusively: "He is a genius. He understands perfectly everything that goes on within the complex systems of an aircraft." Borman, at the time, head of Eastern Airlines, was convinced by Beteille to become Airbus's first American customer in 1975.

Beteille, a polyglot, also managed to unite the different nationalities within his company. Even today, German experts celebrate him as someone without whom the Airbus program wouldn't exist. But for those who succeeded Ziegler and Beteille, it has not been so positive; they have always been in the shadow of their great predecessors. Bernard Lathiere came and went, as did Jean Pierson. Of the German managers, it was Franz-Josef Strauss who in particular had a crucial impact on Airbus Industrie's development. A primarily political man, he was also well informed about his business. As a hobby pilot he could hold his own when the cockpit experts engaged in small talk; and everyone knew that Strauss would always be able to take political advantage of circumstances and, if need be, fight for certain plans.

Otherwise, the Germans became more the technological—or more precisely, the production-technological—driving forces behind the Airbus project, as befitted their historical role and political situation. Engineers such as the MBB founder Ludwig Bölkow and the later DASA chairman Johann Scheffler were among Airbus's first strategists. And Felix Kracht was head of production in Toulouse for many years—later in his tenure he seemed more and more French, complete with the ubiquitous Gauloise cigarette dangling from the right corner of his mouth.

Another remarkable German at Airbus was former VFW manager Hartmut Mehdorn. As a native Berliner, at first glance the vivacious Mehdorn hardly appeared to be an ideal partner for the French. But because he also was a technician, he easily fit the bill. In 1966, at the young age of 24, he had started out in airplane development at Vereinigte Flugtechnische Werke (VFW) in Bremen. Involved in the Airbus program from 1974, he was promoted to VFW plant manager in Bremen only two years later. In 1980, he was transferred to Toulouse as head of production. In 1985, he became head of the MBB aircraft conglomerate in Hamburg, where he soon made a name for himself. Hamburg's state government courted him, as he provided jobs. He dealt evenhandedly with the media, which are numerous and omnipresent in the city on the Elbe. After a few years under his direction, the plant was in the black. He so persistently drummed up support for Hamburg that he eventually succeeded in having the small Airbuses shipped from the Elbe River plant. This marked the first time the French relinquished the rule whereby all customers had to come to Toulouse to pick up their airplanes.

Many considered Mehdorn to be Airbus personified—a distinction previously reserved for the French. He was, simply, *the* man of aircraft. But when longtime Airbus president Pierson retired in 1998 and Mehdorn's name came up as a possible replacement, the French again prevailed. Noel Forgeard became the new boss in Toulouse, and DASA director Manfred Bischoff, an old adversary of Mehdorn, was made chairman of the board.

With Forgeard, born in 1946, and Bischoff, born in 1942, the top managers at Airbus for the first time represented a generation that had no firsthand memories of the war, a generation that includes former student rebels and technocrats. Bischoff belongs more to the latter group, even though he resists that classification. Bischoff hails from Calw, a medium-size city in southwestern Germany. He went to law school not far from there, in Tübingen, and studied economics in Heidelberg, which is also nearby.

Between 1968 and 1976, Bischoff worked as a research assistant at the renowned Alfred Weber Institute in Heidelberg, where he earned his doctorate in 1973. At the age of 34, turning away from his academic inclinations, he joined the junior staff at Daimler-Benz AG in Stuttgart. With his analytical talents and persistent nature, he quickly advanced in Daimler's finance department. A bigger change came when he disentangled himself from the company's bureaucracy and joined the managing board of the company's subsidiary Mercedes-Benz do Brasil.

With his talent now apparent to all, he became a board member of DASA by 1989. There he met Jürgen Schrempp, who became his mentor. Between 1991 and 1995, the two had to make their way through thick corporate underbrush. The DASA conglomerate, which had been put together hastily, produced all kinds of aircraft, but, more significantly, losses. Schrempp and Bischoff pushed through the notorious Dolores program, which was supposed to align the cost calculation for aircraft production to an exchange rate of 1.35 deutsche marks to the U.S. dollar. Since then, however, DASA has been making money.

Bischoff, as DASA's director, earned the chair on the Airbus supervisory board through his combination of moderation and strategic insight. And, importantly, Bischoff gets along well with Forgeard.

Like Henri Ziegler, Noel Forgeard, born near Paris, acquired his knowledge of engineering at the Ecole Polytechnique. Subsequently, he worked as a French government official, ultimately holding a post as technical adviser on issues of aviation and armament. In 1981, at the age of 35, he joined the management of the French steel conglomerate Usinor; four years later, he became executive director of the high-grade steel factory Ascometal. After briefly acting as adviser to then–French prime minister (and later president) Jacques Chirac on industrial matters, he went to work for the private French armament and electronics company Matra.

Forgeard had attracted the Airbus board's attention when he was manager of Matra Hautes Technologies, the division that combined the company's departments of defense, aeronautics, and telecommunications. The board members were persuaded that the 52-year-old engineer was well experienced in industry, administration, and politics, and had some understanding of international business. This made him the first choice among all the candidates.

Forgeard, who assumed his new position in April 1998, plans to give the Airbus consortium clear new structures. He and Bischoff are determined to run the conglomerate as a regular company, even before the restructuring is complete. Both also want to merge the conglomerate with the European aerospace and defense industry, which would make it a lot more balanced.

To climb and reaccelerate or to make a stopover, that is the question. It is one Airbus as well as Boeing must answer. Condit's strategic blunder meant that neither company made much money during the economic boom. Thus, both are in weakened positions as they sail into the aircraft market's next slack period. Boeing is more successful in trying to avert disaster by maintaining a steady armament and aerospace business than the Europeans are.

But at age 30, Airbus is no longer an infant, and its most difficult years are behind it. Airbus Industrie is an established company, a conservative unit in the market. In that respect, it resembles Boeing Commercial Aircraft more and more. Conglomerate and counterconglomerate are facing one another. The confrontation is clear, inevitable, and perhaps permanent. The point is no longer who will succeed in pushing the rival out of the way, but who will be number one. Ultimately, this is a matter of statistics—as well as of propaganda.

Conclusion: Germany, America, and the New World Order

WENDELIN WIEDEKING, tiny Porsche AG's outspoken CEO, likes to say, "If size were the decisive criterion, the dinosaurs would still be alive." But in the world of conglomerates, that's exactly what has happened: The dinosaurs *are* still alive. Of the 10 companies discussed in this book, six represent industrial concerns that were already significant in the last century: Allianz, Daimler, Deutsche Bank, Hoechst, Krupp/Thyssen, and Siemens. Three others—Lufthansa, Volkswagen, and Airbus—were founded later, but their business origins go back to earlier industrial developments in Europe as well. They, too, were big from the get-go—which makes them young dinosaurs. Only Bertelsmann doesn't follow this pattern. True, the company is very old, but it didn't grow until much later. This has something to do with the fact that Bertelsmann is not a technology company.

"Growing through one's own strength," Wiedeking adds, "takes more effort, but it also lasts longer." That may be true as well, but none of today's leading companies have grown entirely through their own strength. At various times in their history they have all received help from outside, and they all have had to deal with the difficulty of combining management styles and corporate culture. According to Mercer Management Consulting, among others, two-thirds of all mergers and takeovers somehow have gone wrong—though that doesn't mean that these transactions weren't completed.

Most of them did take place, whether it was during the big waves of mergers in the late Bismarck period, during the Weimar Republic, or during the waning era of the German economic miracle after World War

II. Everyone knows that mechanically combining revenue and profit rates doesn't in itself a successful merger make. That no merger ever has a mathematically even result is also well known. Strategically, however, the result should be even, even when size is the strategic entity. Whether the accumulated power of labor and capital is ultimately canceled out by bureaucracy and frictional losses is attributable not to size, but to a company's internal structure. It is not a coincidence that the concept of profit centers was invented with this in mind.

A historical perspective on these issues does not always provide a reliable viewpoint. Because the 1926 merger between Daimler and Benz turned out to be successful in the long run does not mean that the merger between Daimler-Benz and Chrysler in 1998 will prove to be successful in the long run, too. Sometimes such combinations blend more smoothly when they have the same linguistic and national background. Economic history tends to follow certain rules. One applicable to the topic of this book says that if markets grow, so will companies. Thus, if markets grow in new legal and linguistic areas, companies will follow suit. The result is that mergers across continents are more common and take place more quickly than they ever did between neighboring factories 30 years ago.

Porsche's president Wiedeking, for instance, reports that his company exports far more than half of its output. It wouldn't be able to do so without the aid of an external organization, which in turn requires the company to be of a certain size. But with that organization in place, large numbers of Porsche staff have to deal with many foreign cultures. That costs money. At some point, an entrepreneur has to ask whether it wouldn't be more cost-effective to transfer part of the company's production and management abroad.

If the answer is yes, the entrepreneur looking toward, say, the United States automatically has to deal with the Immigration and Naturalization Service. Therefore he or she has to hire a native workforce, even for top management positions. In this way, the corporate culture of, in this case, Porsche in America automatically becomes American, albeit with Swabian overtones. Anyone uncomfortable with such far-reaching consequences had better try to buy a foreign company in the same field. That's what General Motors Corporation did in 1929 when it took over Opel. This logic is easy to follow, and thus stringent. As General Motors illustrates, it's not a new way of thinking, either.

The history of economics also has shown us that size has its own dynamics, and that won't change. Simply put, ironworks can no longer be found in the backyards of coal dealers and small farmers. Even Mao Tse-tung's attempt in that direction failed. Henry Ford taught us that there are considerable cost as well as cultural differences between assembly-line production and single-piece production—let's say, the difference between a Volkswagen and a Rolls Royce. Select products can be manufactured individually; popular products cannot.

Munich's automaker BMW is perhaps a good example of a borderline case. A lengthy portrait of that company was intentionally excluded from this book because, with its annual return rate of $35 billion, many (and not only smart alecks) consider it to be suspiciously small. Indeed, it is small inasmuch as its survival was never really threatened only because for decades BMW's management made virtually no mistakes. Consequently, its first major blunder, the takeover of the nonbrand Rover, got the company into trouble.

This is tragic in that it was precisely that acquisition that was supposed to extricate BMW from its microcosmic trap. The attempt failed, and Rover started to become a financial graveyard for BMW. Kuenheim's personally selected successor Bernd Pischetsrieder was forced to leave. While the Rover mess did not put BMW into the red, the company couldn't avoid cutting its most important investments—those in BMW itself. Its superb image can cover a multitude of errors for a time. Even if it decides not to improve this or that model program, it won't make much of a difference—as long as no one notices. But that Audi sold more than BMW in Germany and Europe in 1998–1999 is a bad sign. Though BMW claims that's what it wanted in order for BMW to remain an exclusive brand, no one believes that.

The company no longer has as much in the works as it used to. Daimler-Benz, in contrast, had made enormous mistakes in the past, but was never in danger of cutting essential programs and there was no question that it would survive its list. The big Stuttgart automaker, whose mistakes BMW has been able to take advantage of in the past, has now clearly left its rival behind. BMW illustrates that, in certain markets, companies must have a minimum size.

It was essentially the Americans who started the focus on size. Perhaps because the United States spans an entire continent, Americans have always been enamored of large dimensions. Names such as John

Jacob Astor (trade), Cornelius Vanderbilt (railroads and shipping), Andrew Carnegie (steel), John D. Rockefeller (oil), Henry Ford (cars), Alfred Irénée du Pont (chemicals), John Pierpont Morgan (banking), and Bill Gates (computer technology) exemplify that. Every new area of business has in its wake a new concept of size—the size of a continent.

The names Allianz, Daimler-Benz, Deutsche Bank, Hoechst, Krupp, Siemens, and Thyssen express the identical idea. True, the German conglomerates never viewed themselves as continent-sized businesses—because the country wasn't a continent—but they have all been global companies striving to expand. The thinking of owners and managers of pioneering companies on this or that side of the Atlantic has always been determined by huge units, and so was accordingly "big." Otherwise, those who were big back then wouldn't be big now—a phenomenon, incidentally, that is more pronounced in Germany than in the United States. We'll get back to that.

In the last quarter of the nineteenth century, when conventional mass technologies were being developed, it was America and Germany that were mainly responsible for their growth. The transition from basic industry to processing industry made the Marxist dogma of declining wages obsolete. Increasingly, consumption governed industry. Average wages climbed, and consequently, so did the purchasing power of the masses. Growth spurts became more intense than during the "British" period at the beginning of industrialization. The tendency toward economic "gigantomania" increased considerably. Industry branches and companies that evolved then are still among those with the highest sales figures, even 80 or 100 years later. German companies moving toward America or developing a counterforce to American conglomerates are part of this very old tradition. They were big and they remained big.

In short, size works—per se. On the other hand, it is also subject to zeitgeist. Not too long ago, this zeitgeist decreed that companies be demolished, purportedly because smaller units worked better. But the demolition theory was more a maneuver on the part of so-called corporate raiders. Their business consisted of buying rich companies by way of loans—junk bonds being particularly popular—and later having the captured company pay back the loan.

This was possible only by drastically cutting costs. There were layoffs and other measures to downsize the company. Entire segments were sold until the new owner's loan had been paid off. In the final analysis, typically it turned out that the company had become smaller through the takeover, but also more productive and profitable. The same result would have been achieved if the company had subdivided and structured itself more efficiently, as AT&T and General Electric have done, for instance. The upshot of the downsizing then would have led to an expansion of the company's business rather than to making the raider wealthy.

Another fashionable trend was diversification. In the 1970s and 1980s, conglomerates liked to expand by venturing into entirely new areas of business. This was supposed to allow them to counterbalance a temporary sluggish period in one business area by a temporary boom in another, as in Edzard Reuter's vision of the technological conglomerate. In short, it was an exercise in probability theory, with many unknown factors. Reason dictates that as many different business areas as possible should be involved in such a model. But as always, in the end, this too led to expansion—until someone finally discovered that an enormous administrative apparatus and many different crews would be required to make that diversification model really work. It killed any systematic personnel policy and was thus a huge waste of money. But a countermodel followed quickly. The new direction was now "core businesses."

That's the model most mergers and acquisitions were following at the turn of the century. The fewer the business areas, the new rule went, the larger the profit. This model, too, originated predominantly in the United States. But people are forgetful. Since 1987, there has been no recession, and since 1991, there has been an uninterrupted boom. In such a climate, no longer were there any "strong" and "weak" business areas. Every core business was bound to flourish. On the other hand, any diversification would have worked as well, though it would have been a little more expensive. Still, no matter what the respective zeitgeist, there have always been two invariables: The consulting business declared any trend it had generated to be an eternal truth, and companies kept growing with each new turn.

The European conglomerate pilgrimage into the New World was triggered not only by the laws of pure logic, but also by America's phenomenally stable economic cycle. It wasn't so much the economic boom, which has lasted almost dangerously long, but its general framework. The American economy is ruled by consumption, and not because someone is setting a Keynesian program in motion (which, incidentally, wouldn't be possible, given the country's large national debt), but because it's so deeply ingrained. Even when the economy stagnates, the Americans are more willing to keep buying than are Europeans. One reason for this is that there are more "hard salespeople" in the United States than elsewhere. Being part of that general atmosphere is almost always profitable for companies.

In spite of the United States' horrendous bureaucracy and stultifying laws concerning product liability, the country offers aggressive companies better general conditions than Europe does. Furthermore, it has the largest single-language market in the world in terms of sales. That makes distribution easier, although competition is tougher. Even minuscule U.S. market shares translate into substantial sales: 5 percent of the U.S. market equals the same rate of return as 16 percent of the German market. That's what counts in the long run. But many German companies also have had to swallow at home such short-term vexations as the not-so-reliable Oskar Lafontaine, or the Green Party's demand for a gas price increase to 5 marks per liter (the equivalent of $12 per gallon; in the United States, the price is $1.20 per gallon, so better go transatlantic).

What counts for many U.S. émigrés in the long run, beyond these short-term vexations, is Europe's adherence to the concept of the welfare state. It is their one critical argument against anything they don't like. On the other hand, they don't want to entirely leave Europe, or Germany, either; they want to take the best from both continents: highly qualified labor in Germany and cheap labor in the United States; German corporative security and American corporate culture—all of these being almost antithetical terms, no matter how similar they sound.

Last but not least, the German orientation toward Big Brother America is also a way of distracting them from their pain. Globalization, though often cursed, heals many wounds, which brings us to the next subtopic of corporate mergers: The conglomerates' internationalization is also their denationalization. Companies want a kind of United Nations passport—all the more so because industry doesn't just go where rich buyers live, but also where cheap labor is. Mathematically speaking, this is the golden rule: One can't make money any other way, which is why this trend will continue. Furthermore, it lowers the industrial nations' inflation rate.

Therefore, the status of a global company confers on many a company director the sense of being a Jakob Fugger from Augsburg. Fugger was called "the Rich" because he had more money than Europe's princes and kings. Like Jakob Fugger, conglomerates of the high nobility, such as DaimlerChrysler and Allianz, have more money at their disposal than medium-size states. Their revenue is sometimes higher than the budget, and sometimes even the gross domestic product, of entire nations. That's why the manager of a global company can influence the policies of its host nation or one of its regions. But to do so requires more than selling goods there—they need to have an address there.

Certainly, influencing politicians isn't always necessary, but it sometimes helps a great deal. The more foreign companies act like citizens of their host countries, the less local politicians feel corrupted by them. German companies that have settled in new industrial parks in America have done best, especially in the South.

Under Eberhard von Kuenheim, for instance, BMW managers selected Spartanburg, South Carolina, as a suitable area for manufacturing their Z-3 roadster. The South's old industries—in particular, tobacco—no longer could support the region, and unemployment in the area had reached a disconcerting level. When the people from Munich knocked on the door, they immediately were offered conditions comparable to those granted in the German regions bordering on East Germany before unification. Daimler-Chrysler—at that time Daimler-Benz—fared similarly when it went looking for a manufacturing location for its new M-class. It found a suitable place in Tuscaloosa, Alabama.

Of course, the two automakers did have something to offer—jobs and German training standards, to name the most obvious. In addition, they attracted suppliers to the area, so the transportation business also received a boost. Even distant ports such as Charleston, South Carolina, profited from their move. Noble companies such as BMW and Daimler-Chrysler also embellish their areas' publicity brochures. Americans are not at all uptight about these things. In general, they are not in the least bothered by European investors. After all, investors bring in money, which proves that they are banking on America's future: Foreign investments are a measure of the quality of a region. It's that simple.

Taking all of this together, we are in the midst of a grand polyglot game. For as Germany reaches across the Atlantic, a new global division of labor is emerging, in which the United States is participating in a major way. The textbook example of such a division of labor took place in the eighteenth century, and even then the issue was related to production costs: Inexpensive British textiles and Portuguese wine offered to the consumer the advantages of an international division of labor. But that was still the microcosm of an earlier era.

If we include in this scenario not only labor costs and the natural conditions of a company's location but also technical expertise and innovative capacity, we can discern a fundamentally new division of labor between the United States and Europe, with the Far Eastern industrial nations as a corrective: Technologically speaking and in terms of innovation, we live in a tripartite world. The great inventions and developments of the hardware period took place almost exclusively in Europe, and those of the more modern software period in the United States.

Both periods of innovation determined which industries developed in the various regions. Europe, especially Germany, dominated combustion technology, the chemical industry, and conventional electricity. America became the leading power in the fast-growing micro- and entertainment electronics, as well as in biochemistry. Thus the developmental foci of the European and the American postwar generations have split very distinctly. To Americans, the hardware industry is boring, which is why they stressed its Rust Belt character and neglected it to a certain degree. Europeans, in particular Germans, for a long time threw away their chances in the software business because they wallowed in cultural pessimism for three decades and lost their interest in innovation. They stayed with mechanics, but now made it more sophisticated.

In the Far East, both technological areas were quickly adapted, refined, improved, and made cheaper, but they were not internalized to the degree that they were in Europe and the United States. In that respect, the Far Eastern industries are secondhand cultural carriers, which means that they have not become first-step innovators. Thus, America became the world market leader with strong exports in the software business, while Europe leads in the hardware business. Both have competition in Asia, which keeps consumers from being terrorized by oligopolies.

The move of German companies to America and the expansion of German global conglomerates to U.S. size are almost like textbook examples of these laws. Most of the companies involved deal in the genuinely European hardware business. In this way, German industry is turning out to be the guardian of an old but greatly in demand mass technology, which it helped shape to a great degree and which everyone else has mastered by now, though not quite as well. Its role as guardian can also be viewed as a mark of its ossification, but within the context of a company's organization it has dealt with it well. With the exception of the software conglomerate SAP, no significant companies of the software period have developed in Germany.

Like America's software conglomerates, so the German hardware trusts have led to the development of a network of smaller service businesses, including suppliers and manufacturers of specialty products with larger shares of the world market than many large companies despite their lower revenues. Former Airbus manager Hartmut Mehdorn is the best example. He has made Heidelberger Druckmaschinen AG the unrivaled world leader in integrated and intelligent printing systems. Heidelberger Druck, a part of the Allianz family, had revenue of almost 3.5 billion marks—some $2 billion—in 1998–1999. This may be almost a joke for Jürgen Schrempp, but for Mehdorn it constitutes a major share of the world market.

In short, size does matter, because of cash flow, the distribution network, market proximity, political business games, and the necessary omnipresence in the new free-market world. Thus we are facing a fast-emerging new structure in the world's economy. Simply, the often discussed "new world order" is going to be created by the business community.

The time to deal with that is now. Americans and Europeans understand that. And the Europeans, who were slowed down by the Cold War, have taken an Olympic-size jump.

INDEX